To those who came before us... for their courage and inspiration.

To the ILGO Parade Group and all who, year after year,
supported us in our public protest against homophobia.

And to those now and in the future who will continue
with the vision of a humane world by publicly naming and
resisting all bigotry.

Rock the Sham! is especially dedicated to Maxine Wolfe.

Published by Street Level Press

Cover and book design by Jack Wright

ISBN 0-9729296-3-0

www.rockthesham.com

ROCK THE SHAM!

The Irish Lesbian & Gay Organization's Battle to March in New York City's St. Patrick's Day Parade

Anne Maguire

Acknowledgments

SPECIAL thanks to those readers who so generously took the time to read and re-read my manuscript with thoughtfulness, keen eyes and tact: **Máire Crowe, Marie Honan, Jenny McPhee, Vesna Neskow, Lisa Springer, Grace Suh, Sara Wilbourne,** and **Maxine Wolfe.**

Thanks also to **Ashley Bowers, Rick Prelinger, David Robinson, Sarah Schulman, Ailbhe Smyth,** and **Elizabeth Stark** for their commentary.

I wish to express my appreciation to the photographers and artists who so kindly granted me permission to use their work free of charge. The story would lack a real sense of what ILGO was about and up against without these images. Thank you **Donna Binder, Cecilia Dougherty,** Dyke Action Machine! (DAM! is **Carrie Moyer** and **Sue Schaffner**), **Morgan Gwenwald, James Higgins, Carolina Kroon, Bruce Manning, Carrie Moyer, Margaret O'Flanagan, Alice O'Malley, Saskia Scheffer,** and ILGO member photographers.

Regarding imagery thanks are also due to **Susan O'Brien, Dolly Soto, Joan Vitale Strong, Heide Schaffner** of AP/Wide World Photos, and **Joelle Sedlmeyer.**

For their excellent scanning of photographs, posters and art work my gratitude goes to **Peter English** and **Cathy Maguire,** who despite their newborn son, Liam, hauled out all the equipment and got the job done.

Jack Wright, upon little notice, offered to design *Rock the Sham!* from cover to cover and then talked me into producing a classier book than I had planned. I have only met Jack once, so again I have been charmed to have such generous and talented people supporting this project.

My gratitude is also due to **Aly Walansky** for her excellent copy-editing and proofing of the manuscript (alywalansky@gmail.com). Thanks also to **Nicole St. Clair** for my website. (www.makenew.net).

Rick Prelinger deserves a special mention. From the beginning of my involvement with the St. Patrick's Day Parade he supported me even though I had just started to work for him. He later gave me a computer when I told him I was writing a book. Rick's support has been both political and also very personal and I thank him for his friendship and, mostly, his faith in me.

Marie Honan, I'm still in love with you and it feels good.

Idealists... foolish enough to throw caution to the winds... have advanced humankind and have enriched the world.

– *Emma Goldman*

Contents

CHAPTER ONE

Taking Fifth Avenue

"It is strange that what is now my most vivid experience of mob hatred came not in the South but in New York – and was directed against me, not because I was defending the right of African Americans but of gay and lesbian Americans."

– Mayor David Dinkins,
***The New York Times*, 1991**

ROCK THE SHAM!

E WERE on New York City's famed Fifth Avenue on March 16, 1991 surrounded by cameras, cops and a screaming mob. The force of Paul's grip was making my hand go numb. Just paces behind, Ruth Messinger, the Borough President of Manhattan, gave the order to smile. We tried. Paul was rigid beside me. I turned to look at him. He appeared so strange I wasn't sure for a second if he was, in fact, my 26-year-old friend Paul O'Dwyer from Kilkenny. Clearly, he was furious but that wasn't all—there was something in his expression I had never seen before. I squeezed his hand, hoping he'd turn and reassure me with a familiar look. He didn't. I began to murmur, "Everything's going to be fine, Paul. Everything's alright."

"Okay. Okay," he responded, repeating it like a mantra, without much conviction. Like me, he had no idea whether or not everything was going to be fine. He told me later that he was afraid one of us was going to be killed.

On our heels, a row of politicians maneuvered for position, separating us from our comrades. I was aware of the presence of New York City Police Department uniforms on either flank. Beside them, a fragile line of barricades separated our compact group from the throngs on the sidelines. Ahead were the cameras and a sea of reporters' faces—their mouths in constant motion framing inaudible questions. The vibration of a bass drum in the distance made me shudder. Despite having been denied the right to participate with our banner, the Irish Lesbian & Gay Organization was on Fifth Avenue marching for the first time in the New York St. Patrick's Day parade.

Moments earlier, when we first stepped out at 46th Street where the parade begins, a low rumble of indignation erupted from the sidelines and grew to a full thunder within seconds. "Die faggots! Get AIDS and die." Paul reacted immediately—I could feel him shaking. We kept walking. My senses had been jolted awake by the hostility and I remember feeling shocked and then terrified.

For hours we had waited, expecting to walk onto Fifth Avenue with Mayor David Dinkins, the city's first black mayor. When ILGO applied to march, the organizers of the parade, the Ancient Order of Hibernians (AOH) told us there was no room. The story of ILGO's exclusion hit the presses and caused a furor in the remaining week-and-a-half leading up to the annual event. During that time the mayor had voiced his concern about ILGO's exclusion from the line of march. He had tried to negotiate a deal with the parade sponsors, to no avail. Then Division 7 of the AOH, a liberal Manhattan group, invited ILGO and the mayor to march as their guests. At a packed press conference on Thursday, March 14, Mayor David Dinkins announced that he would march with ILGO. On the day we all turned out to wait in the staging area on 46th Street, cool in the shadow of New York City skyscrapers; all except the mayor. When we finally began to pour out of the obscurity of 46th Street on the afternoon of March 16, to join the parade, Mayor Dinkins was not there.

There had been such a fanfare about him giving up his spot in the limelight, at the head

Taking a stand (for now)... Mayor David Dinkins, Paul O'Dwyer (ILGO), Debra Pucci, me, Joe Hynes, Paul O'Dwyer, Division 7 member, and Pat Clarke © *Joan Vitale Strong*

PREVIOUS SPREAD: With Paul O'Dwyer and Pat Clarke, moving from 46th Street, out on to Fifth Avenue, where a two-mile long monster awaited us © *James Higgins*

of the parade, to march with Irish lesbians and gay men that Paul was incredulous as we stepped off. He kept asking me, "Where's the mayor?" I told Paul and the reporters in front of us, "He'll be here," even though I wasn't convinced. As soon as we were out on Fifth Avenue and actually marching in the parade, I told myself it didn't matter. That would change later.

Paul and I marched up front with Division 7 and the politicians because we had been ILGO's representatives during the fuss of the previous ten days. We had to concentrate on finding our rhythm, putting one foot in front of the other, as we moved at a good clip up the avenue. At 48th Street, the roaring from the sidelines intensified. We were now being booed from behind and ahead. Just before we reached 49th Street, there was a discernable shift in the air as something disrupted the momentum we were slowly adapting to. I looked to Paul for acknowledgement of the change. It was unspoken between us, but understood, that if we were going to go down, we would go down together.

A group of men in suits approached us. The reporters were frantic. For the first time that day I was so shaken that I couldn't help losing my cool. "What going on?" I shouted. From behind there was a powerful surge forward and I lost my footing. Then Paul was no longer beside me. The force of the push from behind lifted my feet off the ground for a second and, to my right, Paul's head bobbed in and out of view. My legs buckled and my throat had tensed so much I couldn't catch my breath. If I could have, I would have screamed. But the disruption ended as abruptly as it had begun. The entourage of well-dressed men was upon us and everything calmed. They broke rank, and David Dinkins, the mayor of New York City, walked toward us, smiling.

The mayor's arms stretched out in front of him, beckoning. We were one block from St. Patrick's Cathedral. I walked towards David Dinkins with an urge so strong to be taken in and held it almost immobilized me. Instead of reaching to greet him, my arms hung heavy by my sides. Even though he was smiling, the mayor's eyes betrayed him—they were sad. He drew Pat Clarke, of Division 7, and me close to him, hugging us for a second or two. I wanted to be held in that embrace for longer than was offered. It felt safe there. This poignant moment is a bitterly upsetting memory. Two years later, Mayor Dinkins would betray ILGO terribly.

Our contingent of about 200 people waited at 49th Street as David Dinkins set about his mayoral duties, exchanging hearty greetings, and slapping backs all around him. He sported a Kelly-green blazer and carried a gnarled and highly varnished Shillelagh walking cane, which I thought was very tacky. His good humor and warm embraces seemed to be an over-compensation for the hostility from the sidelines. No amount of political savvy or scheming could have foretold what the experience of marching would be like. The mayor, along with the rest of us, was part of a historical moment that nobody yet understood. Whether he wanted it or not, he was personally involved.

Paul, now back beside me, was transformed. His relief at the mayor's appearance turned to joy. There was a palpable buzz of excitement as, "The mayor's here," echoed through our group. The mayor's presence made me feel secure, as if everything would be taken care of. I wanted to be happy but was feeling surly. Anger gnawed at me; anger for being so grateful. Paul's plain delight only made it worse. I wondered where the forthright Irish lesbian that had been my persona for the preceding ten days had gone. I wished my girlfriend, Marie, was beside me.

****

IT SEEMED like such a long time since all of this had begun, but, in fact, the Irish Lesbian & Gay Organization (ILGO) was a young group. In the spring of 1990, we had our first meeting in a Japanese restaurant. Since that sunny Saturday afternoon in April, we continued to meet on a monthly basis. Our mission was to make it possible for the predominantly immigrant group to be Irish and gay at the same time. Before ILGO we were forced to choose; we could be Irish if we were closeted (which most of our members were), or we could be lesbians and gay men so long as we gave up the benefits offered by the Irish community to immigrants in this city. ILGO changed all that. Women and men from all walks of life flocked to the group. When spring passed into summer, we celebrated by marching in the Lesbian and Gay Pride Parade in Manhattan. Self-identified Irish lesbians and gay men seemed to come as a surprise to many in the gay community and jokes were made about how our existence was an oxymoron. This made us wonder if Irish people knew we existed at all. We naively thought the St. Patrick's Day Parade would solve everything and sent in our application to march in October 1990, and were turned down. Now it was March 1991, the end of our first winter, but not yet our first anniversary, and we had come tearing out of the closet much sooner than most of us had planned. Now everyone in New York knew about ILGO. What they didn't know was that we were fighting for our most fundamental right; very simply, to live as who we were.

On the morning of the parade I had woken up with a start, knowing, but not yet realizing, what loomed ahead. I turned to lie flat on my back and stared at the turquoise ceiling. Marie lay sleeping beside me. The rhythmic flow of air from her nostrils kissed my shoulder as she slept. We were still getting used to being around each other after her return from two months of travel in Mexico and Guatemala. As I was debating whether or not to go back to sleep I remembered: The parade! My stomach lurched and I leaped out of bed.

Daisy's Restaurant in the West Village was the natural place for us to congregate before our first St. Patrick's Day Parade. It had become our regular diner after our monthly meetings at the Lesbian and Gay Community Services Center (The Center) located a couple of blocks north on 13th Street. In the heady days of the month of March before that first St. Patrick's Day Parade, we had been living on late-night diner food as the row over our inclusion in the most famous of Irish parades grew. As Paul remarked, "If ever there was a replacement Irish bar, it was this little diner in Greenwich Village." Now, once again sitting in Daisy's, on this bright spring morning, the moment we had worked so hard to get to was only hours away. We were far more subdued than was natural for us. Usually we were excited, full of stories, ready to get stuck into a discussion, and having to battle to get a word in edgeways. Today, we watched the grease congeal on our plates of half-eaten eggs. Our tables were strewn with cold bagels, soggy pancakes, endless cups of coffee and, of course, overflowing ashtrays. We didn't know what to do. At about 10:30, we reluctantly left the diner and shared cabs uptown.

We stuck together, fighting our way through the throng in Midtown, until we reached Division 7's staging area on 46th Street. It was already packed though our official take-off time was hours away. Many faces in the crowd were familiar but I didn't know most of the lesbians and gay men who turned out to support ILGO. There were our friends and family as well. My sister, Cathy, came running over and threw her arms about me, and then pulled Marie in. A smattering of Division 7 members, recognizable by their fancy white sashes, was almost lost in the mill.

ROCK THE SHAM!

Because ILGO was marching as invited guests, we were not allowed to carry our banner; we would march behind Division 7's. We had decided on this compromise when the mayor assured us he would march, believing his presence would clearly identify who we were. By the time we were supposed to have taken off we were 200 strong, with many more ILGO people participating than had for the Lesbian and Gay Pride Parade, which shocked me a little. Even then the media possibly outnumbered us. Sound equipment and cameras were lugged from gay man to lesbian to politician and back again. They asked, "Will there be violence?" as if gay people are violent. And everyone wanted to know if ACT UP, the very active and powerful AIDS Coalition to Unleash Power, would be marching. Not one reporter noticed or asked if we were frightened.

The tension thickened the longer we stood around. Everyone noticed the parade spectators, in green, or Aran, wearing plastic hats or sporting bright green hair who walked by to gawk at us—the queers. I turned back to those being observed. ILGO's Father Bernard Lynch wore a satin "Free Joe Doherty" sash and was chatting with a man from Division 7. Bernard, a Catholic priest from Clare, had become well known as "the AIDS priest" for his ministry to people since the beginning of the epidemic. When he testified in support of the city's Gay Rights Bill, in 1986, he remembers been jeered by the AOH who chanted, "Shame! Shame! Put him on a plane," as he left the hearings.

Holding her children close, Rita Higgins, a Belfast native who had founded the Bronx Women's Irish Group, nervously looked about. I saw my friend John Lucas, his blond hair sticking up as usual. Máire Crowe wove in and out of the crowd. She had a spiral notebook and pencil in hand. She had broken the parade story in the *Irish Voice*, a new weekly newspaper in New York. When Máire originally interviewed some of us before the parade controversy for a story in an Irish paper, the *Sunday Tribune*, we had assumed she was a lesbian because she didn't ask any stupid questions.

My girlfriend, Marie, had her arm linked through mine. She was her usual mass of color. She wore a crayon-red fake fur coat and dazzling leggings. Her leopard-print eyeglasses only ever left her face when she lay down at night to sleep. Since our first meeting in Dublin during the mid-eighties, her style had enthralled me. Now, when either of us wandered off, my eye sought her out in the crowd as much for my own comfort as for her well-being. My sister, Cathy, rarely left my side. She was fiercely protective and I knew if anyone tried to hurt me they would have to deal with Cathy first—the seriousness of her mission unmistakable from the expression on her face.

The morning progressed into an afternoon filled with false starts and delays. Not only were we nervous but also starting to get fed up, shivering and teeth chattering after hours in the cold. Remarkably, amidst such high-pitched anxiety, Fergal Doherty, a redhead from Derry with boundless energy and good humor, was organizing traditional Irish céilí dancing. Six people were swinging each other about to the rhythm of their hand-clapping audience. Lucy Lynch, a Fermanagh woman, was beside herself with impatience. She wanted to get out

And a Happy St. Patrick's Day to you, too! © *James Higgins*

there and get it over with. She remembers, "I couldn't wait to walk on Fifth Avenue. I wanted every Irish person I ever knew in New York to see me there saying I was a lesbian. All the time I was in New York I was never myself. Now they were going to see me as I was, at my fullest, as me."

Waiting directly behind us was the St. Raymond's marching band. Every so often they would give us a blast, reminding us what they were there for that day. When the pipes stopped and the only sound was the lone drumming, Lucy would take off in a burst, jumping up and down, arms akimbo. The drumming was militaristic and intimidating. It brought me back to Dublin in 1981 and riot police banging on their shields during the hunger strike marches. The beat of the bass drum had the same ominous effect—it was a warning.

I heard my name called out. "We're moving. Everyone's looking for you." Fergal was shouting into a megaphone, enthusiastically urging us all to enjoy ourselves. At last, the waiting was over. Paul held my hand, which made me feel very young—like he was my brother. Later, Paul described us in this moment as Hansel and Gretel setting off into the dark and dangerous forest. We began to leave the dim street behind and slowly filed out into the blazing sunshine on Fifth Avenue. I had forgotten what a glorious day it was. At last we were where we wanted to be, where we belonged. Then the booing started.

ROCK THE SHAM!

No love lost between New York
City's cardinal and mayor
© AP/Wide World Photos

The jeers from the sidelines acted like a cue for the reporters: "Where's the mayor?" they chanted. But right then all that mattered was that we were on Fifth Avenue. At that moment in history everything else was irrelevant because we had won. Against all the odds, Irish lesbians and gay men were marching in the 230th St. Patrick's Day in New York City.

On Fifth Avenue, watching the faces of people screaming at us with such ferocity both fascinated and horrified me. In spots the police barriers rocked back and forth as pockets of spectators tried to push them over. We had been excited and fearless during the lead-up to this day and hadn't really had a chance to think about what might happen, mostly because it all happened so fast. I don't know if I had imagined or fantasized about how ILGO's presence in the parade would be greeted by spectators. I did know that the idea of death flitted through my mind a lot; I was worried about someone being badly hurt but don't know what I had based that anxiety on. Nothing had been clear at the beginning but now that we were on Fifth Avenue and we were experiencing the crowd's response we knew we had done the right thing and that it was time to tell our friends, families, and our ethnic community that being Irish was not going to keep us quiet about being lesbians and gay men anymore. We were not going back into the closet. A great wall of silence had come tumbling down and what lay behind it was very ugly.

At 50th Street, the sight of St. Patrick's Cathedral stopped us in our tracks. The Gothic landmark loomed before us in all its grandeur and for once there was confusion in the contingent. This structure had come to represent the power of organized homophobia for most of the Lesbian and Gay Community in New York—it was the territory of Cardinal John O'Connor.

He did not want gay people in this parade. He did not want to prevent HIV by supporting safe sex practices. He did not want children and teenagers to receive adequate sex education, not just in Catholic schools but also in public schools, so they might be more able to protect themselves. He did not believe that women had the right to full control of their bodies and he used the pulpit to promote hatred of lesbians and gay men and his other political agendas. "What now?" was my unspoken query. After a couple of fits and starts, and without any direction or instruction, we fell eerily silent. There was a crescendo from the sidelines but it could not penetrate the stillness in our contingent. Keith Moore, a Donegal man who had worked tirelessly on the parade in ILGO, did not march with us. He made it to the waiting area on 46th Street but was frightened off by the glut of media. He couldn't see anyone he knew. He sensed the press wanted something bad to happen—something to spice up the story. Keith fled and went to see a movie, *Sleeping with the Enemy*. The movie was over and Keith was on the sidelines of Fifth Avenue at St. Patrick's cathedral when ILGO arrived. They were shouting, "Faggots. Queers. You're not Irish. Your parents must be English!" People were standing beside him screaming and then turning to him and smiling. "They would've wanted to kill me if they'd known I was gay," he recalled. "Standing in front of the cathedral felt like being raped."

I have no memory of people screaming at us; I was not aware of any noise. I felt like a spectator with a panoramic view that swept from one side of the cathedral steps to the other. The lasting impression was of hugeness and quiet, the mayor only a slight figure in this vast scene. He seemed too delicate set against the physical mass of the cathedral and the bulk of the men who stood in wait for him. I half expected him to be engulfed, never to appear again. All eyes were on David Dinkins. Nothing stirred, the stillness broken only by the mayor dressed in Kelly-green dashing up the steps towards a gathering of men trimmed in crimson, and behind them row upon row of clerics garbed in black. It felt like nobody breathed until it was over. The mayor moved gracefully down the steps ready to continue on the route after shaking several cold white hands.

Traditionally, the cardinal would come down to greet the mayor, who in normal times would be honored by being placed at the head of the parade. These were not normal times. For these two powerful men in New York City, this day would prove to be memorable in their political careers. The mayor, an African American, stood with the Irish Lesbian & Gay Organization. The cardinal, an Irish American, snubbed him for it.

There were no prizes given out that day for guessing when "the queers" were coming. Fifth Avenue was clear for blocks ahead and behind our group. Marie remarked that this tactic seemed to announce that no other contingent was to be tainted by being too close to us. The screaming and roaring seeped in and out of my consciousness. We heard all the usual epithets—the ones we'd been hearing our entire lives: "Die faggots! Queers! Swish! Homos!" Like other lesbians, I was informed by men of all ages, some with children on their shoulders, that what I needed was a "good fuck." Many offered their services. Threats were hurled at us from all directions: "We're going to get you. We know who you are." We were ridiculed as "Perverts. Scum. Child molesters." I even heard cries of "Satan!" One young man, perhaps fifteen or sixteen years old, roared incoherent slurs, tears streaming down his face, while his friends stood in awkward silence beside him. I was distracted again, by the three wiry older women with powdered white faces who screamed, "AIDS! AIDS! AIDS!" with such venom they must have believed they could will AIDS on us. At moments I felt chilled to my core; I knew what was happening was real but it also felt impossible. Men, with rage, spit their hatred at us, shaking their balled fists. Placards, held high, attacked the mayor, "Dinkins... Catholic-Basher," and announced what would be his fate, "One-term mayor." The rest of us were warned, "Beware the AIDS of March."

Catch Keeley, a Dubliner, thought David Dinkins had made a courageous decision. "He stood up for what he believed in and he stood up against the cardinal, a very powerful figure in New York City," she said. "Those people who insulted him should be absolutely ashamed of themselves." Paul felt similarly and during the parade apologized to the mayor, as an Irish man, for the way some Irish people were behaving. Paul remarked, "I don't think the mayor would have cared if he was going to be voted out of office the next day for what he was doing." Of course the mayor cared; he was a politician and, like others in the future, would drop ILGO when we no longer served his purpose. But back then it wasn't surprising we forgot this. Mayor Dinkins was marching with us and going through what we were going through. We believed this experience would bond him with us forever—how could it not?

When beer cans came hurtling across the contingent from the sidelines, Pat Clarke of Division 7 moved protectively closer to me and held my hand. I had to laugh to myself because the beer cans did not surprise me as much as they upset Pat. Lesbians and gay men live with the threat of violence—it is a fact of our daily lives and, sadly, not shocking to me anymore. Umbrellas went up over the mayor to protect him and I wondered who had thought to bring umbrellas on such a beautiful day. Lucy, so wanting everyone to know she was a lesbian despite living in Bainbridge in the Bronx, an Irish and Irish American enclave, was oblivious to the danger until she began to notice how scared some people in the contingent were. This gave her pause in the middle of such a personally liberating moment. Lucy grew up in the north of Ireland which is under British rule. During her childhood the British Army often raided her home. She felt no fear because she cut it off. She explained, "I wanted to be here for all the people who had come to the ILGO meetings and were so scared that they never came back. I wanted to be here for them to say it's okay."

Paul was keeping up with the mayor so I dropped back to where I wanted to be, with Marie. I decided to concentrate on people who supported us. Sally Cooper and Rebecca Cole stood at a prime location along the route, up on a height, placards held high—"England Get out of Ireland" and "Gaylick Pride." Further on I saw an ILGO member's sister jumping up and down. She looked like she was fit to burst. She couldn't make up her mind whether to wave, or cheer, or laugh but she was definitely with us. Her boyfriend stood stony-faced and rigid beside her. I completely missed an episode on the reviewing stand, the image of which continues to encapsulate the Hibernians' stance, when the honored AOH aides to the Grand Marshal turned their backs on us as we passed. "Doesn't that sum it up?" Paul observed. "If they turn their backs then we're not here."

Feeling more secure beside Marie and keeping up with our quick stride, I relaxed a little and was ready again to try to figure out what was going on. I studied the faces of people who were bellowing at us. My instinct was to seek out a person's eyes and look into them to see if they gave a clue to their rage. When our eyes met there were two responses only; either the person stopped screaming, or continued but with eyes lowered or cast in another direction. Others in our contingent held their fingers in the air in the familiar v-shaped peace sign. I couldn't do this; it felt too American. At intervals there were brave bursts of defiance and pride despite the hostile mob when, "We're here. We're queer. We're Irish. Get used to it!" rang out. An edgy and excitable Galway-man, John Lyons, was having fun. "For some reason I felt totally triumphant perhaps because I think I really understood where all these people on the sidelines were coming from," he remembers. "I felt it was just amazing that I could be here screaming my head off as I was saying things like, 'I'm a faggot from Galway and I don't give a fuck about you.'"

Patrick Barker spotted his uncle Jimmy Barker behind the barricades, screaming, "Fucking faggots! Go home!" He was taken by surprise when his nephew appeared in front of him, saying, "Hello, Uncle Jimmy." He looked to his left and then to his right, checking out who might be watching. "He was mortified," Patrick recalled. Marching alongside him was Patrick's friend, Tom Duane, a Democrat who was gearing up for City Council elections, who recognized Jimmy Barker from the Democratic Party machine. Barker had connections with former Governor Carey and was a mover and shaker in the borough of Queens but had no involvement in the parade to that point. He did, however subsequently become involved after that year. He also lied about the incident afterward, insisting it was Patrick who was screaming and cursing!

We moved through the forty blocks of the parade route in record time; we literally dashed up Fifth Avenue. When we arrived at 86th Street the mayor held a brief press conference. Comparing his experience of marching with ILGO with the 1960s Civil Rights marches in Alabama, he said, "It was like marching in Birmingham. I knew there would be deep emotions, but I did not anticipate the cowards in the crowd. There was far, far too much negative comment." Moments later he was whisked off. Along with him went our security. Gone were the extra cops. Most of the politicians and media had dispersed too; we were left stranded.

Four men clad in Aran sweaters and blue jeans shouted they were going to kill us. From the opposite corner of 86th Street the chant, "Fight! Fight! Fight!" rose up. We were being surrounded by groups of furious young men who wanted to harm us. Marie said this was the most frightening moment of the day for her. She could feel how volatile the situation was becoming. Getting through the parade had been our main focus. It had not occurred to us that the most dangerous part of this day would be making it safely off Fifth Avenue.

Our marshals asked the cops for an escort to a train. They refused. Patrick Barker asked a police captain to separate us from the growing mob on three separate occasions, and was ignored. He spotted Manhattan Borough President Ruth Messenger getting into a car and ran to get her assistance. He knew her from election work he had done for Tom Duane. She spoke to a commander who ordered a slew of police officers to take us to the nearest subway station.

Before we began our journey home Tarlach MacNiallais threw his arms around me and sobbed, crying over and over, "I'm so proud of us!" Tarlach's appearance was deceptive—he looked tough, and he was, all six feet of him with his stocky build and big round face. But he was such a softie too. When he was in his teens his photo appeared in a Belfast newspaper after a demonstration against the leader of the Democratic Unionist Party, the Reverend Ian Paisley. Paisley had launched a homophobic campaign to "Save Ulster from Sodomy." (Paisley has spent his career saving Ulster from something or other—usually peace and democracy.) Tarlach's sign responded, "Save Sodomy from Ulster." His mother, brother, and sister-in-law had come from Belfast to march with him in the parade. This was a big deal especially since he'd been kicked out of home in his late teens when he told his family he was gay and now, in New York, he worried about his mother's safety given the violence on Fifth Avenue.

On the train Tarlach led us in song, as was his tradition. "We're here because we're queer," we sang to the chorus of "Auld Lang Syne". We got off at the West 4th Street subway station and came out into the relative safety of the West Village.

By the time we settled ourselves at the Stonewall Bar in Sheridan Square we were completely drained. Father Bernard Lynch sat me in a corner to tell me how proud he was of us. He explained that we were the priests, the true messengers of God's love. Being compared to a priest made me giddy because it was such an absurd idea. I was distracted and couldn't concentrate. Anyway, his words were lost on me—there was no God in my life. Everyone was worried about Keith because we hadn't seen him all day. Nobody knew he'd tried to join us and had gone to a movie and then watched as we were jeered at the cathedral. There was no answer when I telephoned Keith's answering machine.

While those of us in ILGO were exhausted, there were others who had been energized by the experience of marching. John Voelcker, a member of ACT UP, came to marshal the ILGO contingent at the parade. He was excited afterwards and wanted to get drunk but he had so much adrenaline going through him that he drank oceans of beer and it didn't do a damn thing. He hadn't given much thought to what the parade might be like and figured his activist experience would be helpful to ILGO. He had been unexpectedly moved. "I had some sense that this was a moment in gay history. I had that feeling when I was at the AIDS conference in Montreal in 1989," he explained. "All the people with HIV took the stage and we got a standing ovation from 3,000 delegates as we read the proclamation of rights for people with HIV all over the world in three languages. At the parade I remember thinking this is a little bigger

The Ancient Order of Hibernians showing their better sides. © *AP/Wide World Photos*

than I had thought. Afterward, when we were the first on all the news stations, and then the papers the next day, I thought, Wow! Look at this, look what we did."

Marie and I went back to her friend Steve's apartment on Perry Street, five minutes from the bar. We would never have made it back out to Brooklyn where we lived so it was a relief that Steve offered us his place at weekends when he went upstate. Eileen Clancy, with whom I worked, and her girlfriend joined us. They decided to go around the corner to a Japanese take-out. We hadn't eaten all day. Up on the bed I smoothed out the patchwork quilt Steve had made and the four of us settled in surrounded by Styrofoam plates, paper napkins, plastic cutlery, and lots of food. Eileen chattered. I was too shaky to get a spoon of food into my mouth without spilling it so I cupped my hands around the plastic container and drank miso soup. I remember thinking, God, this is delicious. I maneuvered my body around the three women and lay down. It was dark outside. The last I remember of March 16, 1991 is Eileen's voice, receding, as I fell asleep.

CHAPTER TWO

The Kind Of Girl I Was

"I shall state silences more competently than ever a better man spangled the butterflies of vertigo."

– Samuel Beckett

Donnycarney, 1974

ROCK THE SHAM!

THE DEED was done and we survived. The hatred along the parade route was unmistakable and shocking. However, for many of us it was the silence of the vast majority of spectators on March 16, 1991 that was heart-breaking. That silence endured through the years and the parades that followed.

Silence was something I knew very well. The Ireland I grew up in seemed especially devoted to it. In my early childhood I didn't notice it but as I got older it became sharpened. I used to think everybody talked about the weather because it was so dismal but now it seems like it was a safe bet. Between home, school, and the local church, the rules of acceptable behavior were passed on. Because we were never supposed to say what we really thought or were feeling, we became expert in the art of indirect communication—it didn't much matter what the topic was. Trying to find out whether or not someone wanted a cup of tea was often an ordeal. I learned that self-censorship was fundamental to survival. But it never felt right. Since childhood I have been plagued by an urge to say what was on my mind, while simultaneously wanting to be invisible, to fade into the background, quietly, which was almost always what I did instead.

On the streets of Dublin's North Side in the Irish Republic (not the British-ruled six counties in the north), where I was raised, I experienced a sense of freedom, for a while. I loved to run when I was a child; it was exhilarating and exhausting. I remember running to school, to the local shops, on the street where I grew up, in parks, at the seaside—always on the move. But I eventually recognized that life was not carefree, more a delicate balancing act, and that being alert constantly might prevent unpleasant surprises. I rarely knew when or why my presence might lead to or get caught up in a disturbance. It seemed far safer to avoid attention. I became a quiet, observant girl who vigorously applied herself to diffusing tension in the hope that it would prevent trouble. My role was due in part to being the eldest of four children, the one who should always have "more sense." But, in the early days, running around the streets of Donnycarney, I was often stopped in my tracks by the exciting realization that I was a part of the world. My childish belief was that everybody had a place, or a calling, and that living would be about discovering where I fit in. Tucking my striped toweling T-shirt back into my favorite mint-green shorts, I would slowly begin to move again, picking up pace, until I was running, fingers tipping the cool waxy leaves of over-grown hedges.

Belton Park Avenue, where we lived, was a cul-de-sac with fourteen row houses on each side, and next to us were Belton Park Villas, Road, and Gardens. The Beltons were a prominent family. They owned the pub and the grocery shop, named The Packet, and ran the local post office. Paddy Belton was a member of the Fine Gael political party but Donnycarney was a stronghold of the major opposition party, Fianna Fáil. In those days, the parish was split into two sections and my school friend, Noeleen McDonnell, lived in a local authority housing scheme in Donnycarney North, or "new Donnycarney." Noeleen remembers the hi-jinks leading up to elections on her side of the parish. Charlie Haughey, the Fianna Fáil Party boss, who would later become Taoiseach (Prime Minister), came canvassing with bags of plastic sandals for the children. His visit ended in the pub, buying the local men pints of Guinness. That was the beginning and end of what you got from a politician. Women were brushed off with a nod and a wave as they stood in doorways, the only ones not worth a cheap election gimmick. My grandmother, Eileen Maguire, thought that all politicians should be put on a raft and sent to drift at sea.

Even though my parents were not political people, they knew, like many of their generation, what was going on in the world. Politics seemed to be as much a part of life as religion and the weather. The bells of the Angelus at 6pm began our evening ritual—it was the signal to quiet down for the news on the radio. Later, in front of the television, we were hushed again for the main evening news. Like a high percentage of the population, my parents voted on election days. As children we were very aware of elections; for weeks beforehand the lampposts were plastered with posters and on the day we didn't have to go to school. I never knew who my parents voted for and when I asked once, my mother told me that it was a private affair and to mind my own business.

My mother grew up in Donnycarney and my father, in Fairview, a twenty-minute walk away. I loved having grandparents and aunts living within walking distance of home. Several of them liked to spin yarns. My Aunt Tedie, my mother's sister, told us the funniest and wildest stories that were full of youthful devilment and ghostly misadventure. Bodies came alive and sat up in coffins, old ladies were tricked into thinking the Virgin Mary had sent for them, and her childhood had been full of pranks and minor skirmishes. My paternal grandmother, Eileen Maguire, gave me a sense of the history of the city and country in which I was growing up. Her tales were of death, betrayal, grief, hilarity, war, friendship, and growing up—the good times and the bad. Her father, a post office worker, died when a German U-boat bombed the HMS Leinster on October 10, 1918 while he was sorting mail just a month before the First World War ended. Her favorite sister died young, as did her first-born, Una, who died in childhood. It didn't matter how often I heard her stories—I was riveted each time, fascinated by the tragedies, in fits of laughter at her misdeeds, and awed by the events she had witnessed in her life. She saw Countess Markievicz, the nationalist leader and first woman minister in the Irish Republic (or, indeed in any elected democracy), speak in the city. She lived through the Civil War, lost her beloved brother Tom Blake when he went to America to recover from a bullet wound but later died, and her home was on Clonliffe Road when the notorious Black and Tans (WWI servicemen and thugs who were sent to Ireland as paramilitaries to aid the police in quelling the anti-British rebellion) entered nearby Croke Park on Bloody Sunday in 1920 and shot randomly into the crowd, killing

PREVIOUS SPREAD: The hairdo was always important! In my back garden in Belton Park Avenue, Donnycarney

twelve men, women and children, including two Gaelic football players, and injuring 60. Her husband, my grandfather Larry, was a member of the "Old IRA"—he made the distinction, but he never talked about his activities, though when he wasn't around my Aunt Mary showed us his medals and a framed photograph of his battalion. Later on when I began to become politically active, the fact that my grandparents, ordinary people, had been a part of such huge events in Irish history gave me a context for what was going on in the Ireland I inhabited. Being political seemed natural.

My entire education took place in all-girl Catholic schools run by the Holy Faith nuns. The highlight of my primary school years was preparation for our First Holy Communion. We walked up and down the aisle between desks, heads slightly bowed, hands clutched in prayerful pose under the chin, never forgetting to genuflect at the teacher's desk, the altar. However, when my class made their First Communion I couldn't be there because I had whooping cough. I finally had my First Communion, alone, without the usual fanfare, on March 17, 1969—St. Patrick's Day. My most prized accoutrement was a brand new picture prayer book with carrying case which my brother John and I used at home later to say mass using the bed with its pink candlewick spread as the altar.

One spring afternoon, my mother and I were on our way to get bread and milk at the local shop when two middle-aged women passed us on Belton Park Road. I knew they were lesbians despite having no words to acknowledge it then. They were wearing suits, one a tweed skirt and jacket, the other a man's three-piece suit. The woman in the man's suit had sandy-colored hair in a crew cut and she wore men's shoes and a tie. The other woman had shoulder length wavy-brown hair, was noticeably taller and seemed dreadfully sad to me. I wanted to shout, "Oh! Look! Look!" but knew not to. I wanted to leave my mother's side and follow them. I wished they would see that I was a girl dressed like a boy; a nine-year-old tomboy. They never saw me and didn't stay long in Donnycarney. After my initial excitement, seeing them again wasn't the same because they were untouchable. They walked briskly, looking straight ahead, never saying a word to anyone or to each other. I don't remember if they touched or linked arms but it was clear they were a couple.

By the time I was thirteen and entering secondary school, I had started to throw off wearing boy's clothes and wanted to look like a girl again. A year later, I distinctly recall trying to convince myself that it was natural for teenagers to have crushes on older girls and women. After all, it was a well-known fact that we would eventually outgrow this hormonally induced behavior. I worked hard to be "normal." Of course I didn't outgrow my lesbianism, but instead tried to bury it as I got older, which seemed sensible. I didn't know any lesbians, or anything about lesbians, so it never seemed real or possible. Sexual desire was so taboo in the first place that to freely allow feelings of desire for a woman, even in my own mind and body, was much too dangerous. I kept myself busy, mostly physically, running and spending hours on the basketball court. For relief, on the weekends I walked through Dublin's damp streets, usually on my own. Heavy gray clouds hung over the city as wan-faced people passed by in skimpy, drab clothing. At fourteen, I realized I was depressed and figured I probably had been for a long time.

Then I discovered alcohol. At first, getting drunk on Saturday nights was bliss. Among my circle of friends the job of purchasing a bottle of vodka in Belton's off-license (liquor store) was mine because I was tall and could pass for being older. If we couldn't collect enough money, we went through drink cabinets at home and filled up jam-jars with lethal concoctions. On the walk to The Grove, a local dancehall, we drank our bitter booze and ate Polo mints before passing the bouncer's inspection at the main door. Our timing was exquisite—it had to be—we never felt the effects of the alcohol until we were safely inside making our way up the main corridor, Led Zeppelin bouncing off the walls. Being drunk obliterated everything; I felt free.

But that feeling didn't last and turned into numbness, and being at The Grove presented me with new dilemmas. I wanted to look forward to the weekly dance, to fit in, but I hated Saturday nights and would have preferred to be at home watching talk show host Gay Byrne on the television with my parents. I was supposed to be having boy dramas, or at the very least boys should have been interested in me, but they weren't. I was very curious about sex but on the few occasions I ended up with a boy it was tedious and unpleasant and it scared me too. It was never clear to me how my friends were coping because we never talked about anything personal—we were all so intent on pretending we knew it all.

On one of my Saturday afternoon trips into the city, a year before I left secondary school, I got trapped at Trinity College while a huge demonstration passed. The march was in support of prisoners in the north of Ireland who were "on the blanket." The British government had denied political status to prisoners—instead all were categorized as common criminals. Irish Republican prisoners, in protest, refused to wear the government-issued uniform, draping themselves in blankets from their beds. Most of these prisoners had been arrested, en masse, during the period of internment and were imprisoned without a trial. By the late 1970s the protest escalated and became the "dirty protest," after much harassment and humiliation, when prisoners refused to slop out and lived with their own waste smeared on the walls and floors of their cells. That Saturday in Dublin, I became increasingly agitated the longer I had to wait to get across the street. I didn't know what this had to do with us in the south of Ireland. But waiting it out changed my life. A world outside my own in Donnycarney had intruded and I knew I couldn't ignore it. I clearly remember feeling implicated simply because I recognized an internal conflict: If this march was meaningless, why didn't I just barge right through it to get to where I was going? I didn't immediately set off on a journey into political activism but it became increasingly difficult to make judgments and decisions from a position of ignorance, and to do nothing.

Leaving school at seventeen and getting a job in the Department of Labour as a clerical assistant in 1981 (the only fulltime job I ever held in Ireland) sent me further beyond the protective boundary of Donnycarney, which was all I really knew of the world. I had never expected to find that women couldn't do whatever we pleased, like men. When I was very young my mother couldn't explain why letters to her were addressed to Mrs. James G. Maguire, when her name was Christina. Most of my role models had been strong women— my teachers, the nuns who were school principals, along with the women in my family. So, by the time I left school I had an intuitive feminist sensibility and a vague interest in politics. Otherwise I was a socially conservative, non-practicing Catholic, and a non-practicing lesbian. I set off into adulthood with a mess of insecurities and limitless anxieties yet I possessed a healthy reserve of that youthful arrogance and moralism that thrive on a lack of life experience.

I had been working for three months when in May, 1981, Bobby Sands, a prisoner fighting for political status, died after sixty-six days on hunger strike in the H-Blocks of Long Kesh jail in the north of Ireland. Margaret Thatcher was Prime Minister of the United Kingdom, which included the six counties in the north. The struggle for political status ended with the death of ten IRA hunger strikers. Thatcher's response was, "Crime is crime is crime." I had been on a few marches with my brother, John, and thought I was brave wearing a "Smash the H-Blocks" badge at work. I hadn't believed Sands would die and was devastated. It didn't make sense. I went into town with John and stood outside the General Post Office with hundreds of other silent people in the dark. I could not bear to stand there, shivering in the cold in the middle of Dublin, paralyzed, confused and raging. Beyond marching I couldn't figure out what to do.

Along with trying to make sense of what was happening politically I was grappling with how to live true to myself. I told my best friends, Noeleen, Yvonne, and Catherine that I thought I was bisexual. I was nineteen. I don't remember planning to tell them. They took the lie well and said they had already guessed. I wasn't bisexual but I didn't know how to go about being a lesbian: neither did my friends who were straight. So, if a man showed any interest in me, they encouraged me to go for it—better that than nothing! I could have saved us all the awkwardness had I told them I was a lesbian but that took a few more years.

Shortly after my unsuccessful attempt to "come out" to my closest friends at the beginning of the 1980s, an unbelievable thing happened in Donnycarney where I still lived with my family. Noeleen and I were on our way into the city when we spotted a tiny caravan parked outside the church on the Malahide Road. There were general elections coming up and the caravan was the headquarters of Bernadette Devlin's campaign. She was Bernadette McAliskey by then but we always thought of her as Bernadette Devlin, the fierce young Tyrone woman of the Civil Rights movement in the North of Ireland during the late 1960s. We leaned against the yellow-brick wall that surrounded the monstrosity of a church, at the bus stop, mesmerized. The idea that Bernadette McAliskey, whom we idolized, was running for a seat in the south of Ireland, and in our constituency, made us feel so many different emotions from joy and amazement to shock and fear. Even though we were children during the Civil Rights movement we remembered the chaos she had caused. We followed her as she turned the stuffy and bigoted British Parliament upside down, chained herself in protest to the railings outside of 10 Downing Street, punched the liar Reginald Maudling in the face for us all, and generally caused mayhem in the name of justice for Irish Nationalists and Catholics in the north. Amazingly, Bernadette had survived the years in between, including a particularly vicious assassination attempt in 1981. With our hearts in our mouths, Noeleen and I knocked on the caravan door and signed up for election-day duties.

I was reminded of my grandmother's stories about hearing Countess Markievicz speak, and knew how fortunate I was to be working on Bernadette McAliskey's campaign. On the first Election Day (there were three general elections held in the Irish Republic between June 1981 and the end of 1982), Noeleen and I planted ourselves outside our old primary school, the Donnycarney polling station, handing out Bernadette McAliskey election literature. Making our political allegiance so public on our home turf was exciting and nerve-racking. My mother and her sister, my Aunt Charlie, passed us by, arms linked, without a word—I didn't know if it was political or if I'd done something else wrong. After the government fell again, Bernadette campaigned for the second time for a seat in the Irish Parliament. While out canvassing for votes she made a point of visiting my mother to talk to her. She told her that any housewife was more capable of being the Minister for Finance than an elected official given the budgets women had to work with. My mother was charmed and I fancied that she gave Bernadette her number one vote but didn't dare ask.

Working on these election campaigns, even if on the periphery, changed everything. I met people who were activists and radicals, listened to what they had to say, saw them work out strategy and put it into action, and was forced to know what it was about a candidate, and from that, a cause, that made it personally and then politically compelling. I began to learn about the practical aspects of organizing, from talking to people, to writing, and distributing leaflets.

I couldn't have wished for better teachers or role models. I found Bernadette McAliskey to be brilliant, bringing an auditorium of rowdy and disrespectful students to order, telling them to get off their "intellectual arses," to put their privilege to good use. I saw her exhausted, working, thinking, in pain, laughing, and whistling to herself in the conference room while we stuffed manifestos into envelopes at the Crofton Airport Hotel. From my youthful perspective, McAliskey was a flawless, superhuman being who was both intimidating and intriguing. In the many years since those campaigns in Dublin North Central I never experienced that shame and disappointment that often comes with the realization that the hero figure is a human being because Bernadette McAliskey is a rare and remarkable human being. In the 1990s Bernadette immediately supported ILGO when she heard what was going on in New York. She's never marched in the St. Patrick's Day Parade but has said she will make one exception; she'll march when ILGO marches.

It was during McAliskey's second election campaign in 1982 that I met Anne Speed. She was a trade union organizer and a member of the People's Democracy, a small Trotskyist group. At first, I was wary of Anne. She had taken a keen interest in Noeleen and me, and when she wasn't in the middle of discussions about strategy and politics, she'd talk nonstop to us, "educating" us, throwing questions at us to find out who we were. She had a lot of energy, was full of enthusiasm and was a feminist, something I wanted to know about. She encouraged us to attend People's Democracy seminars but they were boring and I didn't see what relevance any of it had to do with day-to-day living. What interested me was doing things, not talking about them or being told what I was supposed to think. Sticking close to Anne meant that I would be active because she wasn't just a talker.

At the time I thought Anne was really old—she was thirty-one. She may have seemed even older because she had so many fantastic stories and had done so much in her life already. She regaled us with memories of the Women's Movement of the 1970s in the Irish Republic— the sit-ins, taking up space in bastions of male privilege. My favorite was the "contraceptive train" story when a group of feminists very publicly "smuggled" contraceptives from the north of Ireland to the south. At the time contraception was illegal in the Republic of Ireland, but not in the British-ruled north. Now I see that Anne's tales completed the link to my grandmother's stories. Anne's memories seemed to pick up where my grandmother left off, bringing me up to speed with the Ireland I inhabited. Listening to and observing Anne helped me figure out that I didn't have to be passive—that I could in fact take political action. It took me longer to realize I could do the same on a personal level. We became good friends. She told me I had a calming effect on her, which I seem to have on many people even though I am not a calm person. I loved Anne's frenetic energy, her directness, and how open she was. I gave her foot rubs, which she loved, and she accepted me the way I was—a quiet, and very guarded young woman. After I left for New York Anne joined the Sinn Féin Party and sat on their national council for a time with Gerry Adams.

I was still living with my family in Donnycarney when a national women's conference took place in the heart of Dublin's inner city in 1984. About a year earlier, the idea for a conference was born at a dinner in Anne's house in Phibsboro. I remember a group of women huddled together around the fire in the damp sitting room. Their excitement fizzed and sparked as ideas and plans were bandied about. I was silent but riveted and found the tension in the room invigorating. Most of these women were a generation older than Noeleen and myself and, like Anne, had been active in the Irish women's movement in the 1970s when gains had been made in areas like employment and violence against women. The backlash came in the 1980s. In the midst of a deepening economic depression the government, in tandem with the Catholic Church, waged a campaign of extraordinary virulence against women's hard-won rights. There were several high-profile examples of how women were being attacked. Eileen Flynn lost her teaching job when she became pregnant while living with a man long separated from his wife. Joanne Hayes was unofficially tried for infanticide during what was supposed to be an inquiry into police procedure. An anti-abortion amendment was added to the Republic's Constitution which gave the life of a woman equal status to that of a fertilized egg. Then came the death of Anne Lovett; she was fifteen when she, and the child she had given birth to, were found dead at a Catholic grotto on the grounds of a church in Leitrim. Seeing a group of women get together for dinner, ending the evening with a plan to address these issues, to fight back, was inspiring. I was learning that this was often how actions or movements began.

"Fighting the Backlash—Defending the Gains," was the theme of the conference. Women traveled to it from all over the country and beyond. Sarah Roelofs, who was a member of the British Labour Party, along with three other English women, rolled out their sleeping bags on the floor of our living room in Donnycarney. My mother made soup and brown bread especially for the visitors and they, particularly Sarah, wolfed down the food with great pleasure. Never before had I seen anyone apply butter so liberally to bread. I made a mental note to buy a couple of extra pounds to put in the fridge. It didn't take me long to realize that these women were lesbians. Because Sarah was a great talker and had an opinion on everything, I hung on to her every word. I followed her around all weekend. It seemed that most sentences out of her mouth began with, "As a lesbian..." After the conference, we began to write to each other and became friends. She sent me cheeky lesbian postcards but I'd not said a word about being a lesbian. When I eventually came out to Sarah she sent three "Congratulations!" cards—one after the other. She told me she'd been waiting a whole year for me to tell her. I was learning to live in a whole new way, but nothing shifted quickly enough, mostly because I was so cautious and anxious. Sometimes the new life I had entered felt as alienating as the one I was trying to leave behind. The scene amongst political activists in Dublin was very confusing. There were Trotskyists, Marxists, Marxist-Leninists, Republicans, Feminists, Lesbian Feminists, Radical Lesbians, and Women for Disarmament, anti-Nukes, Environmentalists, Anarchists, the Militant, Stalinists, and separatists of every hue. Each had its own rhetoric and some were more off-putting and dogmatic than others. At public meetings the same people rose to spout the party line, no matter what the issue was. As a novice I vowed not to join a party, and I never did, preferring to work on campaigns as a free woman. It wasn't due to a lack of conviction that I refused to enlist; it was because I couldn't accept being told what to think as payment for belonging somewhere. I was slowly beginning to change—so slowly I hardly even noticed.

Later in 1984, I moved out of my family home in Donnycarney and into a house in Phibsboro with Rosa Meehan, Hugh Mannion, and Ronan Brady, who had just returned to Dublin after living for many years in London. I was twenty-two. Moving out of my home made it feel possible to truly start coming out. Hugh was gay and Rosa and he were close friends, so I figured they'd be fine with me being a lesbian. Hugh even pointed out that it made our living arrangements more equal, two queers and two straights! I would have to get used to that kind of talk, and way of thinking. Then I set about telling my circle of friends. I called each one and told her over the phone that I had something very important to say but it would have to wait until we met in person. After that all I had to do was find other lesbians. I was afraid of being rejected by lesbians, of not fitting in, and not knowing how to be a lesbian. Within the year I met Siobhán Lennon in the newly formed "Women against Strip Searching in Armagh Jail" group. I came out to her and a bunch of other women, rather awkwardly, after the group's first fund-raising event. Siobhán told me I was very brave and made me see the funny side of my blurting confession and gently teased me, calling me a "baby dyke."

Not long afterward, I fell in love. I was on the lookout for women to join the "Women against Strip Searching" group. Anne Speed introduced me to Marie Honan, who was a student with Anne's partner, Niall Meehan. Because Marie Honan and her friend, Feargha Ní Bhroin, were students, I used what I believed was the only worthwhile ploy, which was to tell them that the group was great fun. Students, in my estimation, were usually a waste of time. So, I was very surprised when they both showed up at the next meeting. Marie was spirited and curious and asked lots of questions so I liked her immediately. Feargha was silent. I fell in love with Feargha.

The fact that Feargha wasn't sure if she was a lesbian was a minor blip. Why she wouldn't hold my hand or even link arms on the street baffled me. Being perceived as a lesbian was very frightening for her, which I didn't understand at the time, having so quickly forgotten how long it had taken me to come out. I was so delighted at last to be in love, it made me bolder. Our relationship was short-lived because Feargha left Dublin for Buffalo, New York, four months later to earn her master's degree. I withdrew and settled into the gloom of nursing my broken heart. Soon after, in 1986, Marie also left Dublin for New York City as she and Feargha had planned long before I met either of them.

Marie and I got to know each other better during her last months in Dublin. She was in the process of coming out. I'd always felt very comfortable with her and was often surprised by what I found myself revealing to her, and even more surprised afterward when I didn't feel humiliated or ashamed for speaking so openly. She thought I was a mess but liked me anyway.

My decision to leave Ireland could hardly be called a decision. Like the job I had worked at for six and a half years as a clerical assistant at the Department of Labour, the offer was made so I took it without giving it a second thought. There was great excitement about a new American lottery for green cards. At work, Betty, one of my colleagues, was giving me a hard time for not being a sport because I thought it was ridiculous. There was a desperation to escape Ireland that was understandable but at the same time, very depressing. We were inundated with news about Americans flying into Dublin to conduct expensive seminars in hotels to advise would-be applicants how best to win one of the prized visas. Some came to collect thousands of applications, which they guaranteed to mail in Washington for a hefty fee. I hadn't the slightest interest in America. In fact it was the one place I had never wanted to visit—Ronald Reagan was President and I'd seen Irish-American tourists in their Aran sweaters and loud plaid pants—that to me was America. To appease Betty, who was a formidable presence in the office, I wrote my name, address, place and date of birth on a sheet of paper and sent it off to a post office box in Washington, DC.

Months later I woke to loud knocking on my bedroom door, "There's a letter from the American embassy here for you," my roommate Ursula shouted from the hall. I had forgotten about the application. However, as soon as Ursula mentioned the American Embassy I knew what it was. I jumped out of bed, tore open the letter and knew immediately that I would be leaving. Nobody in my circle knew anyone else who had been so lucky. My co-worker Betty couldn't get over it—she never let me forget my initial disinterest. I passed all the tests— medical, security, and financial. Kay, a friend at work, gave me a loan of two thousand pounds to put into my bank account in time for my interview at the American Embassy. I transferred the money back to her account a couple of days later. In the packed embassy waiting room, I picked up the phone, raised my right hand in front of a bullet-proof Plexiglas window, and swore to the woman on the other side of the glass that everything I had said was the truth—it felt so American. I had already filled in a form and answered "No" to a question about sexual deviancy because I didn't consider lesbianism deviant. The embassy employee told me to come back at four o'clock that afternoon to collect my papers.

On October 1, 1987, I arrived at John Fitzgerald Kennedy airport in New York. Marie had taken the day off work and was waiting for me in International Arrivals, smoking, when I walked into America.

CHAPTER THREE

Start Spreading The News

"These little town blues, Are melting away, I'll make a brand new start of it, In old New York, If I can make it there, I'll make it anywhere, It's up to you, New York, New York."

– Ebb-Kander

ROCK THE SHAM!

ALMOST A YEAR before the parade Marie and I were late for the meeting. When we discovered we were locked out, we pressed our noses against the tinted glass window of Meriken, a restaurant on Seventh Avenue in Manhattan, to see if there was any sign of life inside. Marie was still on her toes, hands cupped around her eyes to block the sunlight when I knocked on the door. "There's someone coming," she said, jumping away from the window. A handsome Irish man introduced himself as Maurice, pronouncing his name the French way (as opposed to what everyone called him which was Morris), as he ushered us in, while explaining he managed the restaurant and we had a few hours before it opened. Beyond the bar I was surprised to see a large group of men sitting quietly in a circle. However, my gaze was drawn to the only woman in there, Annette Mahon, a woman with a lot of energy and the only obvious spark of life in the room. She sat up, clasped her hands in front of her, and exclaimed, "Thank God, women!" Annette was definitely in charge and she proceeded to gather everyone's attention again to tell us the story of how we all came to be there that Saturday afternoon in April.

One evening Annette and her boyfriend, Niall O'Dowd, publisher of the *Irish Voice*, were dining with two male friends. During the course of the meal one of the men told them he was gay. It turned out that the second dinner guest was also gay.

The news prompted a lively discussion and the possibility that there might be a lot of gay Irish immigrants in New York intrigued them. The *Irish Voice* was still breaking its teeth in the newspaper business and its target audience was the new wave of young immigrants. O'Dowd decided to see what happened if he put an advert in the newspaper. In response to the published notice, nineteen Irish and Irish American gay men, and two Irish lesbians, Marie and me, were now meeting in a Japanese Restaurant in Chelsea on April 28, 1990. Annette sat back, her explanation complete. It was up to the rest of us to decide what we were going to do.

An awkward pause followed Annette's story since nobody was quite sure what came next; somebody suggested we should have a name. A couple of men had already put some thought into it—Cairde USA was their suggestion (cairde is the Irish word for "friends"). This would connect us with Ireland, they explained, because a group already existed there called Cairde, which was a befriending service for people with AIDS. There was also an Irish lesbian group in London called Cairde but they'd never heard of them. "What's the point in having an Irish lesbian and gay group if no one knows what it is?" Marie asked. We both argued, with the agreement of several men, that the subtlety of cairde would be lost in New York. Then Liam (his assumed name in ILGO), an older Irish-American man, wanted to decide which word, gay or lesbian would come first in the title. Marie pointed out that the acronym ILGO sounded better than IGLO and remarked that the pun "I'll go" was better suited to a group of immigrants. The tension in the room eased with laughter at her observation—she had broken the ice. Liam was tenacious all the same. He was afraid if lesbian came first gay men might feel alienated, believing we were a lesbian-only group. (It's funny how this never works in reverse.) His concern seemed a little misplaced, given there were only two lesbians in the room. In the end we settled on the Irish Lesbian & Gay Organization. Our first political decisions were made during the naming process—we would not be a closeted group, and our focus would be on lesbians and gay men of Irish descent. Had Irish and lesbian not been in the title, I wouldn't have gone to a second meeting.

I remember preparing myself for disappointment but the meeting turned out to be lively and productive. The debate about naming ourselves had been contentious and revealing but it got rid of much of our initial shyness and caution. Still, several men did not utter one word and this would be a common occurrence at future ILGO meetings. That Saturday, we began to lay the foundation of our new group. We talked about producing a newsletter and having a party. We decided to participate in the New York Lesbian and Gay Pride Parade in June. Mostly our discussion was about our visibility, or lack of it, in the Irish community. Paul O'Dwyer would contact other Irish groups to let them know about us. He would also ask the *Irish Echo* newspaper, a well-established publication, if they'd print a notice advertising our next meeting. By the end of the afternoon we had a mailing list, someone interested in organizing social events, and Keith Moore volunteered to be our treasurer. We decided to have another meeting on Saturday, May 12, at the Lesbian and Gay Community Services Center.

The first year of the Irish Lesbian & Gay Organization was a journey into a new life. At our second meeting our number almost doubled. We were excited and hungry for information about each other. New friendships blossomed, and roommates and lovers were found. We decided to continue to meet on the first Saturday of every month at The Center. Most of us were so glad to find each other that we spent hours together in cafés or bars after the long Saturday sessions. For most people this was the first time that they had been in the company of other lesbians and gay men who were Irish as many had left Ireland because of their fear of "coming out" or of not being able to live secret lives without being caught. Many refer to this time in ILGO as having a "coming home" feeling. Beside getting to know each other during those first months we also had serious matters to resolve.

From the very start the use of the word political in ILGO's mission statement was a tricky issue. What struck me was that most people were oblivious to the fact that the existence of ILGO was political and for them adding political to our mission statement had some other meaning. Some others, who understood that our name was making a political statement, were not prepared to go any further than that. It seemed that quite a number

PREVIOUS SPREAD: ILGO, formed in April, dances down Fifth Avenue in our first Lesbian and Gay Pride Parade in New York City, in June 1990. *From ILGO files*

of members were worried about turning people off, or of causing "confusion with other political causes such as Northern Ireland" because that's what turned them off. So, most of the tension centered on whether or not ILGO would be a group for those of us who wanted more than a social outlet, personal support and a safe meeting place. Galway man, John Lyons, remembers these early debates clearly, with some irritation: "I thought that the constant bickering over whether it was a social group or a political group was redundant when the two could have co-existed."

Clearly there was confusion about what being political meant. During ILGO's formative months, political was understood as a reference to, or a position on, the North of Ireland; it was not about being lesbian and gay and Irish together. When anyone from the north spoke at a meeting, regardless of the topic, it was assumed they were Provos, or supporters of the Irish Republican Army (IRA). Conversely it was assumed that everyone else held strident anti-Republican positions. Tarlach MacNiallais remembers this with humor as the Green and the Pink split. In fact, ILGO had its share of Irish Republican activists along with American Republicans, Democrats, and the many shades of political opinion in between and beyond these categories. This was normal because all most of us had in common was being Irish and gay. Our understanding of what was political shifted dramatically when we applied to march in the St. Patrick's Day Parade.

ILGO's spring and summer meetings were a hodgepodge of serious debate, play, and laughter as we began to bond. The humor in the air made the group feel safe and relaxed, and for newcomers this was most important—being able to laugh was a huge relief for someone who was terrified or wary. We generally began meetings with introductions. We went around the room telling everyone our names and where we grew up. Finding out where someone was from and where they went to school established an instant profile, mostly in terms of class. There often seemed to be an underlying desperation to make more of a connection, which, unexpectedly, proved to be fun. The game was to find people we knew in common. The small size of the country we left let us do this but the claustrophobia also led most of us to flee, glad to have survived, happier still to have escaped.

Believing we had escaped entirely would have been a mistake. Often, people passed through ILGO who were too afraid to tell us where they were from, or to reveal their last names for fear news would travel, through the immigrant grapevine, to their families and friends in Ireland. This was not an unfounded fear. Most immigrants hook up with family, friends, or someone from their city, town or village upon arrival in New York. This is where contacts for a place to live and work are made. It also creates an instant community for the newcomer as well as the important link to home. But there are rules—being heterosexual is a big one. This traditional welcome was not extended to lesbians and gay men. In fact, it specifically excluded us—there would be no job, no place to live, no relief from loneliness if the community was aware of our homosexuality, and everybody at the meetings knew it. So our options were to either live in the closet in an Irish neighborhood, or as lesbians and gay men with little or no contact with the majority of the Irish in New York.

Knowing there was an Irish gay group was one thing; actually getting to it was another. Keith Moore, from Donegal, remembers being very suspicious, "I thought it was a trap by the Immigration Service." Many ILGO members did not have green cards, so they lived and worked as illegal immigrants. Even though Keith had been in New York since 1985 he'd never met any men at the gay bars who were Irish, nor did he expect to. When he came to ILGO he said, "I was totally amazed that people were sitting around having coffee and normal conversations and that they had grown up in the same country as me, some in the same county." For many, making the transition from the comforts of a world that is familiar, however dismal and oppressive, into a world entirely unknown was extremely lonely and painful.

Peter Kellegher from Cavan caught my attention at his very first meeting. I could see he was terrified. He sat without moving a muscle and escaped before anyone had a chance to talk to him. He never said a word but he came back, month after month, and sat and observed. He wrote a letter called "A New Life" for one of our newsletters:

> *A couple of months ago I saw in the Irish Voice that ILGO was*
> *formed. I don't know how to describe my reaction. I just could not*
> *believe it! I didn't write down the phone number, I just kept the*
> *whole paper. ... Saying the word "Gay" out loud was difficult*
> *for me. ... I can't tell you enough how great it felt to have told*
> *someone else. ... All my life I hated the weekend and couldn't wait*
> *'til it was over. ... Now I can't wait 'til the weekend comes.*

After months of silently attending meetings Peter arrived one Saturday, transformed. His hair was different, slicked back off his face, and he wore a sleeveless T-shirt and tight blue jeans. Before then he seemed to be hiding himself, never showing his arms, or his face. Now, he looked beautiful, long-legged, lean, tanned, and relaxed. For the first time, he seemed comfortable in his own skin. I remember thinking if this was all ILGO ever did, it was worthwhile. Peter and Keith became pals and moved into an apartment together in the Irish neighborhood of Bainbridge in the Bronx.

Lucy Lynch was also living in Bainbridge with her girlfriend, Trish, when she saw the notice about ILGO's first meeting in the newspaper. "I nearly went through the roof with excitement," she recalls. "Immediately I wrote off and said that Trish and I were up here in the Bronx and would be delighted if a group started. Trish was mad that I mentioned her name without asking her but I got so excited that I didn't even think."

I'd spent my first few years in New York trying to find my feet in a strange city. My biggest worry had been finding a job but when ILGO began I had been working as a temporary paralegal for several years. Marie had asked me if I'd like to share an apartment with her when she heard my plan to move to New York—I was so relieved that I wouldn't have to look for a place on my own and of course agreed to share with Marie. After three months living together in the Park Slope area of Brooklyn, we could no longer resist each other and became lovers. At ILGO's beginning we had been together almost two and a half years. My younger sister Cathy lived in Brooklyn too, working as a live-in nanny while she put herself through college. Marie, Cathy, and Paul O'Dwyer, whom I'd hardly known in Dublin but hooked up with in New York, made up our Irish family.

Even with my sister Cathy and Marie in New York the culture shock had been intense. The geography of the city baffled me (I couldn't understand why nobody could tell me where the center of everything, "town" was). The subway system was daunting, and the size of everything, from the buildings to the portions of food, was overwhelming. I went to ACT UP meetings with Marie and Paul and was utterly intimidated; in Ireland hundreds of activists got together for conferences, not weekly meetings. And everyone at ACT UP seemed self-assured and confident even though most of them were gay. I had never seen lesbians or gay men like these before; instead of being excited I felt defensive. I knew I didn't fit in and it was painful. In hindsight I see there was more than culture shock at work; homophobia played a substantial role in my alienation. Seeing lesbians and gay men like those at ACT UP made me face the fact that I wasn't as comfortable being a lesbian as I had thought. The longer I lived in New York, and the more time I spent with lesbians, I began to slowly see the possibility of living more openly as a lesbian, without shame.

When Paul called to tell Marie and me about the notice he'd seen in the paper, I knew I'd been waiting for something like ILGO for a while. I was tired of wandering and looking for a place to belong. I wanted to put down roots. My instinct had been to avoid Irish people and all things Irish but I desperately needed a connection with Ireland. I wanted more than friendship—I wanted a sense of community and ILGO filled that need. Clearly, ILGO had the potential to be my link to the life I had left. It was where I could continue my activism. The prospect of combining my years of experience in Ireland with what I had learned so far in New York, to help create something new, roused me.

Marie and Paul had been excited too in the early days but both had very different opinions about what they expected or wanted from ILGO. Paul is much cooler in retrospect than I remember him when ILGO began. He keeps his distance and describes his feelings about the founding of the organization this way; "The earth didn't move and I didn't think, Oh hooray! I'm in a room full of Irish queers. I didn't feel any need to be validated by the group." While Marie had been very interested in people's stories she inevitably got bored with the threads that bound us together—the rural-urban divide, the Catholic church, and coming out to your family. "That had limited appeal to me," she remarked and explained further, "It wasn't enough to find common ground with people, there had to be something more." Marie didn't have to wait too long.

On Sunday, June 23, 1990 ILGO lined up on a side street off Fifth Avenue, in blistering heat, to march in our first New York Lesbian and Gay Pride Parade. We had a new hand-painted banner and new badges (a green Ireland with a pink triangle transposed over it) to hand out. Most people wore it upside down or sideways because they didn't recognize the shape of Ireland! Kevin, in hot pink shorts, stood waiting in the sun with his bagpipes, ready to lead us into the West Village.

This was the day Catch Keeley joined ILGO. She marched onto the avenue near the New York Public Library, stood behind the banner and dramatically announced, "I'm coming out." Marie and I had met Catch on a women's rowing team at South Street Seaport. We thought she was a lesbian but we never said anything directly. Instead we dropped her pieces of information about ILGO. Ironically—because she was supposedly straight—Catch did a lot of volunteer work at ASTRAEA, at the time a national lesbian organization, and she believed that lesbians there accepted her because she was a feminist. She decided to march with ILGO, not ASTRAEA, when she came out because she wasn't merely going as a supporter of lesbians and gays anymore. As she explained, "To march as a lesbian I felt it would be more committed to go with the Irish group."

Even though Marie had marched in the Gay Pride Parade before, with ACT UP, the idea of marching with ILGO made her nervous. Marie was born and raised in Clonlara, a small rural village in County Clare, where she bided her time until she could escape. Since leaving her home, at seventeen, she had treasured the stark contrast offered by the cities she inhabited and especially appreciated the anonymity. She had come to New York filled with romantic notions—musicians playing soulful saxophones from rusty fire-escapes—and was lured by the fantasy that she could be as free and wild as a cowboy. New York could almost have been the perfect place but now, in reality, everything was different. To publicly identify herself as an Irish lesbian made Marie feel vulnerable.

The impact of ILGO's presence in the Lesbian and Gay Pride Parade wasn't limited to ILGO members—it became very clear that spectators, and mostly gay ones, were genuinely surprised by our existence. The idea that there were Irish people who were lesbians or gay men seemed funny or odd for some reason. I laughed the first few times I heard, "Irish lesbians and gays! No way!" But the friendly jibes became tiresome, and I began to feel angry. That some people thought the existence of Irish lesbians and gay men was a joke haunted me. I wondered if it was Italian lesbians and gay men, would it have seemed so funny? Why was being gay and Irish so odd? I didn't have the answers. When it came to St. Patrick's Day few people were laughing.

ILGO's first newsletter was full of parade buzz and it was in this issue that the St. Patrick's Day Parade was formally introduced:

> *The Irish Lesbian & gay Organization is only a few*
> *months old. But some quick stepping got ILGO into the*
> *Gay Pride lineup for the 21st annual parade. (A question*
> *already raised at meetings is whether such efforts will see*

ROCK THE SHAM!

this new Irish group in the 230th St. Patrick's Day Parade,
or will the establishment attempt to force Irish lesbians
and gays to remain in the closet.)

I don't remember when we began talking about the St. Patrick's Day Parade but I suspect it was after this publication rather than before. Liam, the author of the report, was one of the more closeted Irish-American men in the group, the same man who fought against "Lesbian" appearing first in the group's name. Nevertheless, I got the distinct impression that he, along with a few others, wanted to mold and define ILGO's "issues" while never having to risk any overt or public participation in the work of the group.

By the end of July we had $167.75 in our bank account and our membership had grown to a grand total of seventy-one—fourteen women and fifty-seven men. Our funds were mostly generated at the monthly meetings where we set aside rent for The Center's room and asked for a few dollars extra to cover photocopying and postage—we didn't spend money on anything else. We never instituted a membership fee or specific membership requirements so anyone who attended a meeting, and wanted to be on our mailing list, was considered a bona fide member. We assumed everyone was either Irish, or of Irish descent, and lesbians or gay men, and on occasion, bisexual and transgendered. Not everyone who came to meetings signed the mailing list because they were afraid that receiving notices in the mail from ILGO would cause suspicion among their roommates or family. We learned quickly that we had to be very careful. Making phone calls was nerve-racking because it was hard to know whether or not it was okay to leave a message without having to speak in code. Usually the messages we left on answering machines were cryptic and never mentioned ILGO. One member, a friend of Liam's who used the alias "Conor," went through the minutes before a Saturday meeting and deleted every occurrence of his real name.

Throughout our first year we spent a lot of time trying to figure out what people wanted from the group and where problems might arise. We experimented with the structure of our Saturday meetings. We monitored where new people heard about us, which was mostly through the *Irish Voice*, with some people coming through *Outweek*, a weekly lesbian and gay news magazine in the city. We put together a questionnaire to gauge members' expectations and were disappointed by the dismal number of responses. The most active members tended to be immigrants with the numbers split evenly gender-wise. There were rumblings about how unfriendly the immigrants were towards Irish-Americans, and there was a grain of truth to this assertion and no simple explanation. Paul got very hot and bothered every time the topic was discussed. "When this group started it was an Irish group, not an Irish-American group," he said. "I perceived my identity to be very different to the identity of the Irish-Americans." He conceded, "I didn't know why Irish-Americans wanted to come to the group. When it happened I had very mixed feelings."

The flip side was that many immigrants felt the Irish-American members were patronizing and came with all the usual stereotypes, thinking we were stupid and naive, but cute. At one meeting Ed erupted, as he tended to, and bellowed that we were all just off the boat, coming here barefoot and without green cards. This of course is an extreme example. But just as some Irish-Americans felt left out, the Irish-born were particularly sensitive to being patronized and romanticized.

Father Bernard Lynch noticed something else. "My initial impression was how politically naive everybody was," he said. "I was hearing these people from my own country talk about things that were just wonderful, but without any real idea of the price and cost that was going to be asked of us, were we to bring these into fruition." The Saint Patrick's Day Parade was discussed at our fifth meeting on August 4, 1990. Our minutes are sparse on the topic:

> *St. Patrick's Day Parade: Volunteers to work on the parade are;*
> *Bernard Lynch, Anne Maguire and Marie Honan. Contact KH*
> *who knows the application process. Bernard suggested that we*
> *contact LAMBDA for advice before applying.*

I barely remember the discussion but do know that I thought it was a funny idea. The "KH" mentioned in the minutes had been a member of the AOH parade committee, and was still a member of the Ancient Order of Hibernians, so he could tell us how to formally apply to march. Keith had already informed the mayor's European and Gay liaison staff of ILGO's existence. My job was to get in touch with LAMBDA Legal Defense and Education Fund, a lesbian and gay legal advocacy organization, to see if they had any advice for us if we decided to apply to march in the Irish parade because Bernard thought it was a good idea. I called and spoke to several people who informed me that someone qualified at LAMBDA would call back—they never did, not until it was too late.

Unlike the solid "Yes" mandate for marching in the Lesbian and Gay Pride Parade, the opinions in ILGO were wide and varied on the topic of St. Patrick's Day. Some thought it was a ridiculous idea; others believed it was a dangerous plan. A handful of members were furious we were even considering associating with the St. Patrick's Day Parade for a number of reasons—it was conservative, triumphalistic, boring, and militaristic. However, most seemed indifferent to the idea. I was on for applying to march up Fifth Avenue on St. Patrick's Day, superficially at first, because I thought it might be exciting and fun. Then I remembered ILGO's reception at the Lesbian and Gay Pride Parade and knew it was important that we assert ourselves with as much vigor in the Irish community as we had been doing in the lesbian and gay community. But the parade was by no means high on ILGO's agenda.

After the initial euphoria I associated with the founding of ILGO, the prospect of our monthly meetings started to make me feel queasy. A deep sense of alienation was starting to gnaw at my enthusiasm because I didn't know if I could stand being with the men in the group. Whether in good humor or with a competitive edge, the intensity of the male bonding and machismo that dominated and drove the meetings became oppressive. At first it wasn't such a surprise because the bulk of the membership was male and I chalked it up to excitement that would eventually wear itself out. However, the ritual continued to be the main focus of every meeting and I began to despair. I had not expected to feel excluded by the men in the group. I was angry because anything proposed by lesbians in ILGO was passed, with little thoughtful debate, only because it wasn't considered seriously. Most of my past activism had been with feminists, or in women's groups, and when I worked within mixed campaigns they were always action-orientated; there were tasks to be done and we all pulled together to do them.

Marie and Catch were getting fed up too. "I was used to people being more advanced politically than I was and I thought people would be well informed about Irish and gay politics. It wasn't like that at all," Marie said. Catch was moved to finding a voice for herself in the ILGO environment. "It was out of anger, boredom, and frustration that I had to learn to speak. It was really about shutting the men up."

Of course there were men in ILGO who took both the group and the lesbians in the group very seriously. The lesbians and gay men who felt responsible tried everything to keep the membership happy. We set up smaller groups, like the Lesbian Caucus and the Men's Discussion Group. We cajoled suggestions and ideas out of disgruntled and surly members. Some people wanted more structure and a sense of accountability—they wanted a president. We carried a chalkboard to one of our Saturday meetings so Marie could draw a diagram of her proposal for the group's new structure. We organized discussions, presentations, and invited guest speakers. We planned parties and small fundraisers. We designed and ordered T-shirts. We listened with much patience to nay-sayers and gushers alike.

Essentially, ILGO was like any other group—full of contradictions. We had our ups and downs that first year, and we also had some remarkable moments throughout our time together. The best were making new friends, watching people transform, feeling safe, and laughing together. My particular favorite ILGO activity of all time was our céilí s, which were so much fun. It never mattered what had happened at the previous meeting because the céilí was always about enjoyment and laughter. Once we had a middle-aged couple travel from Long Island to do the calling. Before we started they sweetly asked if we would be offended if they played the "Gay Gordons." Then they produced a bag of neck ties for the men to wear—we all burst out laughing it was so bizarre and it was even funnier because they did not get it. But my sister Cathy was the céilí queen and did most of our calling through the years. The worst of ILGO was seeing people in distress and finding out that some people were devious or mean-spirited. We had moments of great empathy and love along with moments of fierce anger, frustration, and disappointment. I found it impossible to shed my childish wish for simplicity and serenity, and in ILGO, I wished for a coming together of people with joy in their hearts and goodwill towards all, none of which I possess easily myself. Nonetheless, there were times during our first year, despite our frailties and failings, when being in ILGO was simply good.

And while we struggled through these ordinary growing pains there was a storm brewing of which none of us was aware. ILGO was about to burst from quiet obscurity into a public spotlight that we could never have imagined in our wildest dreams, or our worst nightmares.

CHAPTER FOUR

Wheeling And Dealing

"The political arena leaves one no alternatives, one must be either a dunce or a rogue."

– Emma Goldman

NEW YORK POST

LATE CITY FINAL

40¢ in New York City 50¢

AY, MARCH 7, 1991 / ★★ R Sunny, 50s today; clear, upper 20s tonight / Details, Page 2

ST. PADDY'S
DAY
GAY
FUROR

The Irish Lesbian and Gay Organization was told there's no room for th

Homosexua
is barred fr
marching ir

SADDAM
CRUSHING

FORD
NCAA
IS F
Beaten by St. F

ROCK THE SHAM!

O N OCTOBER 5, 1990 Marie sent a letter to Francis Beirne, Chairman of the St. Patrick's Day Parade and Celebration Committee, informing him that the Irish Lesbian and Gay Organization wished to be affiliated with the 1991 St. Patrick's Day Parade. On October 22, 1990 the Ancient Order of Hibernians responded:

Dear Marie Honan:
I am in receipt of your letter dated October 5, 1990. Under all the rules of the St. Patrick's Day Parade and Celebration Committee, all applications for affiliation are submitted to the Credentials Committee. Pursuant to said rule, your letter has been forwarded to said committee.
If you have any other questions, please do not hesitate to write.

Very truly yours,
Francis P. Beirne
Parade Chairman

Now it was official—we had submitted our application and it was being processed. Several people in ILGO claimed that marching in the St. Patrick's Day Parade was their brilliant idea—after the fact, of course. The only person I remember expressing profound concern about the plan was Bernard Lynch: "I knew at a level we were taking our lives in our hands." At the time I thought he was being melodramatic. Bernard believed we were about to embark on a journey that would pit us against one of the most homophobic institutions in the Western world—the New York Archdiocese of the Catholic Church, with John Cardinal O'Connor at its helm. The rest of us paid little attention to Bernard's warning. Undaunted, we waited to hear from the Credentials Committee.

We began to talk about how we felt about marching, or not. Catch saw the endeavor in terms of visibility. She explained, "It was about letting people know that there are Irish lesbians. I didn't want any other women or young girls to have to go through what I went through. I was ambivalent about the parade itself but as an issue it was a really important thing to pursue." In fact, we all felt some of Catch's ambivalence, so the parade became a topic at every monthly meeting.

By mid-November, 1990 we'd heard nothing from the Credentials Committee so I called the Hibernian Parade Chairman, Frank Beirne. This was the only time we ever spoke to each other. He told me we would indeed be hearing from the Credentials Committee. I asked if he had any idea when that might be. He didn't know. When I reported back to ILGO, Keith said he would call Dr. Marjorie Hill, Mayor Dinkins' Lesbian and Gay community liaison officer, to tell her about our plan to march in the St. Patrick's Day Parade. She suggested he keep Debra Pucci, the City's European-American liaison, up-to-date on ILGO's progress. By the time the AOH responded to Marie's letter, she was traveling through Guatemala.

After a year of indecision Marie had finally quit her job at Phillip Morris, where she had worked since she had come to New York in 1986. A month before Marie set off on her travels I handed in my notice at Simpson Thacher & Bartlett LLP where I had worked as a temporary paralegal for several years, because I was bored. I was making a living by cleaning apartments and doing three overnight shifts in a shelter for homeless women while I looked for a permanent job; I was depressed, as I had been on and off for most of my life, but now our relationship of three years was suffering. Marie tried to get me to go to therapy but I refused, not believing there was any need—I felt the way I'd always felt. I knew Marie was unhappy but I wasn't aware I was too. Marie wanted to get away. I admired her get up and go and encouraged her plan to travel. Secretly, Marie believed I wanted to get rid of her. Perhaps I did, unconsciously knowing something was wrong and not wanting to deal with it because that would mean dealing with my deep depression and almost total withdrawal from her. We went out to the airport together and as soon as she disappeared through the departure gate, tears streaming down her face, I wanted her to come home. We hadn't been apart for more than a couple of weeks until then, so the prospect of several months was unbearable—I responded, as usual, by shutting down even further. Marie cried non-stop all the way to Mexico.

The Hibernian's letter arrived on February 1, 1991. ILGO's application to march was declined due to "physical and municipal restrictions." We didn't know what this meant so we wanted an explanation. I called Frank Beirne. He didn't call back. I wrote to John P. Clarke, the letter's author, and asked for clarification, and when there was no response Keith called the mayor's office to tell Marjorie Hill and Debra Pucci. I called LAMBDA, the gay lawyers, for the last time, and again nobody "qualified" returned the call.

ILGO's plans for celebrating our first St. Patrick's Day together were well under way. Whether or not we marched in the parade, it would be an important day for us. There would be Irish nights at gay dance clubs in Manhattan. Fergal Doherty was busy chasing down bureaucrats for permits so we could run an outdoor céilí at Sheridan Square. It wasn't until our Saturday meeting on February 2 that we decided to meet outside of the regular monthly meeting in case we needed to take care of any parade business. In fact, we were so naïve, we weren't certain that anti-gay discrimination was the reason our application to march had been declined. We were still hoping to have the matter of "physical and municipal restrictions" explained to us. Then Keith heard from the mayor's office—ILGO was on the parade's waiting list. This was the first we'd heard of any waiting list so we sent a letter to

PREVIOUS SPREAD: Shocking! Horrifying! Yet, incredibly exciting—ILGO's first front page! The *Post*, as understated as always, on March 7, 1991.

the Hibernians asking for details. As usual, we never heard back. It seemed that City Hall had access to people who knew what was going on. The mayor's people managed to arrange a meeting between the AOH parade committee and ILGO.

The March 6 edition of the *Irish Voice* published the first of thousands of stories about ILGO and the St. Patrick's Day Parade in New York. It was a tiny piece, only a few paragraphs, documenting the story thus far and telling about the upcoming meeting at City Hall on Thursday, March 7. Keith and I would attend for ILGO along with two members of the AOH and some city representatives. The parade was ten days away.

Just before midnight that Wednesday, my friend John Lucas called. Because it was so late I was expecting to hear Marie's voice. She had been trying to get through for days but all I ever heard was "Anne!" and then the line would go dead. John was calling from a pay phone in the East Village. "I just knew it would be you causing all this trouble!" he declared. "Pardon me?" I replied, perplexed. "It's all over the front page of the newspaper," he hooted down the phone. "ST. PADDY'S DAY GAY FUROR!" blared across the entire front page of the *New York Post*. John was reading the early edition of Thursday's paper.

A *Post* reporter had called me at work but I wasn't aware that an article, never mind a front page headline, was in the works. In part this was my own naiveté but the reporter, Joe Nicholson, had told me he didn't think the story merited a mention beyond the *Irish Voice*. I couldn't match John's excitement so when I hung up the phone I sat staring at the receiver, trying to figure out what this news meant. It was too late to call anyone else. I wished Marie was home, not on her way—she was due back in five days. At one in the morning I called Paul. He was still up. I asked if he could guess what might be on the front page of the Post. He couldn't think of anything besides a new Gulf War nightmare. He was astonished when I told him.

On my way to work the next morning I picked up the *New York Post* and felt a thrill of excitement and trepidation at once. Inside, the headline stated, "GAY GROUP GETS IRISH UP OVER PARADE!" Most of the article was background information and Frank Beirne was quoted saying, "Hibernians don't discriminate." I decided to make photocopies at work to send home to my friends and family because they'd get a kick out of it. Little did I know as I turned the key of Prelinger Associates, my brand-new job, that this was only the beginning of the story. I never did get to post any photocopies of Nicholson's story home because it was about to become my life.

Eileen Clancy shared the downstairs apartment of the house Marie and I lived in in Brooklyn and we had become friendly. It was through Eileen, who worked for Rick Prelinger, that I got my new job working 30 hours a week in the office of Rick's film archive. Rick was out of town on business and Eileen was on vacation in Puerto Rico. I could hear the phone ringing as I fumbled outside the office door with keys, coffee, and the newspaper with the big headline. The red light on the answering machine was flashing furiously when I got in. I pressed the "Play" button. There were a couple of business calls but most of the messages were from newspaper reporters and local television networks wanting information about ILGO and the parade. I called Keith. He said media calls were coming through the receptionist at his job so everyone in his office wanted to know what was going on. Until then nobody at work knew Keith was gay. However, with the receptionist shouting, "Keith! It's Channel 11 about the parade," he had to tell them what was going on.

Most of that day was spent on the phone. Keith and I touched base every hour and as the day wore on he sounded more frazzled. We were in constant communication with the rest of ILGO and were set to meet at Daisy's Restaurant that night after the AOH meeting at City Hall. We didn't understand why this story was generating so much interest. I ran around the office in a state of frenzy, pacing up and down, talking myself through my work, writing lists and notes to make sure everything was covered, and cursing every time the phone rang. How was I going to explain this to my new boss, Rick? That afternoon he finally got through and told me the phone had been very busy. I blabbed the entire story and Rick seemed excited, not angry. He said not to worry about anything because what I was doing was important.

Keith called at about 3 o'clock to tell me he couldn't face the strain of the meeting at City Hall that evening. He had already spoken to Paul who agreed to come instead. Then the mayor's office called with a change of venue. They had been inundated by the press all day and didn't want reporters swarming all over us that night. Evan Wolfson, a lawyer from LAMBDA called. He claimed it would be a disaster to go to the meeting without him. I explained there weren't going to be any lawyers. Then he said ILGO had no right to go traipsing off to meetings with city officials on our own. That made me angry. I informed him that ILGO had been trying to get advice from LAMBDA for months and nobody had returned our calls until now, when we were in the news. "Opportunist!" I spat but the phone was already dead.

I felt stoned stepping out onto 14th Street's greasy pavement in the meat market district where Rick's offices were located. What a strange day it had been, and there was still much ahead. Keith, Paul and I got off the train at City Hall and stopped for a moment to get our bearings. Keith came as moral support. As we walked down Chambers Street toward Broadway I heard my name being called out. Without saying anything to each other the three of us decided to ignore it. But the woman's voice continued calling "Anne! Anne Maguire!" I said, "Keep walking." Keith and I had had enough reporters for one day. When we heard the woman's footsteps catch up with us, we stopped. I knew from the hollow sound on concrete that she was wearing high heels, maybe stilettos. It was Rosanna Scotto, a well-known local television news reporter, who stood behind us with a cameraman. She must have been waiting near the original meeting location at City Hall. (I never asked but was curious how she knew we were ILGO. Were we so obviously Irish, or clearly gay, or just out of place in the middle of government buildings?) I gave my first television interview. Paul and Keith stood shoulder to shoulder a few inches from me, smiling and nudging each other.

ROCK THE SHAM!

"We have to go now," I said. We half-skipped and half-ran to our destination, laughing and giggling at the oddity of being chased by a television crew in New York City.

The meeting was a dud. Dick Joyce and Bart Murphy were there for the AOH and of course they had a lawyer, or an observer, as they called Jim Lombard. Joyce remained completely silent. Lombard was a boor. It was Bart Murphy who did most of the talking. He repeatedly assured us that we were not being discriminated against; there simply wasn't room for us. The AOH had their rules and regulations and they never made exceptions. He revealed to us that there were homosexuals in the AOH; in fact some were leaders of various county associations. The room was too small and stuffy and much as Marjorie Hill, of the mayor's office, tried, nothing was being resolved. Every time we asked for solid proof of their claim of non-discrimination, Murphy, jittery throughout, referred to the AOH rules and regulations. Paul asked to see the waiting list and Murphy pulled out a couple of legal-sized sheets of paper with hand-written and typed names on them. The Irish Lesbian & Gay Organization was number 31 on the list and there were a couple of groups after us. Murphy assured us ILGO would march when a place presented itself, which might take a few years. Then Marjorie Hill suggested we have a joint press conference, ILGO and the AOH together. "For what?" I asked. Nothing had been cleared up. In fact Paul and I were far more skeptical about the Hibernian's explanation for ILGO's exclusion from the parade after the meeting than we had been beforehand.

Paul and I had been thrown together at the last minute to meet with the AOH and City officials and for whatever reason we were a pretty good duo. I don't think we were conscious of how we were working—we certainly couldn't have been that very first meeting—but his style and curiosity and love of argument and debate made my job so easy. I had the luxury of observing, something I'd been doing since I was a child, and then of analyzing what was going on. Paul could have worked with many people in this exact situation where I could not.

Just before we left Paul suggested the AOH allow everyone on the waiting list to march, which would resolve the dispute. The mayor's people were desperate and jumped at the idea, and the Hibernians said they would take it back to their leaders. The meeting ended with an agreement not to talk to the press. A follow-up meeting was set for Monday, March 11. Keith, Paul, and I headed for Daisy's diner where ILGO waited to hear the news. The 230th St. Patrick's Day Parade was a little over a week away.

The next day at work, journalist Máire Crowe called to tell me she didn't think the parade news would be confined to New York. Perhaps Máire sensed our lack of awareness—she was certainly looking out for us and later on Máire and I became good friends. She suggested we prepare for the media in Ireland to swarm all over the story. This changed everything and led to huge personal upheavals for many of us in ILGO. The thousands of miles of ocean between New York and Ireland were no longer going to be our closet.

Suddenly many of us were faced with making a rushed, life-altering decision—whether or not to "come out" to our families in Ireland. My parents knew I was a lesbian but I had to let them know to expect some publicity. Lucy had already been through the mill with her family because she told them she was going to be interviewed for the *Sunday Tribune* article Máire Crowe was writing. Lucy's mother knew her daughter was a lesbian but the prospect of it being public knowledge made a big difference. Her mother called her up and said, "Don't do it or I'll never talk to you again." Lucy didn't expect this response. "Our family had been involved in political stuff in the north for years. Two of my brothers were in jail so I didn't understand why they couldn't understand that I was standing up for my rights."

Paul had stepped into the role of spokesperson for ILGO without giving it a second thought. But Paul's parents did not know they had a gay son. He called home and tried to tell his mother. He asked if she'd heard about the trouble with the parade. When she said she had, Paul told her he was involved with the group. His mother was incredulous. She wanted to know, why of all the Irish groups in New York, Paul had chosen to get involved with ILGO. She asked if he was aware that everyone would now think he was gay. He hung up without being able to tell his mother that, in fact, he was—it was heart-breaking to see him so upset.

After ILGO marched in the Lesbian and Gay Pride Parade in June, I sent a copy of an *Irish Voice* photo of the group to my parents and never heard anything back, which was not unusual. Now, in March, I had to ring to let them know what was up. My father answered the phone. I was excited telling him about the hoopla in New York, when, out of the blue the conversation turned sour. My father asked me how I expected ordinary people to understand what ILGO was about given the way we looked in that newspaper photograph, wearing sunglasses and looking like a bunch of fascists! And I was so proud of that? I froze and then got off the phone fast.

I didn't understand my father's reaction. It didn't make me angry—instead it frightened me. I wasn't sure how I was going to get through the parade ordeal but knew not to risk speaking to my father again, unless I was prepared to quit. I hadn't realized how precarious I felt about being a lesbian, particularly in terms of my parents' approval or disapproval. Before this phone call I hadn't acknowledged how scary this parade business might become. I was very conscious of how it might affect my parents. I guessed the worst scenario for them would be if everyone they knew found out they had a lesbian daughter. In my view back then, this was tantamount to "outing" them. In a letter I tried to explain why I felt ILGO was important, how the parade story had happened, and how crucial it was for ILGO not to run for cover.

Ultimately, by not talking to my father until after the parade, I had made my decision. In theory, it wasn't a difficult decision—this was my life and I had to fight to live it. In reality, I was aware of the great risk of loss involved. But so many people in ILGO were risking everything. Two weeks earlier most of these women and men would never have considered telling their parents they were gay. Two weeks earlier most people in ILGO were still getting used to their new lives themselves. Now, regardless of the pain, and the rejection, the decision to "come out" was being made. It took a lot of faith in people, and a lot of guts, and that's a thing that's rarely acknowledged—how courageous lesbians and gay men are.

Marie was due to arrive back at Kennedy Airport at 3:30 PM on Monday, March 11. She had no idea what she was returning to. The house in Brooklyn was squeaky clean for her arrival. Before leaving the apartment, I left a copy of the *New York Post* strategically placed on the bed as a surprise. The reporter, Joe Nicholson, was keeping busy and in a later story he reported that the AOH also refused to allow children who used wheelchairs into the parade, which caused further uproar. I would have to concentrate on keeping quiet about it all on the journey home from the airport.

It was bitterly cold and I was late. I was excited and anxious about seeing Marie again. Maybe it would be strained between us because we'd been out of each other's company for so long. In the past, being separated for two weeks made me feel shy and awkward. Marie wrote while she traveled, telling me how much she missed me and how she wished I was with her. I had a pile of letters from Guatemala, in blue airmail envelopes with hearts drawn on them, which I used to read over and over before going to sleep at night. When I got to Arrivals, I ran through the terminal, my stomach churning by now, and couldn't find Marie anywhere. I waited by the information desk listening to the paging system direct her there. Marie would be furious and worse, disappointed. I was pacing, hoping she hadn't already headed for home when I saw her. She was tanned and freckled, and her hair was bleached blond from the sun—she looked gorgeous. She wore no socks, just a pair of dusty leather sandals. I moved swiftly across the terminal floor and hugged her; she was angry because I was late. She knew all about the parade, she said, because she had called Paul to find out where I was.

When we got home, we drank pots of tea, smoked cigarettes, and caught up with each other. Marie didn't stay cross for long. Her pleasure was obvious as she displayed the treasures from her journey, unwrapping each item slowly, one by one, and delicately placing shells, tiny ceramic animals, soap, a piece of embroidery in my palm to admire. I felt shy about touching her but I liked us being so physically close, hearing her breathe while she explained where each memento came from. I was still distracted though because of the parade. I couldn't concentrate on what Marie was telling me. I wanted time to be tender and attentive but I had a meeting to go to. Marie gave me a pair of silver, heart-shaped earrings, which I put on, loving their little fat shape dangling from my ears. I didn't take them off again until the parade was over. They made me feel close to Marie; all I had to do was touch the cool silver with my fingers and I felt loved.

Although just off the plane, Marie took on the parade work immediately. Because everyone was so caught up in the furor, she never got to talk about her trip properly. Marie was upset about the *Sunday Tribune* article that Máire Crowe was writing because she wanted to contribute, but was too concerned about her parents' reaction, and was angry at herself for letting that stop her. Her mother and father didn't know she was a lesbian but they knew we lived together. A couple of days later Marie's mother called to say she had heard me on the radio in Ireland. She wanted to know if Marie had been there with me. Marie told her she had. Then Marie sat down and wrote a letter home. Her mother called as soon as she got it and told Marie she loved her and only wished she had known that her only daughter and youngest child was a lesbian earlier so she might have helped in some way.

Letters were being written in other quarters too. Shortly after our first meeting with the Hibernians, Mayor Dinkins wrote a most eloquent letter to Frank Beirne, Chairman of the St. Patrick's Day parade. In the letter he addressed the discrimination faced by the Irish in New York in the past and appealed to Beirne to empathize with the fact that bias crimes against lesbians and gay men in New York ranked highest in the country. He had an offer, following Paul's suggestion at the City Hall meeting:

> *I understand that there is a waiting list of some forty organizations*
> *to gain entry to the parade. I also understand that a waiting list was*
> *needed because the City had restricted the duration of the parade.*
> *After some thought and discussion with the concerned City agencies,*
> *we have decided to extend this grand parade for one hour.*

The mayor acknowledged the additional work this offer might entail and offered the services of City Hall to ensure its smooth execution which would include providing additional volunteers if necessary. At last ILGO understood what "physical and municipal restrictions" meant and it did make sense as did the mayor's offer. We hoped, with the elimination of the city's restrictions everyone on the waiting list would get to march. We thought we'd hear at our next meeting with the Hibernians. However, ignoring our previous pact of not talking to the media, the AOH made a statement for the Sunday papers, saying the mayor's proposal was unacceptable.

The next evening, on Monday, March 11, Paul and I were faced with three new AOH people at the second City Hall meeting. The parade's Vice-Chairman, John Dunleavy, was present along with Margaret O'Rourke, the Recording Secretary, and Jim Mulvihill, a past President of the County AOH. By now Paul and I were familiar with the mayor's liaisons. Debra Pucci of European-American affairs was a tough, no-nonsense woman, with a good sense of humor. The Gay Liaison, Dr. Marjorie Hill, was just as tough but appeared more relaxed. The meeting was very tense. These Hibernians were openly hostile compared to the lightweights who had represented them the previous Thursday. Margaret O'Rourke told us we would never march if we ever sued them—it was AOH policy. Suing the AOH had never entered our heads. Every time Jim Mulvihill spoke his color rose to a deep purple which made his watery eyes seem bluer than they were. He didn't really speak—he spat out his words. Paul passed me a note on a yellow legal pad, "I hope he has a heart-attack."

ROCK THE SHAM!

John Dunleavy was cold. He said very little except to repeat their consistent position that there was no room for negotiation, making it perfectly clear they were not interested in a solution. Not once during the entire meeting did any of the Hibernians say the words "lesbian," "gay" or even "homosexual"—instead they referred to us as "you people." Later, it was reported in the *Irish Voice* that there was no shortage of "queer" jokes at their Sunday meeting where they had decided not to extend the parade for an additional hour so everyone might march.

I didn't often speak at these meetings, leaving Paul to fire out the questions and do the talking. I spent my time observing and trying to establish what was taking place. Working with Paul was great—I knew that in these situations, given the chance to sit and analyze what I was witnessing that my political instincts became razor-sharp. When I did speak I was adamant. As soon as I knew the meeting was a complete waste of time I announced that Paul and I were leaving. Marjorie and Debra tried to pull something out of the air to keep the conversation going. I was furious which made Paul nervous. He gathered his notes, grabbed his coat, and we left. When we were safely outside, away from everyone, I stood still and muttered the worst string of obscenities I could muster until I was so breathless I had to bend over and try to get the blood flowing back into my head again. Paul waited patiently, then lit two cigarettes and handed me one. We rushed off to the ILGO meeting. The St. Patrick's Day parade was only four days away. It wasn't looking good.

By then, the parade story was all the rage in New York and beyond. Our days were filled with meetings, phone calls, and interviews with local, national, and international media, on top of which we had fulltime jobs. We were in constant communication with each other, and the mayor's office, and listened to the opinions and suggestions of anyone who cared to comment. On my way into work on the D train one morning a woman said, "I saw you on television. Good luck!" Another woman announced from her seat, "That Cardinal—he's bad. I've never liked him." People began to stop me on the street to talk about the news. Generally we didn't have time to watch the TV reports because we were at meetings. When I finally saw myself on television I was surprised how much like my father I was. My tone was his and my delivery had his particular self-assurance; it was a very strange experience. We didn't even have time to read the newspapers now, so they sat in a pile in the bedroom. But we seemed to be getting our message across. ILGO's strategy was to decide what we wanted to say in public and then, regardless of what a reporter asked, my job was to make sure I got that message out. We were exhausted, functioning on too little sleep, bad food, and high anxiety with no clue where it was all going to lead. All we kept hearing from the mayor's office was not to give up because they hadn't.

ILGO was fully aware of the anxiety this particular whirlwind caused in certain spheres of the gay community—our group was inexperienced, ignorant on so many levels, and barely out of the closet. From the beginning we felt the strain of the huge responsibility we had to the lesbian and gay community in New York. This was a very difficult position to be in. We knew, too, that no matter what we did some people would end up being angry with us. We were unsure of our footing and of our right to be where we were. However, while we listened to everyone who had anything to say, we also believed this was our battle and we would decide how to handle it. It wasn't simply a gay issue, it was very much an Irish lesbian and gay rights concern and we had to decide how to fight. We dealt with the criticism, and kept our fingers crossed, and hoped that by following our hearts and our political instincts, we would work it out.

Early on Wednesday morning, March 13, Paul and I met Deputy Mayor Bill Lynch for the first of three meetings with him that day. We had been up for hours already answering calls from Ireland, which is five hours ahead of New York time. In Lynch's office there was a framed copy of a *New York Newsday* front-page photo of Nelson Mandela during his visit to the city. I'd heard and read about Bill Lynch in the papers and knew he was important and very well respected. He was gruff, straightforward and calm. I wasn't sure whether or not I liked him. As usual Paul began the conversation. He was nervous but also delighted to be meeting Lynch. Instinctively, I do not trust people with political power so I was wary and watchful, trying to size him up. Lynch told us he had been surprised when he first started this job to find himself listening to gay men tell him how nervous they were of cops; he thought that police brutality was mainly a problem for his community, African Americans, not middle-class white men. After the bonding he got down to business. He told us the situation did not look great but they weren't about to give up hope. He sent us on our way, telling us he'd be in touch. I went to work.

Eileen was back from Puerto Rico and dazzled by the big news story. At work, she got a kick out of answering the phone to reporters and even more of a buzz when they arrived knocking at Prelinger's door with TV cameras. My boss Rick was quiet but clearly supportive. He assured me, and possibly himself, that it would be over in a few days and then everything would return to normal. He was excited too because I overheard him telling people to read the articles in *The New York Times* or letting them know which television channels to watch that evening for the latest news. I couldn't have wished for a better place to work.

I had been back at work a short time after the Bill Lynch meeting when Máire Crowe called with the news that Division 7 of the AOH was going to invite ILGO to march in the parade as their guests. It seemed that the Brooklyn District Attorney, Joe Hynes, an Irish-American Democrat, was upset because the controversy did not show the Irish in a favorable light and he wanted to resolve this. Apparently, he approached his press secretary, Pat Clarke, a member of Division 7, to see if Pat thought there would be enough votes to invite ILGO. Clarke thought it was worth a try, given that many of the division's members were fairly liberal, and handily enough, many were also Assistant District Attorneys and Hynes was their boss. It transpired that Division 7 had met and voted the night before and the motion to invite ILGO passed by a two-to-one margin. They contacted City Hall, shortly after Paul and I had left Bill Lynch, to pass on the good news.

ROCK THE SHAM!

Paul and I were called to meet Bill Lynch again later that afternoon. We pretended not to know about Division 7's invitation so we wouldn't steal his thunder. Because we had not yet seen the letter of invitation we didn't know that there would be impossible restrictions placed on our self-expression. Ironically, our entire conversation with the Deputy Mayor at that second meeting was about how to identify ILGO while marching as guests of another group. Either Lynch had not seen the letter or he was testing the waters to see if ILGO would be happy at that point just to march, even if we had to be closeted. As usual that week there was an ILGO parade meeting scheduled for that evening so we told Lynch we'd get back to him when it was clarified whether or not we could wear ILGO T-shirts. There was a fax copy of Division 7's invitation on my desk when I got back to work, which answered our question. The letter of invitation stated:

> *I must stress to you that we are happy to have the members*
> *of your organization to march with us, but the group ILGO and*
> *Division 7 will march as one unit under our name. Unfortunately*
> *the parade organizers will not allow any other banner, button, sash,*
> *or otherwise signifying your organization, political slogan or other*
> *belief. This includes T-shirts and arm bands. If you do intend to*
> *march I would expect your members to comply with all regulations*
> *set forth by the parade committee.*

Over dinner at Daisy's, ILGO's vote on Division 7's friendly gesture was unanimous—we respectfully declined the invitation because we could not identify ourselves as Irish lesbians and gay men. Bill Lynch was not satisfied and asked if Paul and I would come to Gracie Mansion later that night to talk. Lynch was in the middle of financial negotiations but would be available after 10pm. We got the go-ahead from the group, our rationale being that we had nothing to lose.

At Gracie Mansion, the mayor's official residence, Lynch told us he'd been at a budget meeting where the 300 delegates weren't at all interested in discussing fiscal matters—everyone wanted to talk about ILGO and the parade! The story was now top of the news. We sat in a conference room at a large table and ate leftover sandwiches. Debra Pucci and her assistant Juliann O'Riordan pushed, pulled, and cajoled to see if there was any way ILGO might accept Division 7's offer. We were exhausted and everyone wanted to go home. I really wasn't sure what we were doing at this late stage since we had nothing to work with. We sat quietly, except for Paul who was restless even though it was close to midnight. Bill Lynch picked up a ringing phone, and the caller, Joe Nicholson of the *New York Post*, came to the rescue.

Nicholson had managed to track down the Parade Chairman, Frank Beirne, and had wheedled an interview out of him. Nicholson told Lynch that Beirne was furious with Mayor

Dinkins for interfering in his parade. Beirne had said, "Ask the mayor if he will go to bat for the Ku Klux Klan to make sure they are not discriminated against if they apply to march in the Martin Luther King Day Parade." None of us were privy to this conversation as we sat silently watching Lynch. When he hung up he said nothing but dialed a number. He spoke in very low tones. Debra whispered, "He's talking to the mayor." The mayor was furious. Lynch put the receiver in its slot and turned to Paul and me. He said the mayor has decided to march with ILGO and Division 7 instead of his usual spot at the head of the parade. What did ILGO have to say to that?

The drama was only beginning. Paul and I mulled it over, thinking this might be a solution. We took out our address books, settled in at different locations and started to make the calls to ILGO's parade committee members. It was very late but we managed to talk to the majority of the group. Asking people to make a decision over the phone when they were exhausted, confused, and running on emotional energy was not the ideal situation but we had no other choice; or if we did we didn't know it at the time. The overwhelming response was to go for it, but everyone I spoke to stressed we would have to be very clear this was not what we wanted, it was a compromise; in future we wanted to march as ILGO with our own banner. The decision was made to accept Division 7's invitation as long as the mayor marched with us because then everyone would know we were ILGO.

Debra gave Paul and me a lift to Brooklyn. On the journey home I began to get a sinking feeling that we may have made the wrong decision. Nothing was clear anymore and the response from the ILGO parade group had not made it clearer. Nobody shouted "Bingo!" when they heard the news of the mayor's offer. There was no sense of elation or even relief. Marie had waited up for me and I fell asleep as soon as she put her arms around me in bed. We had to be at City Hall the following morning for an 11am press conference to announce the plan.

Through all the years of ILGO's battles the only time members of the group entered City Hall, up the front steps and through the main door, was on Thursday, March 14, 1991. On our way there, Marie sat on one side of me in the cab and Paul on the other. The traffic was terrible and we were cutting it close. I was unconsciously humming the theme tune from "Mission Impossible;" we got out of the cab laughing. There was a line of people waiting outside City Hall so it took us a few minutes to get in. Paul and I watched as Marie settled herself into a seat in the public gallery and then we were escorted into private offices.

The doors opened into a huge room inhabited by men wearing smart suits. I thought we were in the wrong place until some faces started to look familiar. Everybody seemed to be relaxed, except for Debra Pucci and Jennifer Kimball, the mayor's press secretary. Jennifer gave us a copy of the statement and after reading it we went looking for her because we wanted her to change something—neither of us can remember now what it was but at the time it was very important. She was upset and frantic as we listed our objections. She pulled the offending sentence out of the statement.

ROCK THE SHAM!

Paul and I moved about the room as one unit, never leaving each other's side. I wanted to hold his hand but resisted because I didn't want any confusion about our sexual orientation. The room was lavish, lots of dark wood, high ceilings, and elaborate drapes of velvet and satin. There were heavy-framed paintings and plaques hanging on the walls. It reminded me of a grand old drawing room from a British TV series and I could picture Diana Rigg, sitting in one of the beautifully upholstered armchairs, introducing the drama to come. I was too jittery to drink coffee. The introductions began and we met several members of Division 7. Joe Hynes was there along with Al O'Hagan, President of the New York State AOH. We were also introduced to a former City Council President, and former grand marshal of the St. Patrick's Day Parade, Paul O'Dwyer. We swapped banter about the coincidence of both Pauls having the same name. I was delighted to meet Paul O'Dwyer. I knew he was a decent man. Unlike the new generation of "Irish leaders" O'Dwyer was charming, had solid progressive political beliefs, and was genuinely supportive of ILGO. This was important because he was very well respected, not just in New York City and Irish political circles, but well beyond them too.

I was still enjoying chatting with O'Dwyer when we were interrupted. A City Hall employee handed me a note sent in to us from Marie. Bill Dobbs from ACT UP was in the public area and he told Marie that ILGO was making a huge mistake. He said we should not agree to the compromise. Later we found out that ACT UP had never even discussed the parade. But we were vulnerable and Marie got nervous, so she sent us in a note to tell us what he had said. I was furious and thought this whole parade business was going to drive me crazy. Paul and I panicked. We tracked down Bill Lynch and told him some people were having second thoughts. He was cool as a cucumber and instructed us to do whatever we had to do. I asked if there was someplace where Paul and I could speak in private. He showed us into a tiny kitchenette and we took deep breaths and tried to think clearly.

I calmed down and systematically asked Paul a series of questions: Who were we here for? Whom did we represent? What was the decision the group had made? ILGO had decided this was the best of a bad deal, we didn't know how it was going to turn out, but we were willing to take this risk with the understanding that we would never compromise again. We hugged and braced ourselves for what was ahead.

Bill Lynch fetched the mayor. David Dinkins came up the stairs, said a few "hellos," shook a few hands, and then it was time to start. Two huge doors opened into a massive room that was full to capacity. There were cameras and mikes everywhere. I froze. I'd only ever seen anything like this on television. "Where are we supposed to go?" I loudly asked nobody in particular. Ruth Messenger, the Borough President of Manhattan, who had been completely invisible and non-committal about the parade thus far, was behind me. She prodded me in the back, telling me to keep moving toward the top of the room. "You will have to get used to this," she laughed as she coaxed me with her finger in the direction of the podium. Mayor Dinkins stood in front of the microphones and the rest of us lined up behind him. With my arms folded across my chest, hugging my body, I felt how bony I had become. I was momentarily horrified by an image of my rib cage cracking and falling to the floor in little pieces of white bone. I pulled myself together and loosened the grip on myself so I could breathe again. Who was this stupid Bill Dobbs anyway? I wondered as the mayor began to speak. Who the hell was he to show up out of nowhere and mess with us like that? I knew I was supposed to be listening and I tried to concentrate. I looked into the crowd, in search of a familiar face and spotted Máire Crowe, who was focused on the mayor. I couldn't see Marie or anyone else from ILGO.

I recall only words and tiny sound bites about New York's "beautiful mosaic" from the mayor's statement. The senior Paul O'Dwyer followed David Dinkins. I concentrated on him, admiring the shock of his full head of white hair, his bushy eyebrows and beautiful powdery skin, and did not hear a thing he said. Pat Clarke from Division 7 explained their gesture of inclusion and the philosophy of the AOH's rallying call—Friendship, Unity and Christian Charity. Everyone turned and looked at Paul and me. We were so inexperienced and so out of it that it hadn't occurred to us to have a statement prepared. Paul nodded at me as he stepped forward and explained that we had compromised but everyone would know who we were because the mayor would be our banner. I said a few words about being a lesbian and an immigrant, and how it was important to me to be able to give something back to where I came from, and visibility as an Irish lesbian was part of that contribution. Then the press conference was over.

I caught up with Máire Crowe. "Did we do the right thing?" I wanted to know. She was noncommittal; she didn't know. I had to get out. Marie was looking sheepish. She wanted to know if I was angry because of her note. I was but more than anything I was tired. I felt myself shut down, right there on the steps outside City Hall. The protective zone around my body was almost tangible; I could definitely feel it and could see it in my mind's eye—sheets of thick steel. I wasn't aware at the time that this was how I usually was, it was just so intense at that moment I happened to notice it. It's not easy to be in a relationship with someone who has so much protective armor, which I was soon to find out.

In the few remaining days before the parade much of the media coverage concentrated on whether or not politicians were going to march. New York City Comptroller Elizabeth Holtzman was on our side and City Council members Robert Dryfoos, Virginia Fields, and Ronnie Eldridge said they would only march too if disabled people and gays were included. Each day the list got larger. The media hype was so intense that the papers and television reports were making daily announcements about who supported ILGO, and who did not—we had a lot of support.

Our answering machine was always full of messages when Marie and I got home at night. We divided them between us and called everyone back. We used our home to sleep, shower, and make telephone calls. It was a mess. There were clothes on the floor, thrown across the bed, hanging out of the chest of drawers, and endless pieces of paper strewn everywhere with telephone numbers and messages on them.

Late one night I sat on the floor surrounded by this mayhem listening to the machine, scribbling down information, when I heard my father's voice. He called with some handy hints about future interviews after hearing me on Marianne Finucane's popular radio program, which airs daily in Ireland. He said I referred to the mayor as "Dinkins" instead of his full title, "Mayor Dinkins", which, in his opinion, was better for an Irish audience who didn't know all the players. It was an astute observation, which I didn't appreciate at the time because I believed it was a criticism. Siobhán Lennon, the first Irish lesbian I came out to during the Women Against Strip Searching days in Dublin, also heard the interview. She wrote to tell me she thought she was hallucinating when she walked into her work place to be greeted by my voice over the airwaves. She said she was getting a bit nervous about me becoming a radical lesbian, which amused me because I knew she was serious. Everyone close to me in Ireland was worried about my safety. Being in New York was dangerous enough, they thought, without drawing attention to myself as a lesbian.

I spoke regularly to my sister Laura to see how they were all doing in Ireland. My parents would never tell me if anyone said anything bad or mean to them, nor would they report any gesture of kindness so I needed Laura to keep me grounded. I knew my brother John and my sisters, Cathy and Laura, were very proud of me but wondered if my mother and father felt any pride at all, even a scrap, for my courage. I was so afraid of their anger and resentment and blamed myself, not their homophobia, for any discomfort they might be feeling.

Marie worked on the parade from our apartment in Brooklyn. There were lots of loose ends to be tied up so she took charge, answering the phone and organizing what needed organizing. On the eve of the parade she had a remarkable phone conversation with the governor of New York, Mario Cuomo, who had steered well clear of ILGO. He made rambling statements about the parade but managed to clearly state his intention to march: "I certainly plan to march and now it looks like I may be marching with our friend Steve McDonald, a great law-enforcement hero, and the Irish-American disabled children." In other words, despite, or perhaps because of his liberal credentials he made the political decision to align himself with McDonald and the "wheelchair kids" as they were patronizingly called, while refusing to make any statement about the exclusion of ILGO. When Mayor Dinkins made his announcement about marching with us, the *New York Post* reported the governor was happy because he wanted everyone to honor and celebrate the contribution the Irish had made to this country. We were infuriated by his refusal to tackle the homophobia of the AOH and we mentioned the governor's avoidance of the issue at every given chance.

On Friday, the day before the parade, we got a call from a Cuomo aide. He said the governor would like to come meet us before we marched and then take his place in the parade. Marie returned the call after she clarified our position with the rest of the ILGO parade group. She told the governor's liaison that it wasn't appropriate for Cuomo to be seen with ILGO because he had not been supportive of our efforts to be included in the parade. Enraged by this, the governor himself called us at home in Brooklyn. I sat on the floor of our bedroom and listened to Marie's end of the conversation. She was curt but polite, and she didn't back down once. She talked to the governor about his political opportunism. She told him he was not welcome to turn up for a photo opportunity because ILGO did not want him there. Marie explained he had had ample time to make statements about what was going on but he had said nothing in support of us. Did Marie realize to whom she was speaking, the governor wanted to know? Marie continued, undaunted, even when he began to shout. She told him he hadn't risked anything politically but wanted a piece of the action now. She asked him how he thought this would be perceived. He lost his temper completely and told her not to talk to him about perceptions; he had heard things about us, he intimated—did we know how we were being perceived? Marie didn't much care nor did anyone in ILGO know what he was talking about. The governor hung up.

I jumped up and down on the creaky wooden floor with something close to pure delight. Marie had been fantastic. Fierce! But she was shaking with rage. Nobody else would have handled a big-shot like Marie had. We all would have been far too polite when there was no reason to be. Had Marie not taken the call Governor Cuomo may well have been at the parade mugging with ILGO and everyone else—we were very lucky. Unfortunately, Marie didn't get the same kick I was getting—she was nervous about what other people in ILGO would think. In fact, some were appalled she had been so forthright. However, Marie had clearly let the governor know that ILGO had integrity and we were not in the business of playing games with anyone, regardless of their position and power. And 1991 was the last time Governor Mario Cuomo marched in New York's St. Patrick's Day Parade even though he remained governor of New York State until 1994.

CHAPTER FIVE

The Fallout After The Parade

ROCK THE SHAM!

WOKE ON Sunday morning, the day after we had marched in the 230th Saint Patrick's Day Parade, confused, forgetting we were still at Steve's on Perry Street and not at home in Brooklyn. Marie was already up, sitting at the butcher-block table, drinking a take-out coffee with the Sunday newspapers spread before her. There was a white paper bag beside her and that bucked me up—she had bought pastries too. Sunshine filled the room from the long windows at her back. Even though we had marched the day before, today was St. Patrick's Day. Whenever St. Patrick's Day falls on a Sunday, as it did in 1991, the parade is held on the Saturday before. The AOH never parades in Manhattan on a Sunday. I was cranky. I shuffled across the cold floor to Marie and sat down beside her. She pulled me close but didn't lift her eyes from the papers she was scouring for news of the big story from the day before.

There was plenty; the papers were full of the parade—the booing, the mayor, the beer cans, and the AOH turning their backs on our contingent. I was very curious about how the story would be told but couldn't concentrate. I flipped through the glossy pages of *The New York Times* magazine and tried not to get involved while Marie gave me little bits of information. She said the compromise had worked—that ILGO marching as invited guests without our own banner was clearly better than not marching at all. This was a huge relief. But I was in no mood for analysis; in fact the last thing I wanted to think about was what had happened. I leaned against the wall, watching a man who lived in the opposite building potter in his garden. We sat for hours like this, Marie eating up the news while I tried to keep my mind blank, willing away the memories, observations, and flashbacks from the past week. I'd been waiting for the parade to be over for what seemed like an eternity and now; in its aftermath, I felt hung-over and exhausted—I didn't want to hear anymore.

Long before the furor over the parade, ILGO had made plans for our first St. Patrick's Day together. So now, the day after we had marched, we had our outdoor céilí at Sheridan Square, a five-minute walk from where we were. The thought of leaving the apartment and having to be sociable was unappealing. Marie stacked the newspapers; I packed up our weekend bags, and we both fussed about, getting on each other's nerves. It felt very strange being out in the world again. It was another beautiful spring day.

There were green and pink balloons bobbing from the railings of the tiny park opposite the Stonewall Bar at Sheridan Square. At last we got to use our banner, and it flapped in the mild breeze. Blue police barriers cordoned off the surrounding streets. Women and men filled the square tapping their feet to a recording of Sharon Shannon's melodious accordion. The festive atmosphere was thick with an exuberance I couldn't rise to. I felt completely detached from the hubbub and wandered around in a daze, smiling and nodding at people because it was easier than talking. A woman from Trim in County Meath, Anne Reynolds, introduced herself. She had been following the story in the papers and on the television from Rye in upstate New York, where she was a part-time student and full-time nanny. She said she'd never felt so proud in her whole life and was amazed to see a gay group with a lesbian representative. She didn't know anyone but had traveled into Manhattan to "come out." I introduced her to a group of lesbians from the Bronx who was hanging around waiting for something to happen. The next time I saw Anne Reynolds, she was dancing.

During a break in the piped music from the Stonewall bar, Stanley Rygor played his accordion. He had come to the céilí with this son, Robert, who was a member of Queer Nation and ACT UP. Following the recent experiences many of us had with our families we were charmed and surprised that it was possible for father and son to be at a gay event together. Stanley was a big hit. Paul moved through the crowd, talking and laughing. He was still high from the parade. Trish, a dancer and a schoolteacher, tried to get people to concentrate on her instructions but she couldn't control the freewheeling improvisation of jigs and reels. Her bossiness only made everyone giddier so she gave up. For the first time in ages there were no reporters around so we could relax. Paul pulled at my cardigan to get my attention as he excitedly pointed towards Seventh Avenue to where Bill Lynch, the Deputy Mayor stood. Catch was by his side and they chatted. Lynch puffed on a fat cigar. We had invited all kinds of people to our céilí but didn't expect politicians to show up. It was funny to see the deputy mayor there, surrounded by dancing Irish lesbians and gay men. I did my duty and had a word with Lynch—I was beginning to warm to him; I would never learn.

He pulled the stub of cigar from his mouth and leaned close to tell us the mayor would probably pay us a visit. He was in the middle of a game of tennis, Lynch said, but he was expecting a call from him soon. Paul looked like he'd just been told he'd won the lottery. Word spread quickly but nobody really believed it was going to happen. We continued our dancing. But Adrian Milton from Queer Nation played it safe. He wrote out a brief statement thanking the mayor for marching with us and moved through the revelers asking people to sign it. We swung each other around Sheridan Square, not caring that the céilí purists were being driven to distraction by our clumsy dance moves. We didn't want to get too excited in case we were let down.

At 3.30pm, David Dinkins arrived wearing a sweat suit, a towel around his neck, and a Giants baseball cap. The dancing stopped. The crowd went wild. Pocket cameras were clicking and flashing as people jockeyed for a place beside the mayor to have snap-shots taken for keepsakes. His name filled the air and drowned out the music, everyone was shouting, and then a chorus of "For He's a Jolly Good Fellow" rang out. Men and women were crying and laughing and the mayor had tears in his eyes too. Above the din a man's voice roared, "You did the right thing!" Dinkins responded, "We all did the right thing!" Stanley didn't miss a beat and began to play "We Shall Overcome" on the accordion.

PREVIOUS SPREAD: Top: Me and Paul O'Dwyer and Deputy Mayor Bill Lynch.
Bottom: Mayor David Dinkins surrounded by reporters after he joined our céilí the day after marching with ILGO. *From ILGO files*

ROCK THE SHAM!

Suddenly, Sheridan Square was full of reporters, television cameras, and press photographers. Passersby on Seventh Avenue stopped to check out what was going on. The mayor was interviewed and said, "How can people have so much hate stored up? I don't ask them to like me or to like gays or lesbians. You don't have to like them. But you should treat them civilly, treat them fairly." Trish pulled the mayor of New York into a circle and we wrapped our arms about each other's waists as the tune for the "Siege of Ennis" blared from the Stonewall Inn. The mayor was a bit taken aback but he did his best to master the foot work and laughed as he was dragged through the motions—the perfect photo opportunity. Long after the mayor had gone, when our céilí was finally over, nobody wanted to leave—we didn't want to break the spell.

On Monday, March 18, two days after the parade, the ILGO story was still making the front pages of the New York dailies and it would continue to take up many columns for the entire week, and the following months. Monday's news was about the mayor dancing with ILGO at Sheridan Square and continued reaction to his participation in the parade on Saturday. *New York Newsday*'s editorial stated:

> *By revisiting and dancing a jig with gay and lesbian*
> *marchers from the St. Patrick's Day Parade the day after*
> *the event, Mayor David Dinkins boldly affirmed this city's*
> *deep and abiding commitment to tolerance. ... Only the*
> *spiritually and morally bankrupt would interpret his*
> *gesture to lesbians and gays as anything less than a*
> *vindication of New York itself.*

David Dinkins was everyone's hero. Reporters were dispatched to his church, and to the Abyssinian Baptist Church in Harlem, where the mostly African American congregation praised the mayor's actions. The Reverend Calvin O. Butts III, of the Abyssinian Church, made a point of stating his belief that, "...the divine imperative does not allow for homosexuality." Nevertheless, he supported David Dinkins and was critical of Cardinal O'Connor's handling of the parade fiasco. "This march was for a patron saint and some of these people acted as if they had no God at all," Butts commented, and stated further, "It's an absolute disgrace, and I think the Cardinal should condemn that kind of behavior. I think that those of us who are religious leaders ought to condemn that behavior." However, Cardinal O'Connor, the Irish American leader of New York's Catholics, chose to remain silent about what had taken place during the parade. Even the day after, in his St. Patrick's Day sermon, he did not address the violence targeted at ILGO and Mayor Dinkins. The Cardinal had been taken by surprise by the public outrage in 1991, but the Archdiocese swiftly enough regrouped and figured out its spin on ILGO, the parade, and the mayor for the future.

For weeks, the New York press continued to review and analyze what had happened when ILGO and the mayor marched up Fifth Avenue on March 16. The story had gripped the imaginations and souls of the city's scribes and took on a life of its own. The involvement of New York's political machine, and organized religion, only added flavor and depth to what was at stake, and the opinions were wide and varied. For a change the analysis wasn't simplistic or explained away as a clash between Irish American culture and new Irish immigrants, or lesbians and gay men versus the heterosexual norm. At least in 1991 many journalists tried to grapple with the complexities of what had happened in political, social, cultural, and religious terms. In ILGO, we didn't understand why the story was still alive but the impact of what we had done would be slowly revealed, sometimes at great personal cost.

Being the flavor of the month got ILGO invited to the city's Irish night at Gracie Mansion. For most of us, this was our first time in the mayor's official residence. Paul and I had been there for one late-night meeting, and Keith had been there before, on a job laying the carpet! We were having fun. The mayor began his public remarks with a cute story about how smart his wife is and then went on to more serious matters. He listed what he had been doing for the Irish community, which included writing a letter supporting Seán and Philomena Mackin's request for political asylum. He followed the applause with an announcement that he would be going to visit Joe Doherty, the IRA prison escapee, who was being held in the Metropolitan Correctional Center in Manhattan, awaiting an extradition decision. He mentioned practically everybody in the room, either by name or affiliation, except for ILGO, which I thought was odd. Still, we were happy and sipped our drinks, basking in our good fortune in these friendly surroundings.

On Saturday, April 6th we had our first general monthly meeting after the parade. The room at The Center was packed. Catch was facilitating. There were many new faces and when the meeting began people sat on every available surface or stood against the walls. The now familiar "parade high" filled the air, touching everyone whether or not they had marched. ILGO was news—good news.

We had a full agenda and many visitors to get through in two hours. Chris Robson from the Gay and Lesbian Equality Network (GLEN) in Ireland introduced himself. He was in New York promoting a book GLEN and the Irish Council for Civil Liberties had co-published, entitled, *Equality Now for Lesbians and Gay Men*. The same law (criminalizing male homosexual acts) that put Oscar Wilde in jail was still on the statute books in Ireland. Next we joked with Ron, a gay Italian American, about marching in the Columbus Day Parade and he was a little miffed given his group had no interest in marching. Keith reported there were plans to set up ILGO groups in Philadelphia, Boston, Los Angeles and San Francisco. Tarlach sang the ballad of ILGO, *Two Miles of Hate*, that he had co-written with Eilis Heller, about marching in the parade. This wasn't his debut as he'd performed it already in Paddy Reilly's bar with the popular band, Black 47. Adrian Milton of Queer Nation had been patiently waiting for his moment on the busy agenda. He presented ILGO with a painting he had made in honor of our marching in the parade. The spirit of his gesture caught us completely off guard—we didn't know how to thank him. Then there was talk of making an exhibition about marching in the parade and a group huddled together to arrange when to meet.

We had never had so many visitors or so much interest in our small group. Trilby de Jung from the New York City Human Rights Commission (HRC) told us the Commission was interested in conducting an investigation into the Ancient Order of Hibernian's parade committee. Since the passing of the Gay Rights Bill, the City Charter was bound to protect lesbians and gay men against discrimination and the HRC was figuring out if there was enough evidence to sue the AOH. She asked for our support, and I got the impression she wanted ILGO, rather than the HRC, as the Complainant if there was a case.

We didn't make a decision either way at that meeting. But several members of ILGO responded immediately with clear expressions of anxiety, specifically about our mailing list becoming a public document. This was never going to happen because we would have destroyed the list to protect people, their privacy and indeed, their immigration status in the U.S. I balked at the idea of legal action. If the city wanted to sue the AOH, they should go right ahead; they had the resources and time. ILGO had never considered a legal challenge, perhaps because everything had happened so quickly, but far more likely because it wasn't what our group was about. We planned to talk more at another meeting because our brief discussion had generated enough worry and interest amongst the membership.

Wrapping up the meeting, we decided to return to Meriken in April, where ILGO held its very first meeting, to celebrate our first anniversary over dinner. We would go to Long Island for its first ever Gay Pride and Freedom March. Finally, and typically, a disgruntled man said he wanted to talk about ILGO's structure! We weren't allowed to have one celebratory meeting, not even this one, where we should have been able to sit back and be glad and pleased about what we had done. People's eyes glazed over. Catch called a halt to the meeting and we got out of there fast.

Brendan Fay went to work as usual on Monday, March 18, still a little tired after a tumultuous few days. His face was one among many that appeared in city newspapers over the weekend. Brendan had taught religious studies at The Mary Louis Academy, a Catholic high school for girls in Queens, since September, 1988. Brendan's employer was aware he was gay and also aware that his photograph had previously appeared in the *Irish Voice* newspaper when ILGO marched in the Lesbian and Gay Pride Parade in June, 1990. Yet his life was about to take an unexpected turn. He was summoned to the office of Sister Joan Petito, the principal of the school, and asked to "explain himself" with regard to marching in the St. Patrick's Day Parade. Brendan told her his decision to march "was a matter of conscience consistent with the Church's teaching that discrimination against lesbians and gay men is immoral." Sister Petito claimed she was worried about the reaction of parents to an openly gay man teaching religion in a Catholic high school. She told Brendan she had been "bombarded" with phone calls denouncing him, although Brendan was having the opposite experience. During the Academy's Open House that week, Brendan met a lot of parents and nobody made a negative comment. On the contrary, many praised him and expressed shock at the reaction of the parade spectators.

There were many meetings at the school that week, and on March 20, one student was removed from Brendan's class because her parents complained. In response to "confusion" among students, the Mary Louis Academy decided to teach a class on homosexuality and the Catholic Church. Some of the material distributed to students was progressive but much of it was strongly condemnatory. One leaflet stated: "The teaching of the Roman Catholic Church is that all homosexual activity is evil and immoral." Another leaflet debunked myths about homosexuality stating that not all gay men are effeminate, or lesbians masculine, and that heterosexuals were far more likely to molest children. There was a handout to help students formulate an ethical response to homophobia. It stated: "Violence against gay persons ('gay bashing') can never be justified" and it used the 10% theory, proposing, "Some one hundred people in an average parish of 1000 families are gay … there are millions of gay people in the U.S. and millions of gay persons in the Church." "Being gay is not a disorder," according to one document, which was contradicted by another—"Homosexual acts are intrinsically disordered and can in no case be approved of." If anything was going to cause confusion among the student body, it was the Academy's panic.

Toward the end of March 1991, Brendan Fay had his annual meeting with Sr. Joan Petito to review the academic year at The Mary Louis Academy and to determine if he planned to teach the next year. Petito informed Brendan at this meeting that she had "some reservations" about him because of his "lifestyle." She said that some staff members had expressed concern about him, and she mentioned that he lacked discretion in his conversations. Then, on April 8, just after ILGO's first big meeting following the parade, Brendan was fired. He received a letter from Sr. Petito notifying him that his contract with the Mary Louis Academy would terminate at the end of the semester because of his unsatisfactory performance in the areas of "time-management, organizational procedures and pedagogical skill." Brendan's previous reviews had been glowing. Now he asked Petito for clarification. She told him there was no need for an explanation. He was distraught.

At ILGO's monthly meeting in May Brendan told the entire group what had happened. Everyone was stunned. However, when it came down to supporting Brendan and meeting to figure out what we could do, only Eileen Clancy, Marie, and I showed up. Brendan was bitterly disappointed and especially hurt because no ILGO men came. Brendan had put his energy into forming bonds with the men of ILGO through a support and discussion group. He wasn't interested in lesbians and he reasonably assumed that ILGO would come to his aid in a time of crisis. ILGO did, but for Brendan it wasn't enough that lesbians took on the task. It was a dismal response and an indictment of the male membership. It also partially explains how it was that lesbians were rapidly filling up the leadership roles in the group—of the many men in ILGO there were only a few willing to take responsibility for running an activist organization.

Brendan took his case to the Human Rights Commission and eventually, years later, settled out of court. By that time in the mid-nineties he had formed a new Irish gay group, the Lavender and Green Alliance, in opposition to ILGO. I felt deeply betrayed by Brendan and believed his actions were divisive and hostile—the meetings and insults hurled at some of us before he left, with a smattering of ILGO members, made Brendan's position very clear. I think that instead of being honest and acknowledging the bitter disappointment that ILGO, or the men in ILGO, had turned out to be, Brendan directed his frustration and anger at the easiest target—lesbians. It's possible that an equally vibrant male leadership would have lessened the hostility towards strong women in ILGO, but it is just as likely to have had no such impact. I repeatedly tried to speak with or interview Brendan to get his side of the story but after a year of going back and forth, Brendan told me that did not want to be interviewed for my book. Unfortunately, recently when I called he has been traveling as he is busy working on a documentary—I would have loved to speak to him about what happened all those years ago.

From ILGO's beginnings I knew there were misogynists among us, as there are everywhere else. ILGO's membership reflected the world we lived in—we were no better or no worse in most instances. There were racists and anti-Semites in the group too. At first, some people felt quite at home saying whatever they pleased because they felt safe amongst their own people. Nothing went by unchallenged, and most often the challengers were women, and it became increasingly clear that ILGO was not the kind of place some had thought it was, on many levels. Our growing pains were not over and the group's dynamic was in constant motion, becoming more complex as time passed. With few exceptions, the male membership didn't seem to have any vision for the group or much staying power. If debates or decisions didn't go their way they were more inclined to leave. While a lot of male energy was spent on impressing each other, a core group of ILGO's lesbians, along with a handful of men, were doing the bulk of organizational work. Because most of the men paid so little attention to what lesbians in ILGO proposed, or wanted to achieve, everything we ever suggested was given the go-ahead. At first I felt insulted but then realized it wasn't worth getting upset about when those who were dedicated to the group, women and men, were making the decisions and doing the work. It is unusual in a mixed gender group for women to emerge as leaders, regardless of the group's power structure, but this is what happened in ILGO.

Since first meeting in March I'd kept in touch with Anne Reynolds, the Irish woman from Rye who had come out at our St. Patrick's Day dance at Sheridan Square. Because she was living quite a distance away, most of our contact was over the phone, except for the times she got to borrow her employer's station wagon to visit the city. Once Anne decided to come out, she took on telling her family in Ireland. Marie and I met her for dinner one

The Fallout After The Parade

evening in Panna II, an Indian restaurant on First Avenue in the East Village. Anne had an intensity about her that was sometimes very disconcerting. She left herself open and vulnerable telling us hair-raising stories about her brutal childhood in Ireland. Still, she got excited when she talked about eventually going back to work the farm she had inherited from her mother. That night she handed me a gift. I tore off the wrapping paper and uncovered a blank journal. Her inscription read, "To a woman of vision and might. Write." I told her I would. I had already started to jot down some thoughts about what had happened to our group since we first began meeting.

Every time we thought it was over for the year, the parade crept up on us again, often through newspaper stories. An article reported that Michael Burke of 221 Harrison Avenue in Nutley, New Jersey, was sentenced to 40 hours of community service in the Lesbian and Gay Division of the Mayor's Office. The beer can throwing attack during the parade, of which he was found guilty, was officially categorized as a bias crime.

Our exhibition, "The Stone Walls of Ireland: St. Patrick's Day 1991", opened at the Irish Arts Centre on Sunday, June 23, where it remained for the duration of New York's Lesbian and Gay Pride week. Sandy Boyer, our contact at the Irish Arts Centre, was instrumental in the decision to allow ILGO to hang the exhibition there. The Irish venue was incredibly important to us, especially for Gay Pride. (Years later, Sandy suggested that we teach a class on Irish lesbian and gay history, which we did, and it was a big success.) Catch, Marie, John Lyons, and Anne Reynolds had done a fantastic job. Large blow-ups of newspaper quotes hung on the borders between céilíng and wall, covering the entire perimeter of the space. Catch had mounted, and meticulously framed, a large selection of photographs from the parade—they hung in long panels on the walls. Seeing so many images and words together in one place was overwhelming; I was only beginning to understand and appreciate what it was we had done. Within half an hour of the opening the room was packed—we were very pleased.

The day before New York's annual Lesbian and Gay Pride Parade in June, 1991 ILGO, who had been completely unknown the previous year, spoke at the Gay Pride Rally in Union Square Park. We had four minutes but we insisted on having two speakers; the lesbians in ILGO had a position we never strayed from—where a gay man went to represent the group so went a lesbian. The following day, at the parade, all we had to do was wave and smile. Marie and I went all out and dressed up for the day. We were out to enjoy ourselves and weren't disappointed. Anne Reynolds, down from Rye for the weekend, Dave O'Connor from Boston, John Lyons, and Catch beamed all the way down Fifth Avenue holding the banner. Our small contingent received tremendous support from onlookers, and there were no more remarks about how there couldn't be lesbians and gay men who were Irish; everybody knew we were here now.

At the intersection of Sixth Avenue and West Fourth Street, Aldyn McKean leaped from the sidelines to serenade us with "When Irish Eyes are Smiling," making a point of stressing the line, "All the world is bright and GAY." I was still wary and humorless when it came to sentimental references to Ireland but we knew Aldyn now and waited for him to hold that note on "gay" in his beautiful tenor voice. He was making it a tradition to sing this to ILGO every time he came across us in public.

We finished off our second summer together as a group on July 14, with a wild fundraiser at Paddy Reilly's on Second Avenue. Black 47 and the Chanting House performed and the bar was hopping for hours. Larry Luby, a member of Division 7 of the AOH, the group who'd invited ILGO and the mayor to march in the St. Patrick's Day parade, showed up with a friend. When Larry, famous in Irish American circles, is referred to, it's always as Larry Luby, octogenarian. We chatted at the bar and remarkably, it turned out that Larry grew up in Donnycarney where I was raised. He'd been in New York for decades and told me he had lived on Christopher Street with his wife for a long time and they always watched the Lesbian and Gay Pride Parade.

The good times ended that autumn. Marie and I received several phone calls from friends in ILGO to tell us that Anne Reynolds seemed to be missing. I had a bad feeling when nobody knew where she was, including the family she worked for in Rye. Anne usually put up a brave front but it was clear that she was in a lot of pain, always struggling, and often inconsolable. She had borrowed her employer's car, set off, and never came back. Within a week of her disappearance Anne's body was found in a wooded area near the college she attended. She had shot herself. Many lesbians in the group who were close to Anne were devastated and angry and several eventually moved away from New York.

Life in ILGO continued. We never thought anything could be as hectic as our first year but we were mistaken. By November a separate parade group met outside of ILGO's monthly meeting. The events surrounding the 1991 St. Patrick's Day parade had merely set the pace; now we were dealing with a more drawn out process where making last-minute decisions would become a necessary habit. Mostly, the same people who had worked on the parade in 1991 came back to plan the 1992 event. But we had lost people from the general membership. Some ILGO members had been scared off by the public profile of the group. However, we also gained many new members. ILGO members who hadn't been so engaged became active precisely because of the challenge of working on the St. Patrick's Day parade. We were a little wary of people we didn't know. A man whose name we didn't recognize was leaving messages on our telephone hotline because he wanted to get involved. When John Voelcker walked in to our meeting I relaxed—I recognized him immediately. He had been one of our marshals during the 1991 parade. John is pretty conservative in appearance. He laughs when he remembers coming to his first meeting. "I think you all thought I was a cop." He wasn't far off! We settled down and began to plan.

Toward the end of 1991 Marie and I moved into Steve Menges' apartment on Perry Street when he returned to live in his original home in Livingston Manor; he had AIDS and was dying. He wanted us to live in his apartment because he knew we loved it. The landlord refused our application for a sublet. We had a couple of months to pack up and leave. This began months of moving from one place to another. We spent two months in one sublet on 28th Street, which was a great relief. Marie loved this huge loft apartment but the anxiety of constantly living out of bags and never knowing where we were going to end up next was taking its toll. I don't remember our discussing why it was that we weren't actually looking for a permanent place to live.

It seemed like everything had changed between us and I blamed the rupture on the stress of the parade. However, our trouble began long before March 1991. I had thought everything would be fine when Marie left her job at Phillip Morris, because she hated it so much. But Marie had left the job and instead of getting better, everything seemed to get worse. Marie was depressed and stuck, with no plan. I felt overpowered by her loneliness and couldn't fill the void in her life. I had hoped her trip to Mexico and Guatemala would fix everything, which, of course, it didn't. After the excitement of the parade I believed we would settle down again and everything would be okay. Clearly, we loved each other but we were so unhappy, independently and together. I was extremely depressed but was unwilling or unable to acknowledge it which was suffocating Marie. With no home, we drifted further and further apart, living out of suitcases, not knowing what was going on, or how to connect or talk to each other.

Shortly after New Year's Day of 1992 Marie and I split up. She had had an affair and I was devastated. Marie was the first person I had ever opened up to. She loved me and I had trusted her. I cried with Marie like I hadn't ever cried before. I had felt safe. She had too. But we had come to a standstill and were very lonely despite being together and neither of us knew what to do. I started to look for an apartment. John Lyons told me about a studio in his building on Broadway and 196th Street. It was affordable, far away from everyone I knew—perfect. Marie moved into a house in Williamsburg where she rented the top floor and lived above the owners who were Italian immigrants.

It wasn't a clean break—we couldn't seem to stay away from each other. It was a mess of tears, rage, grief, confusion, and loneliness for both of us. I remember lying on Marie's cold bathroom floor sobbing for hours and then getting up, taking a shower, and going to work. I felt raw, like my skin had been peeled away from my flesh. I wanted Marie to comfort me but when she tried, it was unbearable. Being held in her arms was much too dangerous now. The one thing I had been sure of was Marie. Now nothing felt safe. I had to scrutinize everything. I felt like I had to start over again, from scratch, but wasn't sure how. I couldn't trust Marie and I didn't.

CHAPTER SIX

The AOH Goes Berserk

(And More Telling Tales)

"When will it stop, this unbenign contempt for gay men and women – their existence, their most basic civil right, their very attempt to express their joy and pride in their daily lives? Until it does, we will not stop. This grotesque St. Patrick's Day ritual must end."

– Terence McNally, proudly gay Irish-American playwright (except on St. Patrick's Day)

ROCK THE SHAM!

THE FOUNDATIONS of traditional Irish Catholicism in America had been deeply shaken by the spectacle on Fifth Avenue on March 16, 1991, and the crisis within the Ancient Order of Hibernians became more convoluted as the year advanced; it would take a long time for the Hibernians to recover and unite again. Their downward spiral began with a shocking announcement in May 1991, when Al O'Hagan, President of the New York State AOH, suspended Parade Chairman, Frank Beirne, for one year because of the mess he made of the parade. This suspension would mean that Frank Beirne could no longer act as the St. Patrick's Day Parade chairman.

The AOH is a large, bureaucratic, national organization with local chapters, or divisions, all across the United States. George Clough was the national president in the early 1990s. Below the national body were the state organizations and Al O'Hagan was New York State's president. The next organizational tier are the county groups and below them again the many local divisions. For example, Division 7, who invited ILGO to march, was only one of many Manhattan-based divisions answerable first to the New York county body, then New York State, and finally the National Assembly. The parade committee was under the jurisdiction of the New York county AOH with Timothy Hartnett as its leader.

The entire AOH structure is burdened with archaic rules and regulations, which often confused everyone, except the brothers of the order. Suspensions and one-year disciplinary procedures were common enough in Hibernian circles but outright expulsions were rare. However, the backlash in response to the inclusion of ILGO in the New York parade had just begun. Following on the heels of Beirne's punishment, Division 7 was expelled outright in perpetuity by the New York County Board AOH because they had invited ILGO to march. It no longer mattered that Beirne's Parade Committee, along with the state and national Presidents of the AOH, had supported Division 7's invitation to ILGO. In fact, the AOH was trying to recover from what it deemed *the* major blunder in terms of the parade—Frank Beirne's acceptance of ILGO's application to march in the first place.

Regardless of his suspension, Frank Beirne was on solid ground. He had an army of supporters and every attempt to oust him from the parade committee failed. Cardinal O'Connor (who had joined Frank Beirne's division of the AOH right after the parade) immediately inserted himself into the fray. He instructed Bishop Thomas Daly of Brooklyn to contact Al O'Hagan, New York State's AOH president, to account for Beirne's suspension. So, the upheavals began within the Catholic fraternity, and because ILGO and the AOH were by now joined at the hip, their turmoil would be ours.

The Irish press was having a field day with the story and the *Irish Echo* began publishing a series of op-ed pieces on the topic. George Clough, national president of the AOH, kicked off the trend and surprised everyone when he stated: "It has to be decided now whether continued sponsorship of the St. Patrick's Day Parade is in the best interest of the Hibernians." It seemed as if the AOH national leadership was going to wash its hands of the New York troubles. Frank Beirne dismissed rumors there might not be a parade in 1992. Contrary to all evidence, he stated that he believed the national AOH would support and fight for its principles. In his op-ed, Frank Beirne shirked all responsibility for what happened at the 1991 parade. He even denied issuing a public statement in March 1991 in which he affirmed that ILGO's application to march had been approved! And he got away with it! Beirne ended his op-ed with a great flourish: "During the parade, through various stratagems and ploys, this parade became a showcase for sexual perversion. ... It was more than a great scandal, it was an abomination."

Division 7 then responded with their op-ed: "Our intention was to resolve a conflict peacefully. We complied with parade rules and regulations, AOH protocols and with the instructions of Mr. Beirne and Mr. Hartnett, respectively." We figured it was our turn now but, after much negotiation, the *Irish Echo*'s publisher, Claire Grimes, refused to print ILGO's opinion telling us that there was no room. We had to wonder if Grimes' long history of involvement with the parade had anything to do with silencing ILGO. Her late husband had been the parade's Grand Marshal in 1971. Grimes herself was a member of an elite fifty-member fundraising group called the Knights of St. Patrick, each of whom contributed the sum of $1,000.00 annually to finance the parade. Back then, the members of this group considered themselves the stuff of grand marshals and through their generous funding felt assured of and entitled to the prestigious title one day.

The *Irish Echo*'s main competition, the *Irish Voice*, gleefully published our op-ed in their newspaper. We did a little "gay" education and corrected the record, stating that contrary to what the AOH was saying; ILGO had not been set up in order to disrupt the parade. Rather, "Marching in the St. Patrick's Day Parade was seen by ILGO as an appropriate cultural activity for the group to celebrate its Irish heritage." We also challenged the AOH's narrow definition of what constitutes being Irish, which in their terms is limited to men who are practicing Catholics. "We see this as a fight for the full participation of all Irish people in the annual celebration of our heritage. The parade committee shouldn't be trying to determine who is Irish enough to celebrate St. Patrick's Day."

Shortly after the publication of everyone's opinion—except ILGO's—in the *Irish Echo* we read a report hidden in the back pages of the newspaper that was very disturbing. The Police Department's Emerald Society, a fraternal organization for Irish American cops, had unanimously approved a resolution "to bar homosexual and other 'alternative lifestyle' or 'counterculture' groups from marching as 'units' or 'organizations' in the New York City St. Patrick's Day Parade." Their resolution also stated:

PREVIOUS SPREAD: Beward the AIDS of March – fundamentalist Catholics show their immaculate placards at every gay event, including the St. Patrick's Day Parade. © *Donna Binder*

ROCK THE SHAM!

By using political clout, members of various extremist homosexual groups, who now call themselves the "Irish Lesbian and Gay Organization," muscled their way into the last St. Patrick's Day Parade for the purpose of degrading the spirit and intent of the parade and thumbing their noses at Cardinal O'Connor.

ILGO's parade committee immediately wrote to the New York City Police Commissioner, Lee P. Brown. We were appalled by the implications of the resolution—how could police officers who promoted such virulent bigotry be trusted to provide equal protection to lesbians and gay men? Openly lesbian New York State Assembly Member Deborah Glick, also wrote to the Police Commissioner and stated, "This most recent action takes the Department to a new low. It is incredible that a fraternal organization made up of members of the Police Department feels free to openly embrace and encourage extreme homophobia."

The Chief of Department, David W. Scott, responded and told ILGO he was gathering facts about the issue and that he would "have more to say about it soon." Three months later the Police Department had not responded. We didn't let it go.

We hand-delivered a letter asserting that by its silence the Police Department was condoning homophobia. Chief Scott's position was that the Emeralds had "acted within their rights under the First Amendment." We knew all about free speech but didn't see why it precluded the Police Department from making it clear that the sentiment of the resolution was not the position of the entire New York City Police Department, unless of course, it was. The police brass would not budge, so by refusing to publicly state that the Emerald Society's resolution was not NYPD policy the Department gave the distinct impression that bias against lesbians and gay men was acceptable.

Parade business continued among Hibernian ranks and when election time rolled round, in October, 1991 Bill Burke, a former grand marshal and the president of the Bank of Ireland, made himself available to challenge Frank Beirne's chairmanship. Burke looked like the ideal candidate to heal the rifts within the AOH but, like Beirne, the parade regulations ruled him out. Even with an impressive group of AOH supporters behind him Burke's nomination failed because Burke was not a parade delegate. Frank Beirne's power base, the parade delegates, revolted. At the very same meeting that Burke was told he was ineligible, the equally ineligible and suspended Beirne was given the all clear to run again for the chairmanship position. Upon hearing this news, the national president, George Clough, stepped in and ordered the elections postponed. Nevertheless, on October 10, 1991 Beirne ran uncontested and was voted in as parade chairman! All parade committee officers were re-elected except for J. Barney Ferguson who was critical of Beirne's style of leadership. Beirne was on a roll and next stop would be the AOH National Board meeting in St. Louis.

It was highly irregular that a suspended member be allowed to attend the St. Louis meeting, especially one who had been openly defying the national leadership. However,

Beirne was indulged; the dispensation was granted because the leadership was baffled by Beirne and wanted to know why he was challenging them. The national board pronounced the results of the recent parade elections null and void. Then Beirne spoke. It was reported that he quickly launched into a tirade that lasted fifteen minutes. His language was colorful and foul in defense of his actions—he called his brothers in Division 7 the "Fag Division" and referred to ILGO as "scumbags." He vowed that neither group would ever march again. According to news reports the gathering was visibly shaken, angered and embarrassed by Beirne's outburst, and National President, George Clough, declared him out of order. In response to the New York troubles the convention constituted a five-man board to oversee the workings of the Parade Committee, dumping Frank Beirne and his committee. The 1992 St. Patrick's Day Parade was effectively put on hold.

The national leadership obviously wanted to be rid of Beirne but the rank and file in New York, with the support of the Archdiocese, stood squarely behind their man. Shortly after his return from St. Louis, Frank Beirne was honored by the New York County Ancient Order of Hibernians at a function in the Roosevelt Hotel. There he denied reports he had used anti-gay epithets at the National Board meeting even though a tape recording of his remarks exists. The cardinal did not attend the dinner but he sent a message to the gathering: "There are few who are so deserving of our accolades as is the extraordinary son of Ireland whom you honor tonight. Following in the tradition of the faith by our forebears, Frank Beirne has demonstrated a remarkable willingness to the Church in both word and action." Beirne read O'Donovan Rossa's motto, which, he confided to the gathering, guided his actions—"I hate evil, untruth and oppression and hating them I'll strive to overthrow them."

Continuing to thumb their noses at the Order's national leadership, the New York County Board defiantly nominated Beirne for the John F. Kennedy Award, the highest AOH honor. This had become quite a circus and I waited with bated breath for the next installment in the Irish weekly papers. The New York Parade Committee mailed affiliation cards to every marching unit, except Division 7. The notices proclaimed the 1992 parade would be dedicated to the 200th anniversary of the United Irishmen, and to the First Amendment to the United States Constitution, which protects free speech, the freedom of religion and the freedom of the press.

But the State and National AOH were not about to be railroaded by an unruly New York faction. They had been talking with the mayor's people and agreed to host an inclusive parade if the state Hibernians were awarded the parade permit. On January 9, 1992 the Police Department issued the St. Patrick's Day Parade permit to the State AOH over the local County Board who had been running the event for years. There was uproar.

A little over a week later everything shifted again, on Saturday, January 18, when the full might of the National AOH came down on ILGO. At a meeting attended by the National AOH President, George Clough, State representatives, and New York County officers, it was announced that ILGO would be banned from the 1992 parade. This came as quite a surprise to ILGO and even more so, to the mayor's office. They had been assured the State body would be willing to host an inclusive parade—this was the reason they were granted the parade permit. Mayor Dinkins said; "We had hoped—indeed, we had been led to believe—that through conversation and consultation, the 1992 St. Patrick's Day Parade would be an inclusive celebration of Irish heritage. ... Regrettably, it has become increasingly clear that such a prospect is increasingly remote." The mayor's office had been outwitted and it wouldn't be the last time this occurred at the hands of the "leadership" of the Irish community. The Hibernians issued a press statement blaming ILGO's "outrageous behavior" during the 1991 parade for their decision. Patrick Farrelly of the *Irish Voice* hit the nail on the head in his Citizen Kane column:

> *Messrs. Clough and Coggins know very well that despite*
> *the most extreme provocation from supporters of the parade*
> *committee, the ILGO conducted themselves along the route*
> *with admirable restraint. Far more, indeed, than the aides to*
> *the grand marshal, the sight of whose backsides, along with*
> *cans of beer flying through the air, are the enduring images*
> *of the 1991 parade.*

Within days of the AOH statement barring ILGO, the New York City Human Rights Commission filed charges of illegal discrimination on the basis of sexual orientation against the Hibernians. ILGO signed on as an interested party so we might have some input in the case. This was happening too quickly for us and we met very regularly now to keep up with developments and make decisions. Paul approached an Irish lawyer he knew, Clare O'Brien, about contacts she might have for pro bono (free) legal representation. Clare had worked with the Irish Immigration Reform Movement and her day job was with Sherman & Sterling, a powerful corporate law firm. Paul hadn't considered asking Clare, or her firm, to represent us but after a meeting with a partner, Paul Wickes, Sherman & Sterling offered their services. We were very nervous about the Commission hearing. We already felt submerged in unknown waters and the world of the law could only complicate matters further.

The Commission's charge of illegal discrimination against the AOH drew much media attention and the ire of well-placed and well-established institutions—the general consensus was that city agencies had no right to go poking around in privately run public events, especially the St. Patrick's Day Parade. The New York Civil Liberties Union (NYCLU) was outraged by what it saw as the city's political expediency "at the expense of time-honored principles of constitutional law." For the NYCLU, parades are the ultimate form of expression, the bedrock of freedom of association. It didn't seem to matter that New York City was obliged to protect lesbians and gay men against discrimination. Bill Dobbs, the gay activist who had told ILGO through Marie not to accept the 1991 compromise because it was a cop-out, popped up again for the press. *The New York Times* reported, "Bill Dobbs, a gay lawyer who is a member of several gay rights groups, including ACT UP, said he found the Hibernians' refusal to let the gay group march together repugnant but found the city's effort even worse." Then the press piped up with newspaper editorials sounding warning bells and charging the administration of treading on thin ice. The Lesbian and Gay Community had fought long and hard to pass the city's Gay Rights Bill. But now nobody seemed to be of the opinion that here was the perfect opportunity to enact the city's law to protect lesbians and gay men against discrimination—it wasn't even suggested. What was suggested was that ILGO be given "separate but equal" treatment by allowing us to march before the official parade on Fifth Avenue. This may have let First Amendment purists off the hook, had it worked, but after 1992 ILGO was never again allowed to hold a pre-parade protest before the St. Patrick's Day Parade, and more importantly, participation in the parade was our goal, not protesting our exclusion.

It was around this time that, as Marie describes it, the "I" was taken out of ILGO. Civil libertarians and the non-Irish media began to describe and define ILGO as a gay group, not an Irish gay group. Analogies, which unmistakably supported the Hibernian's exclusion of ILGO from the line of march, began to pop up in articles where ILGO, for example, was compared to the Ku Klux Klan. We had not anticipated this blow. In essence, these analogies proposed that being lesbians or gay men was the antithesis of being Irish. The most shocking aspect for me was the way these comparisons seemed to make sense to so many people. Mentioning ILGO and the KKK in one breath seemed to switch on a light bulb that was followed by a big "Oh! Of course! Now I get it." But ILGO doesn't hate Irish people—we are Irish. We wanted to march in the St. Patrick's Day Parade because it's Irish and so are we. ILGO never applied to march in any other ethnic parade.

So, out of one side of their mouths most editorialists applauded the mayor for standing by ILGO: out of the other they supported the AOH. It was so easy and acceptable to deny ILGO was Irish only because we were lesbians and gay men too. Homophobia united guardians of the constitution, liberals, and religious fundamentalists alike. Norman Siegel of the New York Civil Liberties Union (NYCLU) offered to represent the AOH. This shocked not just the AOH but many others. Siegel, like other civil libertarians, believed all that was needed was more speech so ILGO could speak by having a counter-parade and then all would be hunky dory. He didn't see any problem linking ILGO with the KKK so long as ILGO got to "speak." This kind of first amendment argument always ignores power differentials and assumes that there is a level playing field. It also advocates speech and more speech regardless of whether or not that speech is ever heard or can have any impact. The AOH declined the NYCLU's offer but paid attention to Siegel's legal argument for keeping ILGO out of the parade and used it with much success.

ILGO was never discouraged for long, and clearly we couldn't afford to be. Despite the recent Hibernian statement banning us from the parade we decided to go ahead and meet with the permit holders, the state AOH, on February 6, 1992. Lots of people from ILGO attended, including Marie, Paul, and Eileen from work—who had become a central figure in our working group now—Brendan, John Lyons, Tom Kieran and me. Debra Pucci and Marjorie Hill were there too with a few other City Hall employees. Several AOH men showed, including Kevin Coggins, the new AOH State President (taking over from Al O'Hagan) and the Chemung County Deputy Sheriff from Elmira in upstate New York, who had driven for several hours to attend. At every available opportunity during the meeting, he brought up his arduous journey; it turned out to be his only contribution. Nothing was gained by the encounter though we tried every imaginable idea we had to resolve the dispute. I asked several times to be told exactly what ILGO needed to do to march and was blown off. Brendan was eloquent in his explanation of why we wanted to march and the Hibernians may have been impressed; but they were otherwise unmoved. They had nothing to offer and nothing to say for themselves. It was another stupid meeting in a series that ILGO sat through with the AOH, who never once attended in good faith. The state AOH had other things to deal with besides ILGO.

Frank Beirne and the county AOH were on the warpath because the parade permit had been robbed from under their noses by the superior state body. They took their case to the State Supreme Court and sued the State Board of the AOH, the mayor, and the police commissioner for the return of the permit. This caused much internal mayhem; the Manhattan brothers were in violation of Article 18 of the Hibernian constitution, which prohibited them from suing other Hibernians without first exhausting all internal channels. More suspensions and expulsions were predicted. And as always in moments of crisis, people show their true colors, so the betrayals and backstabbing began.

Following a slew of negotiations between AOH lawyers in the office of Monsignor Henry Mansell, the Chancellor of the Archdiocese, a deal was struck. Frank Beirne was to relinquish his position as chairman of the parade. Everyone involved knew they needed Beirne's agreement because without it they would have no parade given his support amongst the rank and file. Beirne told the lawyers to do whatever they wanted—he didn't care. What Beirne hadn't anticipated was the decision of his friend, AOH County President, Timothy Hartnett, to sell him out. Hartnett agreed to remove Beirne from the position of Parade Chairman. This wrenched all official, financial, and structural support from Beirne. While the parade delegates supported Beirne they would be more likely to march than not, to make the point that the controversy around ILGO would never stop the historical parade from taking place.

Not for the first time, I was seriously beginning to wonder what on earth we had gotten ourselves embroiled in. The internal workings of the AOH belonged to a different era and the more I tried to follow what was going on, the more surreal it became. I remember, at pre-action meetings, trying to explain the latest AOH shenanigans but having to stop because of people's absolute confusion. In the midst of these parade eruptions the security and daily routine of work comforted me. However, work was not immune to the parade madness because Eileen Clancy was there and she had become very caught up in it. Even though Rick was extremely supportive I felt guilty about all the time spent on ILGO during work hours and worried he might think I was abusing his good will. So we came to an agreement that the time could be made up at weekends when the parade was over again for the year. Things were tense with Eileen for several reasons – I didn't want to work on the parade during the day at work and she did. I wasn't convinced that a legal strategy was something ILGO should pursue and she was. Often I got the distinct impression that Eileen was trying to win me over; she knew, and I was beginning to understand too, that my opinion held a lot of sway in ILGO whereas hers did not. The power dynamic between us was intense and complicated; Eileen was my boss at work.

Aside from my job, my life felt very fragile and unpredictable. My new studio was large and bare; I had a bed, a tiny bookcase, an ugly kidney bean-shaped coffee table the previous tenant had left, and a large heavy desk. Pictures and photographs remained unpacked in cardboard boxes and stacked in the closet. I felt lost without Marie. She visited on rare occasions and hated the studio; she said it was depressing and looked like a waiting room. I liked that it was free of clutter and mayhem, probably because the rest of my life felt so out of control. I set up little routines to help pretend I was coping. I got up at exactly the same time each morning, ate the same food for breakfast, lunch and dinner every single day. Marie, on the other hand, sat at home with a fridge bursting its seams with food, drinking beer, and crying into her pasta dinners. Neither of us knew what to do. I rejected Marie constantly because I was so frightened of being hurt, so I hurt her over and over again. I couldn't bear to be with or without her and began to have panic attacks. I had fantasies of fleeing New York, the parade, and Marie. In February, the fantasy became a reality.

My youngest sister Laura was having her twenty-first birthday on February 25, and I decided it would be a great surprise to arrive in Dublin for the party. It would have been had our aunt, Tedie, kept it to herself! When Catch heard my plan she decided to visit home too, so we flew to Dublin on February 22.

The terminal at JFK was packed and I stood in one of the many queues to check in. Catch had gone out for a cigarette. After five minutes of waiting and attaching name tags to my luggage, a man in his mid-thirties walked the length of the line and stopped close by me, looked in my face, and walked away. Within seconds he began to speak very loudly from his line: "It is that bitch? Who does she think she is? She's not getting on the same plane as me. It's that fucking lesbian bitch. She's not getting on my plane!" I was frozen to the spot and, like everyone else in the immediate vicinity, pretended not to hear him. I knew he wouldn't physically attack me only because he wouldn't have the nerve to in such a public place, but I was terrified and couldn't think of what to do. I assumed he recognized me from the news. In more normal times, when I wouldn't be feeling so vulnerable and exhausted, my reaction would have been to dump my bags and march over, stand right in front of him and make such a scene he would think twice before doing something like this again. At the check-in counter I decided I'd make sure not to be seated near him on the plane. While I planned and panicked, feeling humiliated and scared I heard someone behind me saying, "Hello, Anne." It was Bill Burke—the Bill Burke who had challenged Frank Beirne's leadership by putting himself forward as a candidate for the position of parade chairman. He was the manager of the Bank of Ireland in Manhattan, where I had been recently to pick up a loan, and we had chatted about the parade. We used to laugh about it in ILGO, joking that the only reason I was given a loan was so Burke could pick my brain. Whether or not he realized it, he had come to my rescue; the couple of sentences that passed between us diffused the tension because someone had spoken to me, "the lesbian," which made me human. This was the first time I felt terror because I was recognized in public—it wouldn't be the last.

Before Catch and I left New York, ILGO was in the middle of heated discussion about whether or not we should go into federal court, which would mean a constitutional case, to do battle with the AOH. The Human Rights Commission hearing was scheduled for March 6. Understandably, some people in ILGO were angry with us for abandoning them at this fraught time but I didn't think I'd make it through a second parade without a break. Also I wanted to be there for Laura's party.

It was a great success. We all gathered in the local pub, The Jolly Beggar Man. The place was buzzing and it was difficult to pay attention to anyone for more than a couple of minutes—I was looking forward to the party back at the house where my mother and Aunt Charlie were holding forth in the kitchen, their domain. The night was awkward because I was aware people believed I was a different person now because they all knew I was a lesbian. I wished we could all talk about "the parade," which really meant talking about me being a lesbian but it didn't happen. In a way I was relieved to be spared painful or ignorant opinions about homosexuality but had I been in the spotlight in New York for any other reason everybody would have been excited to talk about all the details. In the meantime Laura was getting very drunk and obstreperous on Southern Comfort and black currant juice and my father looked like he was trying to out-do her. Later at home, my mother, Ina, kept the food flowing. I enjoyed hanging out in the kitchen with the women; I missed that in America.

Meanwhile in New York tensions were running high in the ILGO parade-working group. Those left behind were still in the process of making the colossal decision of whether or not to sue the Hibernians in Federal Court. For the first time the decision would have to be made by a vote because the group couldn't come to a consensus. Marie was the lone clear voice in opposition while others in the group were still unsure. She was up against Paul and Eileen, who otherwise never saw eye-to-eye. Fighting on constitutional grounds was a daunting prospect. Marie knew constitutional law had no record of protecting lesbians and gay men and wondered why Paul and Eileen thought it might now. The odds were stacked against us.

The AOH Goes Berserk

In my gut I didn't want to be in any kind of court and did not want to go ahead with a federal case feeling so ill at ease. No reason or argument had convinced me that the law was a viable option. Marie and I talked on the phone, me sitting on the green couch in my parents' house, looking out at the long, narrow back garden I once believed a vast adventure ground, and Marie sitting on her bed in Brooklyn, cigarettes and ashtray set up on the floor beside her. Both of us worried about lawyers and the law overwhelming everything we were trying to do. We both decided to vote against the move. It's always struck me that such a basic freedom, the right to live as who we are, is a bizarre issue of law—to put it very crudely we go to court and ask to live like everyone else and the court says we have no right to. The law is very tricky and has always caused a lot of tension in ILGO.

Finally, the vote took place—ILGO was headed for Federal Court. Immediately what Marie and I feared happened—the lawyers put their foot down on a political decision and ILGO went along. Even though our previous meeting with the AOH had been fruitless, one final meeting was scheduled. Marie had called me in Dublin to tell me the news, which I passed on to Catch. She said they were all there, waiting and waiting for the AOH to show up when Deputy Mayor Bill Lynch arrived with a startling announcement—the AOH had left the building; but the real shock lay in why they had left. Lynch said the AOH representatives had received a message from a Monsignor at the Chancery ordering them not to meet with ILGO and to "stand firm." Indeed the State President, Kevin Coggins, admitted in the *New York Post* that the Cardinal's advisors, Monsignors Murray and Monsell, had "urged the group to battle the Irish Lesbian and Gay Organization." Naturally, the Archdiocese denied any such messages or statements had been made.

Now ILGO had evidence of something we had known all along but had never been able to prove—that Cardinal O'Connor was calling the shots. I usually smoked in the garden at home because my mother hates the smell of smoke in the house, but I was so excited hearing this news from Marie, that I lit up without thinking. Now we could release a press statement and the media would ask O'Connor to explain his meddling. But Marie was very subdued in response to my great plans. She told me to listen; the group had decided to keep quiet about it, she explained, despite her efforts, because our lawyers didn't think it was good strategy to go public with this information. I was stunned. I wanted to know if all our political decisions would have to be vetted by the lawyers now that we were set to sue the Hibernians.

Paul called me in Dublin later that night and was very forthright, insisting he had never said Catch and I shouldn't vote because we were in Ireland. Those ILGO members who believed in the merit of a legal strategy had suggested this during a very heated debate, which had turned downright dirty. I didn't want to talk about that now. "What about the Cardinal?" I asked him. When he started to explain what the lawyers said I rudely cut him off. I was furious and disappointed. I believed the integrity of how we worked as a group had been badly shaken, and didn't like that Paul had either agreed, or caved in, by accepting the lawyer's advice to keep quiet about Cardinal O'Connor's involvement. I did something

ROCK THE SHAM!

I had never done before, or since; I actively went against the decision of the group and told Paul I was going to talk about the depth of the Cardinal's involvement in banning ILGO from marching in the St. Patrick's Day Parade.

A press conference was already in place. The Gay and Lesbian Equality Network (GLEN) in Dublin had organized it for ILGO. This news would not have the same impact in Ireland because the press would not understand its relevance; it was something that needed to be aired in New York, not Dublin. I went ahead and talked about it anyway. As it turned out, I didn't have to worry that the full story would never be told; the following year Cardinal O'Connor made it perfectly clear how far he was prepared to go to keep ILGO from marching in the parade.

So, one year later, for better or worse, everyone would finally show their true colors. Unfortunately, by then there would be times in ILGO when we forgot who the enemy was, so intent were we on our internal power struggles. In the lead up to our second St. Patrick's Day Parade, in 1992, our small group was having its first real crisis.

The worst had yet to come.

OPPOSITE: Poster from 1997 *Courtesy of Carrie Moyer*

THE *fifth* YEAR
IRISH & QUEER

IRISH LESBIAN AND GAY ORGANIZATION

DEMONSTRATE
WITH THE IRISH LESBIAN AND GAY ORGANIZATION

ST. PATRICK'S DAY
FRIDAY MARCH 17 8:30 am
NYC PUBLIC LIBRARY, FIFTH AVENUE AT 42nd STREET

PRE-ACTION MEETING
THURSDAY MARCH 16, 8PM
THE LESBIAN & GAY COMMUNITY CENTER 208 WEST 13TH STREET

ROCK THE SHAM
The Sequel

ILGO HOTLINE: (212) 967-7711 EXT. 3078

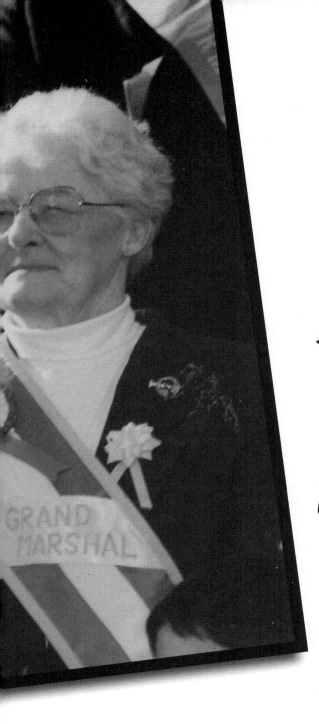

CHAPTER SEVEN

Sex, Lies And A Myth Take Shape

"Every form of bigotry can be
found in ample supply in the
legal system of our country."

– Florynce Rae Kennedy

ROCK THE SHAM!

CONSTITUTIONAL law and the Bill of Rights are a bit like the Ten Commandments. People can't say what they are exactly, for others they seem irrelevant to their lives, and some become zealots or cynics in following them to the letter. Those who are most invested often use, abuse, or mold the rules to suit their particular purpose. This explains why for many Christians in America the commandment "Thou Shalt not Kill" does not apply to capital punishment. So when the Human Rights Commission (HRC) embarked on its discrimination case against the Ancient Order of Hibernians, the Irish Lesbian & Gay Organization began a surreal trip into the highways and byways of the law. The twists and turns in this story would be comical in their absurdity if where they were headed wasn't so damning.

ILGO's experience has been that the law does not work for openly gay men and women; on the contrary, it is punitive. We have testified, submitted briefs and memos in cases where we may as well have rattled off nursery rhymes or presented shopping lists for all the difference they made. I've watched lawyers, new to our case, become convinced of victory when faced with the apparently progressive track records of judges, the opposition's incompetence, shoddy paperwork, missed deadlines, and incomprehensible presentations to the court. And yet, over and over again they are stunned when the ruling comes down so definitively against us.

ILGO's first brush with the law began in March 1992. The Human Rights Commission case laid the foundations for all the legal positions and decisions to come in the years ahead. During the hearing the Ancient Order of Hibernians successfully revised what had taken place on St. Patrick's Day the previous year. This was where being gay was firmly posed, and established, as the antithesis of being Irish, thus robbing ILGO of an intrinsic part of our identity.

Back in 1992 our every spare moment was taken up with ILGO between our monthly meetings, organizing social activities, and the continual reinvention of the group as new members joined. Though it seemed impossible we had even more meetings to attend because of the court cases. We moved from Daisy's, The Lesbian and Gay Center, and our apartments to the grand conference rooms of Sherman & Sterling to meet with our new lawyers, Clare O'Brien and Paul Wickes. Sitting in upholstered chairs around a large, immaculately polished dark wood table, we grappled with the intricacies of the law of the HRC case, along with the contentious federal lawsuit we had voted to pursue. Eileen was very focused and diligent—she carried a laptop computer to meetings on which she tapped out notes. The rest of us weren't quite sure how we had ended up in such plush surroundings.

For the purpose of both lawsuits the Hibernians had redefined the St. Patrick's Day Parade as a Roman Catholic event, as opposed to an Irish celebration, which proved to be a very astute strategy. But this definition ran contrary to any previous descriptions of the famous parade, hence the "Kiss me, I'm Irish" paraphernalia and not "Kiss me, I'm

Catholic." In the entire preamble of the AOH parade handbook there isn't a single mention of the Catholic Church or homosexuality. Rather the Hibernians described the parade as a "broad-based community event" which "celebrates the fact that all Americans, native and immigrant alike, enjoy the 'freedom of the city' on the streets of New York." The handbook also stated the parade committee does not discriminate against groups wishing to march on the bases of "race, color, creed or sex."

So, in our federal lawsuit, filed on March 2, 1992, ILGO challenged the AOH's new assertion that the parade was inherently Catholic. Our legal brief argued that the AOH could not claim that this very public parade was, all of a sudden, a private Catholic affair for the sole purpose of keeping ILGO from marching. I made the mistake of assuming the law would prevent the AOH from redefining themselves at will in order to ban ILGO. The lawsuit was assigned to Judge Pierre Leval. But first, we had to deal with the Human Rights Commission's suit against the Hibernians.

On March 3, 1992, two weeks before the parade, Catch and I arrived back in New York from Dublin. The following day at the Human Rights Commission offices, AOH lawyer Ernest Mathews took my deposition while Maura R. Cahill questioned Paul in a separate room. I was jet-lagged and had no idea what to expect, which made me nervous. Sunlight filled the conference room and I noticed there wasn't a speck of dust on the wall-to-wall shelves packed with immaculate legal tomes. Debra McCullough of Sherman & Sterling and the stenographer sat in with Mathews and me. Within the first few minutes I decided Mathews was smug. I wasn't sure yet whether or not he had a nasty streak. We warmed up; I insisted Mathews refer to me as a lesbian and not a homosexual, and then we got down to business.

Most of the questions Mathews posed addressed the function and history of ILGO as well as details of our application to march in the St. Patrick's Day parade. It was easier and less contentious than I had expected. However, he did liven up a little with a series of conspiracy theory questions when he inquired if two prominent gay activists in New York, Ann Northrop and Andy Humm, had been the movers and shakers behind ILGO's attempt to march. The suggestion was so preposterous I burst out laughing and felt a bit sorry to have to disappoint the AOH lawyer. When I left to go back to work Paul was still being grilled. The following day, I was scheduled to be a witness at the Human Rights Commission hearing.

When the few of us from ILGO arrived at the Commission's office in Lower Manhattan at nine o'clock the next morning, we were refused access. A couple of reporters joined us at the elevator bank and used the opportunity to try to get interviews. I was cranky because I

PREVIOUS SPREAD: The two biggest losers at the 1991 parade... Parade Chairman, Frank Beirne, and Grand Marshal, Mary Holt Moore. © *James Higgins*

was anxious. I wanted to get inside and settled before the grueling session began. Over the security man's shoulder we could see reporters, a CNN television crew, and I recognized Frank Beirne from newspaper photographs. But the hearing room was so packed that the security service continued to keep us outside, even after being told the case was about our group. I became more agitated and started to feel hot with rage and then panic because I didn't know what to do. I paced, trying to calm down. A thought flashed through my head and I decided to leave. "Stupid people," I muttered, when the door opened again and our lawyer, Paul Wickes, nonchalantly drew us in, as if there was nothing to be upset about. We followed him through the crowd into a dingy room where we waited. I knew how nervous I was because it was only when we settled into this room that I became fully aware of other people. When ILGO was called I dunked a smoldering cigarette into a paper cup and rushed to the courtroom.

Judge Rosemarie Maldonado was in charge of the hearing. She was business-like and confident, which was reassuring. She laid out the ground rules, accepted an unsolicited amicus brief (friend of the court argument) on behalf of the AOH from the New York Civil Liberties Union (NYCLU) which went to great lengths to deny that ILGO was an Irish group. Instead, through its analogies, the opinion cynically portrayed ILGO as the dangerous outsider, the enemy, and most definitely and ludicrously anti-Irish:

> Could the organizers of the Israel Day Parade be compelled to
> accept German born neo-Nazis to its ranks? Would the Gay
> Pride Parade Committee be required to accept heterosexual
> homophobes and skinheads to its contingency? Can the AOH
> exclude on the grounds of national origin an English born group
> which wishes to march with the banner "England Stay In Ireland"?
> Must the AOH include non-Catholic groups who wish to express
> their anti-Papal beliefs?

Norman Siegel of the NYCLU played a central role in stripping ILGO of our Irish identity. For their legal argument to work the Irish Lesbian & Gay Organization had to be defined solely as an organization of homosexuals because the fact of our Irishness made a sham of their premise. No lawyer would have had the stupidity to assert that ILGO was not a lesbian and gay group. However, for some bizarre reason, taking away our Irish identity was not scrutinized or perceived to be just as ridiculous. Siegel suggested the city award ILGO a permit for a separate parade so our views might also be heard on St. Patrick's Day. According to his theory the law would then be seen to serve everyone equally. ILGO wasn't buying the separate but equal status. It was of vital importance we were recognized as a bona-fide group of Irish women and men who were also lesbian and gay.

We sat where we could in the packed room, which was with the reporters, and watched the opening action. This was the first time I'd seen Frank Beirne in person and I stared at him when he wasn't looking. During the day we carefully slipped by each other on several occasions and it was strange to be in such close quarters with him. I instinctively felt that regardless of his beliefs, he at least was completely honest about them. But when the hearing was over I was disappointed. The AOH was on a mission from God or next best thing in New York, the cardinal, and they would do whatever needed to be done to keep ILGO away from the parade.

The hearing officially began. My only remarkable memory of the morning was that Kevin McKernan, the lawyer for the National AOH, made a speech that was entirely incoherent. Rolando Acosta, Deputy Commissioner for Law Enforcement at the Human Rights Commission, began the opening statements. Their grounds for suing the AOH were based on the city charter, which protected lesbians and gay men against discrimination. They argued that the parade was a public accommodation, that it was civic and public in nature similar to other public venues, like clubs, parks, bars or marathons. If they proved this the thinking was that the AOH could not ban ILGO because of our sexual orientation. Acosta was tall and good-looking but he was disconcertingly scattered. (I didn't know at the time that a coherent argument was necessary in a courtroom.)

Paul Wickes, grey-haired, debonair, and a quick-witted lawyer then took the floor for ILGO. Compared to Acosta's, his delivery was very smooth. He kept to the point and was eloquent in his reminder of the history of the St. Patrick's Day parade, claiming, "This parade in its roots, in its history, throughout the years of its existence, has been dedicated to eradicating and eliminating discrimination." The attorney who had deposed me the previous day, Ernest Mathews, was the final speaker. He wore a smart blue suit that covered his plump figure, and his thinning wavy hair was brushed back from his forehead. He had a neat moustache, one similar to my grandfather's. He contended that ILGO was treated like everyone else and explained that because ILGO had not reached the top of the "waiting list" the people currently running the parade weren't in a position to either allow or disallow us to march. The fact that the entire AOH had bonded around banning ILGO from ever participating in the parade made this a spurious position at best. Mathews encapsulated the AOH argument by stating, "the first defense that we have is that there was no discrimination. The second defense is that if you should find there is discrimination, we have a right to discriminate." So, they didn't discriminate against ILGO, but just in case they did, it was irrelevant.

As I sat waiting in the witness seat I relaxed my arms and laid my hands in my lap, fingers criss-crossing to ward off any urge to fidget. I remembered watching my friend, Anne Speed, on the *Late Late Show* on TV in Ireland years earlier. She was cross because she had forgotten to keep her hands still. She said it distracted from what she had to say. My palms were sweating. Paul Wickes had told Brendan Fay, the other ILGO witness, and me to answer the question asked and not to expand or ramble. I blocked out everyone, ignored

ROCK THE SHAM!

Frank Beirne and the AOH contingent who were directly in front of me, only feet away. For most of my testimony the only person I was aware of was the man asking the questions. I regretted wearing a Kelly-green woolen sweater; it was too hot, but earlier that morning I had thought it was funny—green sweater, mop of red curly hair, clunky Doc Marten boots, definitely Irish and definitely lesbian. I looked down at myself and felt enormous.

During his cross-examination Ernest Mathews was sometimes feisty and a smart aleck. My mouth was so dry the carafe had to be refilled several times. The sensation of water traveling past my throat was a relief but as soon as I placed the glass back on the table my tongue thickened and felt like it would have to be pried from the roof of my mouth. After being assertive with Mathews during the deposition, he did not refer to us as homosexuals during the hearing but as lesbians and gay men. He asked questions about the experience of marching in the parade and when I was describing the scene and mentioned that ILGO people were "walking along, waving," he interrupted. He was beginning to establish the AOH spin—which was that ILGO, and not the AOH or some spectators had behaved inappropriately in 1991.

> Q: You didn't see anyone making obscene gestures?
> A: I did not, no.
> Q: You did not see anybody fondling each other as they walked?
> A: I did not, no.
> Q: You did not see anyone shouting obscenities as they passed the Cathedral?
> A: My recollection is complete silence at the Cathedral.

There was much whispering and barely muffled comments in the hearing room. Judge Maldonado snapped saying she would clear the room unless the noise ceased immediately. The AOH's underlying thesis was that ILGO was treated like every other group but we weren't satisfied because we wanted an "exception" made. Invoking special treatment, when "special" is a code word used to undermine the validity of a claim of unethical or unequal treatment, is pretty typical. Mathews gave several examples even suggesting I would expect to jump to the top of the line at the supermarket! He didn't bother me—I remained calm and didn't let him get away with anything. Then came a retired Court of Appeals Justice, Jacob D. Fuchsberg, acting as Frank Beirne's lawyer. This man really confused me.

Marie was waiting outside with a couple of other ILGO members. They couldn't get in until there was a break in testimony. A reporter for one of the Irish weekly papers told them I was being hammered—that the Hibernians were really going after me. Marie was frantic. She had run out of her office at NYU on an early lunch break and had to be back soon. Even though we were no longer together I had stayed with her the night before the hearing and she knew how scared I'd been leaving that morning. There was nobody there to tell her I was holding my own.

However, I was in no position to gauge how it was going. When I caught Clare's eye I couldn't read her expression; she was concentrating. Jacob Fuchsberg began. He was aggressive from the start and quickly worked himself into frenzy, roaring questions at me. I thought he might be unstable and wanted to ask Judge Maldonado if he was supposed to be shouting at me. I wondered why she didn't stop him or why our lawyers didn't object. I tried to stay focused, adamantly refusing to answer any questions where he referred to ILGO as "your friends." If he could not say lesbian, gay, or even ILGO, I was not going to answer his questions. His style rattled me nonetheless. Fuchsberg's cross-examination was a dud, as was Kevin McKernan's, another AOH lawyer. Brendan Fay took the stand.

Ernest Mathews was pugnacious to begin with but gradually became more respectful. Upon hearing the Mary Louis Academy knew Brendan was gay when they hired him but didn't fire him until after the parade, he seemed perplexed.

> Q: You don't accept the position of Cardinal O'Connor, for instance, who has preached that homosexual activity is wrong?
> A: Well, I think that it's important to remember that the Church has been consistent in its teaching that to discriminate against lesbian and gay people is wrong.

Brendan talked a lot about his personal experiences as a gay man in Ireland. Much of his testimony centered on theology and Mathews engaged him, eager to show off his bit of knowledge. But Brendan was an expert and ran rings around him, which I thoroughly enjoyed. After Brendan's testimony there was a break before Frank Beirne, the parade chairman, took the stand. At last we got the feedback we were waiting for—Paul Wickes told us we had done superb jobs and he couldn't have wished for better witnesses. Now we could relax and listen to what the other side had to say.

Frank Beirne settled himself and looked composed. He had a great big nose and his black hair was slicked from left to right over his bald patch. His skin looked weather-beaten, like he had spent most of his years working out of doors when, in fact, he had worked for the Transit Authority for twenty-nine-and-a-half years. When he spoke it was softly, with a distinct Leitrim accent. He'd left Ireland in 1956. An insight into Frank Beirne's attitude and understanding of lesbians and gay men was given during his deposition. He explained, "We do not discriminate against any individual. Regardless of who they are, race, creed, nationality, color, sex or *creature* (emphasis mine). He went on to state, "We never asked anyone whether they are male or female or anything else." Beirne talked of his childhood, saying, "The way I was brought up in Ireland as far as gay or homosexual, it is a sin. ... At home in Ireland a fag meant a queer or a gay." He agreed "fag" has a derogatory meaning but insisted he hadn't come up with "Fag Division" to describe Division 7 who had invited ILGO to march in 1991. However, the term "Fag Division" didn't appear in print until he coined the term during his outburst at the AOH's national convention.

ROCK THE SHAM!

...do Acosta of the HRC had first dibs on Beirne but was so muddled he gave up
a... d the witness over to Paul Wickes who asked Beirne about ILGO.

Q: What do you know their agenda to be?
A: Well, homosexuality is a mortal sin in the Church.
Q: Do you know what ILGO's agenda is?
A: They are gay and they are lesbian and they are against the teaching of our Catholic church.
Q: That's their sexual orientation, but as an organization, what do you think they are?
A: I don't understand the question.
Q: Why do you think they get together as a group?
A: I don't know.

Wickes then tackled the recent AOH position that the parade is non-political and does not allow groups with a political agenda to march. The testimony established that Beirne did not consider the likes of the New York City Council, trade unions, or the Irish Immigration Reform Movement to be political in nature or to have political agendas—so they, and other similar groups, were allowed to participate in the parade. He also made it abundantly clear that as long as he was Chairman ILGO would never march.

Though Frank Beirne was the parade chairman in 1991 and watched the parade from the official reviewing stand he could not testify from his own experience about ILGO's bearing during the event. However the parade committee regrouped following the disastrous 1991 parade and developed a strategy that would haunt ILGO. They revised what had happened by inventing the myth of ILGO's "outrageous behavior." (There was not one complaint in any AOH or parade documentation to back up the falsehood though many other violations by other marching units were noted and written up, with recommendations to censure and in some cases, remove the units from the parade.) During his deposition Beirne described what he meant by the alleged "outrageous behavior."

We got complaints that there was girls holding hands
kissing one another, and in front of the reviewing stand
they stopped and they used four letter words starting
with 'F.' They even shouted up at one woman, "We
are not after you. We are coming after your children."
And they put their finger up at the people in the
reviewing stand.

Jacob Fuchsberg, consistently ineffectual during the hearing, despite being a former

Court of Appeals Judge, should never have come out of retirement. He stood tall and questioned his client. I assume his plan was to portray the parade chairman as a "salt of the earth" immigrant unlike those of us in ILGO, who after all, were not even recognized as Irish anymore. Instead he managed to imply that Beirne was a "thick Paddy." But Beirne didn't bat an eyelid when Fuchsberg said, "Perhaps everybody will agree with me, you have a kind of a charming Gaelic accent. Now, I want to ask you did you get any education in the United States in English after you came here?"

At the time of the commission hearing, Margaret O'Rourke, a heavy-set woman in her sixties, was in charge of the parade waiting list. When ILGO originally saw a copy of the list in March 1991 at our first meeting with the Hibernians and City Hall officials, we were number 31. O'Rourke had since typed up a new list for the commission hearing and ILGO now came in at number 43. We were staggered by the chicanery. O'Rourke proved to be elusive even for Paul Wickes. He was trying to elicit some procedural information about the waiting list when, exasperated, she burst out, "I am a one-man stenographer army and I have many, many other pressing things that must be done."

Like the other AOH witnesses, she wasn't too busy to remember to mention ILGO's alleged bad behavior during the parade. In her deposition on February 28, 1992, O'Rourke gave the reasons why ILGO would not be permitted to join the march on Fifth Avenue again. She explained, "Well, the disorderly way in which they participated in the parade. Their discourtesy. Their ... what I would call ... outrageous behavior." When the Credentials Committee held a special meeting to decide that ILGO would not march in the 1992 Parade, O'Rourke cited stories she heard from people about the "outrageous behavior" in 1991, as well as accounts in the print media. But no such accounts exist in any newspaper because there was no substance to what the AOH was claiming. The Hibernians either deliberately lied or actually believed Irish lesbians and gay men marching in the St. Patrick's Day Parade, in itself, constituted outrageous behavior.

The seeds of the lie began with a letter. Frank Beirne had come under attack within Hibernian circles following his mishandling of the controversy and he probably solicited letters of support, one of which came from Mary Holt Moore, who was the Grand Marshal in 1991. In the letter, she lavishes praise on Beirne and comments on the "sad spectacle" created by a group of people whom she alleged marred the "beauty and dignity of a glorious day by their strident, vulgar, and outrageous behavior before me in the reviewing stand." It's safe to assume she's referring to ILGO and not the Fire or Police Department Emerald Societies.

The ground work was in place but it was not until a joint press statement issued by the Parade Committee and the County, State and National Boards of the Hibernians in America on January 20, 1992 that their accusation really took root. Their statement announced that they were "of one mind, one heart, one determination" to take "all necessary steps and measures to insure that no organization or organizations are allowed to use the parade as a vehicle to publicly insult any person or group watching or reviewing the parade." The punch line of their statement read: "The outrageous behavior and conduct of ILGO mandates that ILGO not be permitted to participate in the 1992 Parade."

Unfortunately, the ploy worked and became as real as the designation of ILGO in violent opposition to everything Irish. Reporters began to ask us to comment on our outrageous behavior during the 1991 parade. ILGO responded to the charge, saying it was false. Some reporters, most of whom had marched with ILGO in 1991, challenged the AOH's position. Jim Dwyer, a *New York Newsday* columnist wrote, "All this was very curious to me, since I had marched up Fifth Avenue with the gay group, and while many beer-boiled red-faces on the sidewalks were screaming that the gays should die quickly of AIDS, and using their middle fingers, I didn't see the marchers doing anything besides walking with their arms around each other."

Reports also appeared in the Irish weekly newspapers denying the AOH claim, to no avail. We were witnessing a replay and knew the damage it was causing: the first myth was that because we were gay, we were not Irish, and now, even with the facts on our side, there was something about this new lie that was sticking. One explanation is that the fabrication was generally accepted as true because it's what people expected—because we are lesbians and gay men. Or perhaps the raw abuse hurled at ILGO on St. Patrick's Day was so distasteful to the general population that it chose not to accept what had really happened. Maybe it was easier to blame ILGO rather than acknowledge the very public display of hatred targeted at lesbians and gay men. I believe some people think we deserved what we got for being gay and open about it. Finally, the AOH became the victim—a position far more palatable to the public, it seemed, in this instance.

This wouldn't be the last time ILGO was expected to accept the burden of hostile action taken against us, an expectation ILGO has never once caved in to. But once accused of bad behavior it seemed we were no longer innocent—the charge was made and the truth proved to be no defense.

Now, sitting in the Human Rights Commission witness chair was Mary Holt Moore, the originator of the outrageous behavior myth. She is a tall, handsome woman with perfect posture. She had the air of a primary school principal, not merely a regular teacher as she had been. For all her manners and primness she stood out in that she was the only witness who managed to say "fuck" during the hearing, not once but twice. She feigned coyness but as soon as she was asked about ILGO passing the parade's reviewing stand she took off:

> Q: *And when they passed in front of you, what did you observe?*
> A: *Outrageous behavior. They gave the finger ... which I believe is the same as, well, I will use it, 'fuck you.' Is that right?*

In case we didn't get it the first time she repeated it: "...it's hard for me to bring out the word because it's not used. ... they (ILGO) used 'fuck', 'shit' and 'garbage.'"

Mary Holt Moore had the distinction of being the second woman to hold the position of Grand Marshal in the 230-year history of the St. Patrick's Day Parade in New York. This grand achievement was overshadowed by the controversy in 1991. Her disappointment and bitterness was understandable and palpable. She'd had plans. She was especially pleased that she would lead the parade that commemorated the seventy-fifth anniversary of the Easter Rising against the British in Ireland. Ironically, in Ireland, the organizers of the Dublin parade refused to admit a float commemorating the Rising supposedly because there was no room! St. Patrick's Day in 1991 was supposed to be Mary Holt Moore's shining moment, but she blew it. In her letter to Frank Beirne, she blamed ILGO for her ineffectiveness, saying, "This single-issue organization denied the Irish-American community the opportunity to be heard on many valid issues of human rights and social injustice which are unfortunately generally ignored by the media. I had high hopes of reaching the American people and enlightening the media in such neglected matters." But Mary Holt Moore could have addressed these issues; she had the perfect forum, especially in 1991 when the media was all over the parade. She saw the conflict and knew she would not be able to address human and civil rights violations in Ireland with integrity without having to comment on the discrimination against ILGO in New York. Rather than rise to the occasion, she chose silence. Her hostility to lesbians and gay men destroyed what could have been her glory.

In conjunction with the alleged verbal profanities, "outrageous behavior" included dress code, body language, affection, and what we did with our fingers. One of the more amusing depositions was that of Lieutenant Shalvey of the Police Department. He was the Chairman of the Line of March Committee and a member of Division 9 of the AOH. Lieutenant Shalvey had much to say about what constituted men's wear and women's wear. His particular expertise was kilts. He told the court, "I saw one, possibly two people, males in female attire. By that, I mean they were wearing skirts." Shalvey got very excited when asked to explain how he knew they were skirts and not kilts. He talked about the specific cut of a kilt, which he noted, was originally designed for male wear. To stress the point he announced, "They were not kilts. I have worn kilts. I know what kilts are."

Lieutenant Shalvey went on to describe the ILGO contingent with colorful language. "They were playing and they were all theatrically swishing around trying to incite the people on the sidelines watching the parade. I observed some males reaching out and grabbing their crotch area and shaking their crotch area, along with other people chanting, 'We are gay and we are here to stay!' I observed other males patting each other on the rear end ... As this type of behavior was continuing up the avenue it was inciting people on the sidelines and they started throwing sandwiches and paper cups and what have you ... and it was reaching the point where they thought people were going to spill over the barriers onto the street." Paul Wickes was interested in Shalvey's charge that the ILGO contingent was inciting the onlookers. He asked:

Q: What was thrown back into the crowd by members of ILGO?
A: To my knowledge, nothing.
Q: Is inciting a riot a crime in New York City?
A: Yes, it is.
Q: If one of those 3,200 police officers had seen people inciting to riot, would they have been obligated to file reports?
A: They would be obligated to effect an arrest.
Q: Were any arrests made?
A: No, because no one incited to riot, counselor.

In fact he testified that, "At one point in time, in order to protect the mayor, a one- or two-star chief of the New York City Police Department left the mayor's contingent and actually jumped over a pair of barricades into a crowd of people." Shalvey said that as Chairman of the Line of March Committee one of his duties was to ask for written reports of improper behavior from his colleagues working the parade. When asked how many written reports he received about ILGO's improper behavior after the parade in 1991, he said, "None."

Under Paul Wickes' cross-examination Monsignor William Smith admitted that there is nothing in Church teaching that requires a good practicing Catholic to leave Fifth Avenue because there's also a homosexual there. The hearing was close to ending. The final witness was David Marr, a video producer who had been quoted in a news article denying ILGO's alleged bad behavior. It turned out that out of Marr's six hours of video footage of the parade, only 90 seconds included ILGO marching. This was the dud that ended the proceedings. The decision was now in Judge Maldonados' hands and ILGO was very hopeful, and from what we had experienced, we had every reason to be.

Beyond this courtroom, ILGO's struggle to live, not as one dimensional human beings (homosexuals), but as the complex multi-dimensional people we are, continued for years. The Ancient Order of Hibernians was never in the position to define what constitutes being Irish. They cannot claim the St. Patrick's Day Parade is Irish while excluding those Irish they don't happen to like. What everyone seems to forget is ILGO would not have applied to march in a Catholic procession.

The heart of the matter was that ILGO asked to be treated just like any other group in the line of march. Every other group is allowed to express its own special affiliation or affinity with their Irish heritage except ILGO. We were penalized for daring to be open Irish lesbians and gay men. But the Ancient Order of Hibernians was not acting in a vacuum. We lived in a country where Bill Clinton, the self-proclaimed pro-gay president, instituted the farcical, "Don't Ask, Don't Tell" policy in the U.S. military—the government's version of "Love the sinner, hate the sin." It got worse in his second term when he signed DOMA – the Defense of Marriage Act in 1996 which stated that marriage is "a legal union of one man and one woman as husband and wife." ILGO's legal battles would prove that the United States Constitution neither upholds the right of lesbians and gay men to say who we are with impunity nor does it even attempt to treat us with equality. While the Irish Lesbian & Gay Organization may have had the moral high ground, the AOH had everything else.

MY IRISH EYE
are BRIGHT & GAY
BUT... THEY'RE
NOT SMILING

CHAPTER EIGHT

A View From The Barricades

"I do not want to be tolerated nor misnamed. I want to be recognized."

– Audre Lorde

ROCK THE SHAM!

FIVE DAYS before the 1992 parade, with no definite plan in place, ILGO was in court again. When we appeared in front of Judge Pierre N. Leval of the United States District Court in our lawsuit against the Ancient Order of Hibernians and the New York City Police Department, we were still awaiting the Human Rights Commission's decision. In the meantime ILGO was seeking an order to disallow the AOH's discrimination against us or, alternatively, to prevent the Police Department from issuing a parade permit and closing a public avenue for a religious procession—the separation of Church and State.

Judge Leval said that while the constitutional arguments were very interesting, he felt the Hibernians had a point because ILGO had not yet reached the top of the waiting list; he wondered why ILGO might expect to leap over the groups ahead. Paul Wickes pointed to the testimony of AOH witnesses during the Human Rights Commission hearing. Both Margaret O'Rourke and Frank Beirne of the Parade Committee had said that ILGO would never march. O'Rourke admitted ILGO remained on the list for historical record only. The waiting list was a ruse—it couldn't have been any clearer.

Again, Norman Siegel of the New York Civil Liberties Union (NYCLU) spoke for the Hibernians' right to exclude ILGO. He felt the problem was political rather than constitutional. The NYCLU's main point hinged on the constitutional guarantees of any private organization to define its message, which oddly, in his thesis, did not apply to ILGO. For the NYCLU, the AOH's right to be homophobic outweighed ILGO's right to say we were gay and Irish, which was central to our message. I couldn't help feeling cynical about the ACLU, given their history of defending anti-Semites, white supremacists and homophobes just to prove the purity of their philosophy—nothing is ever that pure. Judge Leval said he would do his best to have a decision by March 17, St. Patrick's Day.

The following day, on March 13, we received news that moved the parade issue out of New York. The Irish-American Gay, Lesbian and Bisexual Group of Boston (GLIB) had sued and won the right to march in the Boston St. Patrick's Day Parade. In New York, the Hibernians responded by threatening to cancel the New York parade if ILGO was allowed to march. We were pleased for GLIB and I was thrilled that the impact of what ILGO had taken on had reached beyond New York. The controversy that had begun in New York's Irish community one year earlier had spread its wings to Boston and would travel even farther a field before the day of the parade.

Across the Atlantic Ocean, plans for St. Patrick's Day were well underway throughout cities and towns in Ireland. When I was a child, everything closed down for the national holiday except the churches. St. Patrick's Day was always fun. We got to eat sweets even though it was the middle of Lent and we were supposed to be abstaining for 40 days and nights. If we didn't go to the parade we could watch it on television. People didn't wear green the way they do in New York but adults pinned wilting clumps of shamrock to their lapels or small rosettes of green, white, and gold. I now often wondered what it would be like to be in Dublin again for St. Patrick's Day.

Katherine O'Donnell, who had spent several years in Boston as a student, had moved back to her native Cork, the second-largest city in the Irish Republic, often considered the real capital by its natives. She was involved in a lesbian philosophy group that met throughout the Winter months. In a café, after one of the meetings, the St. Patrick's Day Parade came up. "Petra and Orla said we should get a lesbian float because the biggest problem for lesbians was our invisibility," Katherine remembers. "But we decided to be very generous and to invite bisexuals and gays as well!" So while ILGO didn't know whether or not we'd be marching in the 1992 New York parade, lesbians were all set to march in Cork.

When news of the Cork group reached us, my response surprised me: I was upset. I knew I should be happy. I didn't understand my sadness or why the news had immediately made me cry. This hadn't happened when we heard about the Boston group; in fact, along with my excitement I had felt a bit envious of them. The news from Cork had something to do with "home." In ILGO we felt so proud that what we were doing in New York had started an ebb and flow of connection between our new home and our old. It took me a long time to figure out I was saddened by what I had lost by leaving Ireland, and worse, grieving because I knew I'd had to leave; there are so many reasons that it hadn't seemed possible to me in 1987 to survive in the country I was reared in and loved, one of which was that I was a lesbian.

The irony of what was happening wasn't lost on anyone. Here was ILGO in New York, the city of all cities, a haven for lesbians and gay men, having fled our homes in search of freedom, and we couldn't march in a silly parade. But in Cork, lesbians were being welcomed with open arms. Parade official Kieran Murphy, proudly announced, "I suppose you could say we are fairly progressive down here in Cork. The Junior Chamber of Commerce, as the organizers of the parade, recognized that this group are a part of our society and have as much right to march as anybody else." Next we heard two lesbians from Dublin and two gay men from Cork were preparing to fly to New York to support ILGO on St. Patrick's Day.

The phone rang at work. The Human Rights Commission was ready—Judge Maldonado's recommendation was about to be announced. Eileen and I grabbed our coats and told Rick what was going on. It was four days before the parade. We would be back in the office in a couple of hours. Rick's patience seemed endless. We were constantly on the phone, running off to meetings, typing up press releases, faxing them out, photocopying and generally leaving him in the lurch. Eileen and I had worked out a routine to cope with the massive work schedule around the parade. Our days at Prelinger Associates were spent juggling our time between our paid work and ILGO. When television interviews were

PREVIOUS SPREAD: There wasn't much to smile about in 1992. We were duped by the NYPD, and ended cooped up like animals on Fifth Avenue. © www.carolinakroonphotography.com

requested we staggered them about fifteen minutes apart and took turns. We tried to fit them into our lunch hour to give some semblance of a regular work environment. The news crews thought Rick's office was ILGO's headquarters! Now we were abandoning Rick yet again. He sent us on our way, wishing us luck. It was Friday, March 13, a bad day for the superstitious.

Although standing in front of a camera with a microphone shoved in my face had become second nature, I was never entirely at ease. I learned to rattle off neat sound bytes, which was all the press was interested in, but this news item was real life for us. The responsibility was nerve-racking. While it was never overtly acknowledged we were aware of the advantages and appeal of having a lesbian with curly red hair and an Irish accent representing the group—it clearly defined who we were. But it was also complicated for a whole host of reasons, not least of which was my growing status as ILGO figurehead.

Being such a visible and recognizable lesbian caused an unforeseen invasion of my privacy. I could no longer walk the streets in peace and started to feel like every minute detail of my life was under intense scrutiny. If I didn't behave appropriately—a standard that is absolutely subjective—it reflected on the group. The strain of having to be so self-conscious wore me out. I never knew when or where I would be approached or accosted. Sometimes it was in the local bodega, on the train, in a restaurant, at a cinema, the supermarket, in a bathroom or an elevator. I might be standing in line minding my own business when someone would call out, "Hi." I'd look, not recognize the person, but return the greeting because I'm not rude and because I was never sure whether or not I should remember this person from somewhere. Then they would invariably mention the parade.

The closer the parade drew, the more frequent the news stories became and I was sometimes stopped several times a day. In subway stations I began to stand further away from the platform's edge and always directly behind a pillar when the train approached, and I still do. Nobody ever tried to push me under a train but I had reason to be cautious. On my way into work one morning a car ran a red light when I was crossing an intersection, the driver leaning to scream about the parade through his lowered passenger seat window. Another time a van drove up onto the sidewalk, on a busy block in broad daylight, and drove straight at me. I sidestepped into Dizzy Izzy's, bought a cup of tea, a banana, and a bagel and went back to my job and worked. Everything was normal except I couldn't stop shaking.

Every time something frightening happened I knew exactly what had taken place but I was protecting myself by shutting it out; otherwise how would I get out of bed to go work every day? Once, someone witnessed one of the incidents. A truck driver, staring directly at me from the high seat of his cabin, slammed on his accelerator and came screeching out of a loading dock on 15th Street, missing me by a breath. Right before, everything went into slow motion and I thought, *Shit, I'm dead!* I knew it was purposeful because I looked into his face as he drove at me. A man on the street said, "Jesus! What did you do to him?" Then he laughed nervously, stating the obvious. "He did not like you." I didn't answer him but when I got back the office I was unable to work. The man's acknowledgement of what had happened somehow made it harder for me to recover. I didn't understand this kind of hatred. I didn't even know if it was about being a lesbian but what if he had hit me? Killed me? His life would have been changed forever, in the space of a second or two, and for what? I still jump and duck at the noise of brakes screeching, horns blowing, even a car door slamming.

Usually the only person I told what had happened was Marie, often very matter-of-factly. I didn't want to scare anyone in ILGO. But I wasn't just protecting ILGO. I felt a profound sense of shame that such violence was directed at me.

However, strangers also stopped to talk about their vacations, families, relationships and the kind of day they were having. I had conversations with men about their wives, or girlfriends who'd run off with lesbians, and listened to a host of others working out their ambivalent sexuality. An elderly Irish woman who'd lived in New York for most of her life called me at work over a period of years to talk about her late husband's bisexuality and his artistic friends, always stressing what decent people they were. People stopped to chat as if they'd known me all their lives, like we were long lost friends. I don't know what I represented for them but being asked to be kind and intimate, or to have empathy, wasn't such a hardship, more an unexpected surprise.

Time for anything other than work and ILGO was very limited. Compared to our first parade, we had months to organize ourselves in the lead up to the 1992 event but we also had much more to contend with. We were tying up loose ends for a rally we had planned at Sheridan Square and we had to take into account that we might not win the court case. Those who didn't have the same freedom that Eileen and I went about their parade responsibilities surreptitiously at their jobs. A core group of about five of us worked non-stop for weeks and months. Our days began at seven or eight in the morning and continued through to the early hours of the following day. We had a parade calendar to keep track of meetings we had to attend, either our own or ones in the lesbian and gay and Irish communities. We had lists of times, dates, and locations for distributing our flyers, including a regular weekend spot at Sheridan Square. We set up schedules for wheat-pasting (bill-sticking) and had maps of areas to be covered and re-covered with posters announcing our plans for St. Patrick's Day. We were in constant physical, emotional, and creative motion, trying to keep up. Contrary to the popular belief that ILGO was a huge, powerful, and well-funded organization, we were a small group of activists trying to pull off something big. There was no stopping us—we only took breaks in between to sleep.

Within half an hour of receiving the phone call, Eileen and I arrived at the Human Rights Commission on Rector Street. Paul, John Voelcker, Tarlach, and John Lyons were already there, looking solemn and nervous. I made a joke about it being Friday the Thirteenth. All was quiet. We waited impatiently in a conference room, aware of the bustle of busy staffers beyond the door. One copy of the judge's recommendation was sent in and a moment passed before our hands reached out to touch it. We huddled; the pages turned before I had finished reading them. At first it looked good but the preliminary scan revealed we had lost. It didn't make sense. The judge said the AOH had discriminated against us. She even ruled that the parade was a public accommodation. According to her findings the waiting list was a sham. But ILGO could not march.

I did not understand. Either the parade was a public accommodation and under the jurisdiction of the city charter or it wasn't. The recommendation was infuriating and baffling. We kept thinking we had missed something so we divided the pages between us and pored over them to see where the mistake was. More copies of the decision were dropped on the table and we became quieter as we realized we had really lost. The atmosphere in the room dulled with our disappointment. Having our position vindicated but under the law deemed ineligible was very confusing. We were trying to grapple with what was before us, trying to make sense of something senseless. Everything we had said was true. We believed that would count. However, in Maldonado's analysis, the right of the AOH to discriminate outweighed ILGO's right not to be discriminated against.

It was three days before the parade and, whether or not we admitted it, we had been depending on the HRC's recommendation to sort out our plan—we had hoped we would be marching. Now we would have to figure out something else to do on St. Patrick's Day. Bright television lights snapped on and cameras flashed as we entered the HRC's press conference. A clump of microphones was arranged like a centerpiece in the middle of a long table. There wasn't room for us all to sit so most of us stood by the back wall and listened to Rolando Acosta break the news. Ernest Mathews was there. The Hibernians had not expected the commission to rule in their favor. It would have been easier for the mayor had the decision gone in ILGO's favor because then he wouldn't have to make a political decision about how to continue to handle this difficult dispute. But a legal decision eventually gave David Dinkins his way out of the mess, even if it wasn't the one he had originally banked on.

Being expected to perform on cue is a lot of what I didn't like about media work —always having to be calm, patient, and reasonable. In the past, being a model of self-control had made me good for the job. But now, as soon as the questions started I realized how furious I was and slid back against the wall, leaving the others to respond. How could everything we said be true but meaningless? I could not accept this. The commission offices were always too hot; tiny dots of perspiration gleamed on Tarlach's forehead, and John Lyons, agitated, incessantly ran his fingers through his hair. Paul and Eileen's energy seemed to be colliding above my head. I started to feel a little out of control and had an urge to tell the reporters about my confusion over splitting up with Marie, and how frightening it sometimes was being a lesbian. People squeezed past me in the cramped space, or leaned over someone's back to speak into the microphones. We managed.

There was always Judge Leval's Federal Court decision, which we expected on Monday March 16, but we weren't feeling hopeful. We had discussed having a protest march before the St. Patrick's Day Parade if all else failed and decided to go with that plan now. Mayor

Dinkins had fallen ill and a news report from the hospital announced he would not march in the parade if ILGO didn't. I wondered if his sickness was psychosomatic. John Voelcker and Eileen, the two active Irish Americans in the parade group, often worked as a team and agreed to meet with officials of the Police Department. The police requested the meeting to discuss ILGO's protest march.

The court battles were drying up Hibernian coffers and they held a big fundraiser in Gaelic Park in the Bronx to help pay their legal fees. But this was not the only area of AOH bankruptcy. Joe Doherty, the IRA prison escapee, had finally been ordered back to jail in the north of Ireland in February. He'd spent over eight years in jail here while his lawyers fought British extradition orders through the courts. Out of the blue the AOH announced that Doherty was to be the honorary grand marshal of the 1992 parade. They had some nerve. The parade committee had never liked Joe Doherty while he was imprisoned in New York. In fact, they did everything in their power to silence anyone who supported him. When people marched in past years wearing "Free Joe Doherty" sashes, they had been ejected from the parade. Now when it was too late to do Doherty any good, the AOH made their cynical gesture in an attempt to divert the bad publicity from the ILGO issue.

On Saturday, March 14, GLIB, the Irish-American Gay, Lesbian and Bisexual Group, marched in the Boston St. Patrick's Day Parade. Twenty-five women and men marched five-abreast in five compact rows for the four-and-a-half miles through the narrow neighborhood streets of Southie, the Irish-American working-class ghetto. GLIB wished onlookers a happy St. Patrick's Day while they were pelted with smoke bombs, stink bombs, food and bottles. Dave O'Connor from Dublin remarked afterwards, "Some people would have thrown their kids at us except they would have been arrested." They were spat upon and jeered and Kathleen Finn, an Irish-American member of GLIB said, "Seeing people who remind you of people in your own family condemning you and yelling at you was really hard." There were no police barricades along the route and police on motorcycles escorting the gay marchers were knocked over, spat upon and covered in food and beer. Kathleen said there was a concerted effort to intimidate them. People used video equipment and took photographs shouting they knew who the gay Irish marchers were and threatened to "get them." Dave, who admits to being a hothead, still doesn't know how they kept calm and focused and never once responded negatively to the onslaught. They were later accused of making obscene gestures but had more success than ILGO in fighting off the charge. "God Hates Fags" was a favorite sign in Southie that Saturday.

The following day, on Sunday afternoon, ILGO had a rip-roaring rally at Sheridan Square. Despite the freezing cold and icy wind hundreds of people showed up and stayed to listen to all the speakers. Eileen's red scarf was nearly blown away as she spoke for ILGO. She got into it, taking her coat off and beaming. She shouted, "The courts have recognized the absurdity of barring women from public places but not the absurdity and immorality of barring lesbians and gay men. Well, what shall we do?" The feisty crowd bellowed, "Fight

ROCK THE SHAM!

back!" Catch and Lucy, holding clipboards, took turns jumping up on the platform to introduce each speaker. My girlhood hero, Bernadette Devlin McAliskey, was on our side. People cheered and nodded their heads after they heard her message, "I will be with you in spirit on March 17 because you are a vital part of the Irish freedom struggle." Maxine Wolfe, a long-time feminist, radical, lesbian and AIDS activist, was dressed in layers, but still looked cold, her nose pink and shiny. She climbed up to the microphone, her trademark backpack strapped to her. "Isn't it amazing that the mere visibility of lesbians and gay men in 1992 in New York is still such a huge issue?" she asked. "It's okay if we're visible as perverts or as disease carriers. It's okay if we're visible as people who are dying. It's just not okay if we're visible as people who are fighting to live. It's just not okay if we're visible as members of all of the communities that comprise the so-called general population. It's just not okay if we're visible as intact, proud human beings who are not sorry about who we are; women loving women and men loving men."

"Yes!" rose the response from the crowd.

I looked around and saw that everyone was stiff from the bitter cold but staying put nonetheless. We asked the remaining speakers to keep it brief. City council member Tom Duane told a parade story. When his colleague, council member Annette Robinson, was a girl she went to a Catholic parochial school and remembered being taught jigs and reels in preparation for the St. Patrick's Day Parade. However, when the exciting day came round she was left behind with all the other black children, who were not welcome in the parade, while the white children marched. Rita Higgins, founder of the Bronx Irish Women's Group, marched with her two young children and ILGO in 1991, which was frightening for them all. But she was with us again and said, "If any of my children are gay, I want you people to be there to support them and me to be there to understand, together." When people stopped clapping she announced, "I marched last year and I'll march again." At last the end was in sight and Candice Boyce of African Ancestral Lesbians United for Societal Change was glad. She shivered, "Yes, I'm freezing. This is not my weather!" She continued: "Marching in the Black African-American Day Parade has been quite an experience. It's a hard thing that we're doing. But every year that I have to go, I go. And every year that you have to go, you have to go." Then it was over. If we didn't get out of the cold nobody would be on Fifth Avenue in two days; we'd all be in hospital with the mayor.

At work on Monday, the day before the parade, we got word from a reporter that Judge Leval did not grant our application. We would not be marching in the parade. Leval said ILGO filed the complaint too late and he also stated we were not entitled to relief because of the waiting list—he would not jump over the 40 groups ahead of us. His decision stated:

> I recognize that ILGO does indeed suffer irreparable harm
> through exclusion from the parade. The harm is of a symbolic
> nature. ILGO seeks, through inclusion in the parade, a

*recognition of status so long denied to homosexuals. Such
loss of symbolic recognition is recognized in law as an
irreparable harm.*

There is no denying that it would have been better to file a complaint earlier. But Judge Leval knew ILGO had been led to believe there was hope of a resolution. ILGO had been in meetings with the State Hibernians to try to solve the problem. It was only when they made it clear that their intentions were bogus that we filed a lawsuit. Also, since the Human Rights Commission hearing it was patently clear that the waiting list was a sham. Essentially, Judge Pierre Leval's decision was a cop out—he did not want to decide the constitutionality of this hornet's nest.

Our plan for the day was set and Leval's decision gave us the opportunity to publicize the details. We would meet at 59th Street at nine in the morning, two hours before the official starting time of the St. Patrick's Day Parade. From there we planned to march up Fifth Avenue to 68th Street where we would continue to protest our exclusion for the duration of the parade opposite the official reviewing stand.

Later that night at The Center a couple of hundred people attended our final pre-parade meeting. People were sitting on the floor making placards. Some of them played on the Hibernians' acronym, "Awful Old Homophobes", "Ancient Order of Hate", "All Odious Hypocrites." We got started and Paul highlighted the details of our plan with interruptions from Eileen, who couldn't wait to get to the podium.

When the media cleared out of the unwieldy assembly room at The Center we had a questions and answers session which Eileen handled expertly. "I want to say to people to keep an eye on each other," Bill Monahan reminded the gathering. He was worried about how dangerous marching before the parade might be. A nurse, Catherine Cusic, stood up so everyone could see her; she said she would take care of first aid if the need arose.

At the end of the meeting Marie used her charm to sell ILGO buttons, smiling and beaming at everyone. Our group had few resources and we needed to pay for all the photocopying and mailings we had done in the past couple of months. Marie single-handedly collected close to three hundred dollars, wandering about the room talking to people. While we were stacking chairs and getting ready to go home, Marie's bag was stolen. All the money was in the bag. She was distraught and inconsolable when the rest of us were more concerned about everything else in her bag. After checking in at the front desk at The Center we took to the street outside. We rummaged in bins up and down 13th Street and poked around in doorways. The bag was eventually found inside the men's bathroom at The Center; everything but the money was recovered. The Center was the last place we expected anything like this to happen—it was sad. We were exhausted, it was late, Marie was upset and we just wanted to go home, but I still had to do an interview. It was close to one in the morning when we got on the L train and headed for Marie's apartment in Brooklyn.

ROCK THE SHAM!

For a pair who had broken up we spent a lot of time together. Neither of us knew how to negotiate our new situation, or the loneliness. I'd always felt like I'd grown up with Marie and didn't know how or even if I really wanted to separate from her. I loved her apartment, which was the opposite of my stark studio. Pictures and odd paraphernalia hung on her walls. She had furniture—tables, a couch and lots of chairs. There were always flowers in a vase in her living room. Her blue bathroom was full of bath salts and musky smelling oils. She had made a home for herself and was distressed because I had not, as she perceived it. She didn't think I was coping; neither of us was.

That night I remember trying to explain to Marie how lonely the parade work made me feel. It didn't seem to matter that we worked so closely as a group. Nor did it matter that Marie and I had managed to continue to work as partners in ILGO, because when it came close to parade day we were all on our own. I was acutely aware of loneliness possibly because of the traumatic shift in our relationship. Most of my defenses had been stripped away. Everything upset me and I couldn't differentiate between a murder story in the newspaper, hate messages and death threats on ILGO's telephone hotline or seeing someone tug on their dog's leash in impatience on the street.

The weather hadn't changed much between the rally and when we arrived at the Plaza Hotel, at 59th Street, on St. Patrick's Day. We cupped our hands around our large coffees to ward off the chill. Stopping off for breakfast beforehand was such a practical thing to do but I never drank the coffee or ate the bagels; it was a trick to try to normalize what was happening. A reporter from *The New York Times* was going to be on my tail for the day—the paper had decided to do two profiles, an ILGO and an AOH one. The *Times* reporter, N.R. Kleinfield, introduced himself. For once I was incapable of being polite. He immediately started asking questions but I was so stressed out and distracted that after a couple of curt answers I ignored him. Grey clouds hung low in the sky and the forecast was for showers. A small group of people was pulling fabric out of a plastic bag, and Marie and I automatically began to tear the black ribbon into strips to wear as arm bands in commiseration with Joe Doherty, the political prisoner who had been extradited. We kept our eyes peeled, looking out for people or possible trouble, calmed by the monotony of ripping satin. Kleinfield hovered wherever I went in the crowd, which made me more anxious. I tried to obstruct him by getting people to stand between us to cut off his access. I must have been his nightmare but he was tenacious, patient, and hopefully did not take my behavior too personally.

John Lyons arrived wearing an exquisite bow tie and jacket. His nervous energy sparked about us and he made us laugh. He'd been hard at work the night before making his own placards; "I Am Feeling Queerish" and "I Am an Out and Proud Irish Fairy." His lover, Josh, stood quietly by him, his arm linked through John's and his eyes visible and calm through the bulky woolen scarf wrapped about his head and shoulders. The crowd began to grow by the minute until there were people everywhere. Marie relaxed. The marshals were fixing their arm bands and planning; Voelcker (as he had become fondly known) had a tight grip on a bullhorn. A beautiful young man gave me a triangular chocolate wrapped in gold paper from the Plaza Hotel shop. I ate it. The politicians began to arrive. The mayor was ill. Governor Cuomo was staying put in Albany. Three thousand cops were scheduled for parade duty—up by 400 from the previous year. Straight Kids USA, a duo of middle-aged men set up to allegedly protect children from the influence of homosexuality, announced they would be holding a counter-demonstration. They did, shouting "Anne Maguire" as we passed.

As it approached ten o'clock the marshals began to usher us out on to the avenue. We were close to 1,000 strong. Brendan, Catch, Marie, Tarlach, Lucy, Kelly Cogswell, John Lyons and I held the banner. Someone handed me a huge tri-color, the Irish flag, and it flapped about wildly in the wind swatting Ruth Messinger and the politicians behind us in the face. Eileen strode back and forth screaming at photographers to get out of the way, her arms punching and flailing the air around her. Tarlach sang our ballad into a bullhorn. "Let's go!" Eileen commanded. A thunderous cheer followed as the banner moved and the protest march finally began. We were flanked on both sides by a line of riot police and, to the side of them, cops on motorcycles. Exhaust fumes engulfed us, and the noise level soared with the roaring engines of the bikes. Their red lights flashed round and round as they traveled, wheel to wheel, in a convoy by our sides. Every once in a while a siren blared. The burly riot police had the visors of their helmets down, covering their faces. This spectacle seemed absurd and out of place in New York City in the 1990s.

I turned to look at the demonstration and all the people behind ILGO's long green banner that Lydia Medina had recently made for us. Posters and placards waved over our heads—"Lavender Emerald Society Oscar Wilde Division," "Don't Parade Bigotry as Morality," "England Get Out of Ireland," "In Honor of Irish People with AIDS." Some were written in Gaelic. Bill Dobbs, possibly our biggest pain in the ass from the gay community, with his endless critical analysis of ILGO strategy at hand for any reporter who'd listen, was there. (Bill was the man who'd told Marie, right before our big press conference, that we shouldn't march with Mayor Dinkins, which was after all, the wrong call.) I couldn't help but admire his outfit; he wore jeans, a sweater, a baseball cap, and jacket over which dangled a perfect string of pearls—so stylish I felt rather fond of him that day! We slowly continued our short nine-block march up Fifth Avenue chanting and blowing whistles to the empty sidewalks. It began to snow. But seven blocks from the Plaza Hotel we were stopped by the police at 66th Street and not opposite the reviewing stand on 68th as was planned. Eileen and Voelcker had been tricked by the cops.

Instead of standing directly in front of the honored guests of the AOH at the reviewing stand we were physically isolated on Fifth Avenue. Nobody was allowed to stand on the sidewalk opposite us or on the blocks to our left and right. We were barricaded in by blue police fencing, and then surrounded by cops. Everywhere around us had been designated frozen zones by the police. We made the most of the situation. At least our visitors from Cork and Dublin were excited, wondering what to expect. Linda Cullen, a television producer and director from Ireland with whom I'd begun a correspondence, which quickly turned into an intense trans-Atlantic crush, if only over the phone, was on the opposite side of Fifth Avenue. She was busy directing her crew. I liked watching her work. Someone shouted, "The parade's coming through!"

Soldiers approached, the Fighting 69th Division. We weren't quite sure how to respond. I was surprised they were so young. Green-uniformed New York City sanitation workers followed behind a contingent of men on horses. Their shovels, brushes, and garbage bins were ready for any horse droppings. I thought of my mother who used to send me out in the mornings to scoop up the milkman's horseshit for her roses. We gave the sanitation men a good warm clap and they waved their appreciation. The mood quickly changed when we saw the grand marshal, Connie Doolan, approach. "Shame! Shame!" rose up from the barricades and out into the avenue. Fingers pointed at Doolan. We were angry—he was in a powerful position and refused our request to do or say anything helpful. "Dump D'Amato!" rang out as Senator Al D'Amato marched by wearing a Kelly-green cap. Wave after wave of police officers and fire fighters passed us, laughing. One member of the Fire Department stepped away from his unit to be closer to the barricades and when he marched past he stared at me and sneered. "How would you like this rammed up you?" He was carrying a flagpole that was strapped to his body in a thick leather holster. His malice and the violence of his threat frightened me and I began to feel trapped. It was as if we were a bunch of animals or freaks, there to take whatever the marchers felt like giving, good or bad. It was not an uplifting experience.

We weren't quite ready to give up yet. "Two, Four, Six, Eight, How do You Know Your Kids are Straight?" (In a newspaper report the next day, Jim Dwyer was appalled by the chant, feeling it uncalled for and distasteful. I've always considered it rather thoughtful and responsible—like a public service announcement.) When the New York City Council passed by we shouted at full volume, "We Vote Too!" Irish Northern Aid, those radicals, took their turn in filing by, gawking. We challenged them; "Two, Four, Six, Eight, Why do You March with Those who Hate?" Our lawyer, Clare O'Brien, stopped by to see how we were doing. Spirits lifted and then floundered again, depending on the attitude of those who freely marched past us on Fifth Avenue. We were in a bad position, corralled and simply reacting. One thing I knew for sure was I would never do anything like this again or expect others to. At about 1:30pm, hours before the end of the parade, we started down 66th Street and away from the nightmare on Fifth Avenue.

Barbara de Lamiere led the way, pounding on her bodhran drum. Mary Ann Wadden kept her company, holding the large green, white, and gold tri-color flag I had long since forgotten. Some of the protesters were still very spirited and continued to sing at the top of their voices. "Oh! When the dykes, Oh! When the dykes, Oh! When the dykes go marching in. I want to be in that number. Oh! When the dykes go marching in." From a window, several flights up, a man shouted, "Faggots!" The response was angry and succinct. "Jump! Jump!" We had police protection as far as the subway station and were followed by at least eight police vehicles. We filed onto the first train that was heading downtown. The singing started up again, "If you're queer and you know it, snap your fingers!" The rest of the people on the car fell silent. Right before we got to the Village, Aldyn McKean, wearing the most incredible green earring I'd ever seen, sang "When Irish Eyes are Smiling." As always, he held the note on *gay* as long as was humanly possible. Everyone on the train applauded him when he finally stopped to breathe, including the previously sullen commuters. Every year I waited for the surprise of Aldyn jumping out onto the street to serenade us with his ILGO anthem during the Lesbian and Gay Pride parade. Sadly, like many men who have been with us on St. Patrick's Days, Aldyn died a few years later after years battling AIDS.

The police said that they were expecting two million onlookers at the parade but estimated the turnout at 385,000. And instead of the usual 250,000 marchers, only 150,000 marched in 1992. For the first time in decades large sections along the parade route were bereft of spectators. An employee of the Parks Department said it was the smallest show in his fifteen years working along the route. In parade terms, it was a flop. The weather was bad, the atmosphere worse. Bigotry is bad for business.

CHAPTER NINE

The Calm Before The Storm

"All things fall and are built again. And those who build them again are gay."

– William Butler Yeats

ROCK THE SHAM!

EVEN WITH our second St. Patrick's Day behind us the parade was never far from our thoughts—or other people's, for that matter—so we never knew when or where it might pop up again. The summer of 1992 was relatively quiet but the action heated up again in the autumn when ILGO's resolve was tested over and over again right up till the morning of our action on March 17, 1993. We would be thwarted at every turn; sometimes we expected it but at others the betrayals were so deep they seemed incomprehensible. Nevertheless, we made it to Fifth Avenue, once again, for our third St. Patrick's Day Parade.

While our 1992 protest had been far from ideal—trapped behind police barricades and ridiculed—some people's lives would never be the same again. We would never know the full impact we were having on people outside of ILGO, but within the group I saw the shift. In the space of one year Keith had changed radically. ILGO's 1992 protest was the first time he marched on Fifth Avenue on St. Patrick's Day. He was the one who had been too fearful to join the group in 1991, so he'd stood and watched ILGO from St. Patrick's Cathedral. His world was changing. "For the first time in my life I felt that ILGO didn't go far enough to achieve our goals," he said, discussing the 1992 protest. "I've always been one to go for the middle of the road but this felt like the end of it. We were like a freak group barricaded in while the parade went by. It didn't give us the dignity we had gained the year before."

Whether or not we were conscious of it, nothing was the same for any of us. "The Parade" was a constant presence on the periphery of my consciousness so I never felt much relief in the aftermath. Instead of marking the New Year in January, mine now began and ended with the parade in March. ILGO had only been involved in two St. Patrick's Day Parades, spanning a one-year period, and I was exhausted. Even when everything was calm I worried about what lay ahead. I used tricks, like pretending I could walk away at any time because I had done enough, and this gave me some room to recover and rest. I needed to feel the parade work wasn't running my life, even if it was.

Two days after being barricaded off Fifth Avenue by the city's Police Department in 1992, ILGO attended the mayor's annual Irish reception at Gracie Mansion on March 19th. David Dinkins looked shaken after his hospitalization but was feeling better. Several ILGO people looked shaken too, most notably Marie. Eileen and I took the train together from work. She wanted to talk about what was going on between Marie and I, but I was never sure what was going on so I couldn't really explain too much, nor did I want to.

When the dust settled after the 1992 protest we studied the newspaper stories about the 231st St. Patrick's Day Parade. Most of the editorials were happy ILGO had not been ordered into the parade by a court decision which, in the bizarre opinion of *The New York Times*, would have been the cure that "looked worse than the disease." So, breathing a sigh of relief the scribes of the city could afford to be genuinely saddened by the discrimination suffered by the "mild-mannered" Irish gays at the hands of the mean-spirited Hibernians.

The editorials dutifully repeated ILGO's charge that anyone who marched in the parade was condoning and supporting bigotry against lesbians and gay men. So long as ILGO (or the LGBT community in general) were denied equality under the law, and so long as we could be portrayed in some way as victims, the press was with us; any shift in the status quo could be tricky.

Jim Dwyer went all out to make ILGO, as opposed to non-ILGO lesbians and gay men, look good. In his column in *New York Newsday* he said the other activists "... spent the day boiling hate on the sidewalk, the evil vapors steaming into the cold morning as they taunted every group that passed." ILGO had publicly called for a boycott of the event so anyone who decided to participate, and so support the AOH's bigotry, was a fair target of our anger. Jim Dwyer's problem, like so many other ILGO well-wishers, was he could only support us if he could feel good about it and he could only feel good if ILGO was being victimized. This type of empathy comes from a position of power—very specifically a position of power those you're feeling sorry for don't have access to. I believe that Dwyer was genuinely upset by what was happening to ILGO but he saw us in romantic terms—immigrants, lonely, persecuted, God-fearing, and from large rural families in the old country. Dwyer's description of ILGO on St. Patrick's Day in 1992 says so much: "They stood as prisoners in a pen and cheered the friendly faces of those who were free to march." He also pointed out that ILGO had been completely marginalized by the Irish community which I believe would have been a far more interesting and complex story to cover. Rather, in order to be supportive of ILGO, Dwyer pitted ILGO, the "good gays" (victims) against the "bad" (empowered and angry) New York lesbian and gay activists.

Clare O'Brien, our lawyer, called to tell me she really liked N.R. Kleinfeld's front page profile in *The New York Times*. Kleinfeld had been generous. The profile of the AOH man, Brian F. Sullivan, President of Division 6 of the Order, was just as good. Sullivan was a registered Democrat, working-class, and a conservative, who voted for Ronald Reagan and George Bush, like a huge percentage of Irish-American New York Democrats. According to him, homosexuals were "weirdoes." He said, "Certain things I hold dear to my heart, God made men and women with different characteristics." When he was asked by the *Times* reporter, Alessandra Stanley, what he would do if one of his children was gay, his first response was, "I'd kill the bastard." He went on to say that he didn't really know what he would do; it would be a major crisis. Sullivan admitted he disagreed with the Catholic Church's fervent position against contraception and abortion. I'm sure he still marches up Fifth Avenue every year regardless.

We were often surprised by where support for our effort came from. *The National*

ROCK THE SHAM!

Catholic Reporter ran an editorial with the damning headline "Homophobic Hibernians Should Read their Hero's History." The editorial reminded its readers of the execution of Irish hero and global humanitarian, Roger Casement, following a turn in public opinion against him when the British Government released his diaries, which revealed his homosexuality:

> *We are dismayed by their (AOH) decision to ban a*
> *contingent of Gay Irish-Americans from the parade*
> *and doubly disturbed by their use of religion to*
> *justify that ban. ... Casement's story shows how the*
> *powerful use homophobia—like other prejudices—to*
> *divide and sometimes kill the powerless.*

An Phoblacht, or *Republican News,* Sinn Féin's weekly newspaper in Ireland ran an editorial that was critical of the Ancient Order of Hibernians. Months earlier, Brendi McClenaghan, an Irish Republican prisoner, came out as a gay man in an article he wrote for *An Glór Gafa/The Captive Voice,* a magazine produced by IRA prisoners which probably paved the way for Sinn Féin's supportive stance. *An Phoblacht's* editorial, "A Display of Intolerance," stated that the AOH should follow the example set in Cork and allow gays and lesbians to march in New York:

> *The decision portrays the AOH in a very poor light*
> *worldwide. It is unfortunate that an organization*
> *which has done so much for justice in Ireland has*
> *allowed itself to be led down this particular cul-de-*
> *sac by conservative extremists.*

Ironically, in 1996, Gerry Adams, the president of Sinn Féin, would make a conscious decision to go "down this particular cul-de-sac" with the same conservative extremists his party had so righteously rapped on the knuckles just four years earlier by marching in that year's parade. To add insult to injury, Adams would send a letter to ILGO, via Federal Express, explaining that Sinn Féin believed in pluralism and wanted to see the issue resolved. Adam's letter arrived on St. Patrick's Day but nobody from ILGO was around to sign for it—we were in jail for protesting against the parade he marched in.

Back in ILGO there was never a shortage of tension or new gripes. While ILGO couldn't have been more out of the closet in the public eye there was still a lot of uncertainty within the group. We insisted on our right to carry a banner up Fifth Avenue in the St. Patrick's Day Parade with the name of our organization spelled out for the world to see. At the same time, in our spring newsletter the editor announced, "ILGO Report was arbitrarily put across the top, instead of the group's formal name, out of consideration for those who may read it on the subway or some other place where they may feel the need for discretion."

Indeed, the bulk of ILGO's membership was not announcing its joyous homosexuality from the mountaintop but I didn't think it was a good idea for the editor of our newsletter to impose his closet on the organization. What about the people who specifically wanted to sit on the train and let everyone know what they were reading? The front page of the same newsletter had a plea "from Allison" for the membership to shape up, and get involved to make the organization work for everyone. She believed too much of ILGO's energy was spent on the parade; indeed this concern was fast becoming a sore spot in the group.

Like most organizations, there was a core group of people who did the work to ensure the survival of ILGO. It had been a natural step for those people to take on the parade work in 1991. Even though I was wholeheartedly committed to ILGO's cause of providing a social and supportive network, it was no longer my main interest. There were more than enough people to take care of everything we wanted to do. But most people were disinclined to take charge of anything. Because ILGO was a lesbian and gay group, the passivity of the membership was even more complicated. Many people were fearful and didn't feel entitled to much more than making it through each day in one piece. Unlike Keith, most never moved from the closet. Their expectations seemed to be that those who had "come out" should care for and cater to their needs. Those of us who wanted ILGO to work for as many people as possible spent a lot of time trying to figure out how to accomplish this goal. We continued to run lots of social activities so that people who would not necessarily attend a meeting, out of terror or disinterest, would have somewhere else to go to meet Irish and Irish-American lesbians and gay men. But ILGO was not a social service agency. At one point or another everybody was frustrated.

In April 1992 *A Terrible Beauty* opened at The Provincetown Playhouse in Manhattan. The play, written by Kevin Breslin, son of New York veteran columnist Jimmy Breslin, starred Tatum O'Neal in her stage debut. Kevin Breslin had been inspired to write and direct the play after watching the St. Patrick's Day Parade in 1991. In an interview in the *Irish Voice* he said, "When I saw Steven McDonald and his wife going up with the handicapped kids, and then I saw the gays and all the white people screaming at them, I thought, this is a wacky parade. And the feeling never went away." The wacky plot—the homophobe is saved and redeemed by the AIDS death of his gay childhood friend—was very simplistic. The cast of stereotypes included a wise old barman; his gentle, soft-spoken nephew from the old country (the queer); the alcoholic, wife-beating brute and childhood friend of the dying gay man; and two recent immigrants with caustic tongues. Breslin called to invite me to the first reading at the Irish Arts Centre. I asked Marie to join me in an effort to distract her from her upsetting trip home to see her father, who'd recently had a massive stroke. The play was so awful, it was indeed distracting—one cliché after another had us squirming with embarrassment and discomfort. We thought we'd never get out of the Arts Centre. It didn't come as a surprise to either of us when the play bombed after its first five performances.

ROCK THE SHAM!

It felt good to leave spring behind and move into summer even though it meant ILGO's third St. Patrick's Day drew nearer; but it loomed far off enough into the winter months to relax a bit and even to try out a new idea. Marie and I met Maxine Wolfe, Ana Simo, Sarah Schulman, Anne D'Adesky, Debby Karpel and Kathryn Thomas at Columbus Circle on the morning of the Lesbian and Gay Pride Parade in June. Already it was blisteringly hot and my hands and feet were swollen from the humidity. We divided up the boxes of bright green palm cards and stashed our share of 8,000 each in backpacks and plastic bags, to hand out to lesbians during the march down Fifth Avenue. Maxine had called Marie and me to invite us to a meeting at Ana Simo's several weeks before to talk about setting up a lesbian direct-action group. She had tried to get one off the ground with Sarah Schulman in the past but the time hadn't been right. The time was right now. The theme of revenge was decided upon. We agreed to start by calling ourselves The Lesbian Avengers and if anyone had any better ideas we'd discuss them later. The opening lines of the palm card that Sarah wrote declared:

WE WANT REVENGE AND WE WANT IT NOW!
LESBIANS! DYKES! GAY WOMEN!
There are many more Lesbians in this world than there are men like George Bush.
But cold-blooded liars like him have all the power.

We were fed up, the message continued, but ready to strike back. There was a phone number on the card to call, and lesbians called. The first meeting was a success and subsequent meetings grew larger as the word spread. We knew at the very first meeting at Ana's that we would have to have an idea for a first action so that there was something solid to work on when lesbians showed up, ready for revenge. Our brain-storming was lots of fun, and after all kinds of wild fantasizing we decided on an action for the first day of school in District 24 in Queens. There, Mary Cummins, chair of the local school board, was leading the fight against the proposed multicultural curriculum for the New York public schools system. Cummins and her school board had a problem with the "Children of the Rainbow" guide which the Board of Education had introduced to foster an understanding of the full diversity of life in New York. There were four books out of over 400 titles on the curriculum that had lesbian and gay themes and so District 24 voted to reject the entire guide. Five years previously the same conservative school board rejected the Board of Education's sex education curriculum and adopted their self-styled Family Living guide in which mentioning homosexuality, masturbation, abortion, and contraception was banned. So, the Lesbian Avengers would go to Queens on the first day of school wearing "I was a lesbian child" t-shirts, and a new movement began.

Marie had met Maxine during her first year living in New York in the mid-eighties. I was invited to Maxine's with Marie for Thanksgiving dinner six weeks after I arrived in New

The Calm Before The Storm

York. I had no idea I was attending a traditional lesbian and gay Thanksgiving—I didn't even know what Thanksgiving was. People arrived, filling Maxine's kitchen with noisy excitement, sorting out if their dish had to go into the oven, the fridge, or needed finishing touches added. Maxine's daughters, Karen and Amy, caught up with their mother's friends, some of whom had known them since they were children.

That first Thanksgiving in November, 1987 I had no idea who Maxine was or the impact she, and our friendship, would have on my life in the future. I recall sitting at the table, being very interested in all that was going on around me, but I don't think I spoke once! The shock was definitely cultural, but this lively group of lesbians and gay men also intimidated me. I wondered how Marie had managed to maneuver herself into this extraordinary circle and was impressed that she had. But Marie was worried she had nothing to contribute. We lost touch with Maxine for a spell, not wanting to disappoint her. I remember encouraging Marie, trying to get her to call Max, because I knew Marie wanted to be her friend and because I was very interested in Maxine and the world she lived in. But I had no idea how to make the connection in an informal way. Eventually, through seeing each other at meetings and protests, we did manage to make our way to finding Maxine and becoming friends, but it was through the Lesbian Avengers that we became very close.

When Marie and I arrived at Columbus Circle for the Lesbian and Gay Pride Parade Sarah was waiting on the steps with Debby Karpel, boxes of flyers at their feet. Sarah told me I looked handsome. Because Marie and I had been so uncertain about our relationship we had come to a weak decision to try to make a break. I told Sarah that Marie and I had split up after talking for a long time the previous night. Sarah said we were being very brave. When Anne d'Adesky showed up I was amused by how different she looked from the meeting at Ana's. There she had seemed conservative and business-like. Now she wore cut-off denim shorts and the oddest bits of clothing layered over her body with all kinds of trinkets and chains and jewels. Anyone else would have looked ridiculous but she was very cool.

When all the flyers were divided we walked up by Central Park together and then went our separate ways. Marie and I were quiet. The last thing we wanted to do was hand out cards. I wanted to go home, afraid I might collapse in a heap if even one lesbian rejected the card I offered. But Marie took charge and told me she was off to do her job and get it over with. I stood, paralyzed. I fantasized about running away, hopping on a train, and disappearing. Miraculously, once the parade began I flung myself into the task; running out into the middle of Fifth Avenue whenever I spotted lesbians, which was often. Marie and I didn't stray far from each other, nor did we speak. It was the most inopportune time to break up, watching everyone march by, in high spirits. When we finished we sat on the curb on Fifth Avenue, in silence, and waited for ILGO. I started crying, and for once, didn't care who saw me. ILGO arrived, waving and blowing whistles. A contingent from GLIB, the Boston Irish group joined us. Marie and I were supposed to be leaders and couldn't be down in the mouth on a day like this. We got up and marched, waving and smiling at spectators, and were festive. Later that evening we went to the Lesbian Dance, which we had never done before, and had a miserable time. Neither of us could wait for the weekend to be over.

Marie threw herself into the Lesbian Avengers. We talked about the strain of working together, given our painful break. Between the two of us we decided I was much more embroiled in ILGO and Marie preferred to be active in the Avengers, and so we chose our separate groups. We would not be seeing each other much now. I knew I was missing out on something very exciting and worried that Marie might meet someone new and fall in love.

Within a couple of weeks of our very official break up I received an invitation in the mail. Marie asked me to join her for a picnic in Central Park. All I had to do was go. The card was so sweet and funny, full of tiny colorful drawings explaining everything from the menu to the meeting place—it was very Marie. I loved the invitation and carried the card with me. Sometimes just feeling it in my pocket, knowing that no matter how many times I looked at the pictures they would always make me laugh. But I was apprehensive too and wondered what on earth Marie was thinking. This could be disastrous. Nevertheless, I accepted. How could I resist?

At the 72nd Street entrance to Central Park Marie was sitting on a green bench surrounded by plastic bags. She had not seen me approach. It had been two weeks since we'd seen each other and I'd forgotten what Marie really looked like. My heart leaped and started to beat faster. This kept happening to me! It was obvious I was in love with her. My head was spinning and when she spotted me I was completely disorientated. A huge smile broke out on her face. She handed me a single sunflower and led me to a secluded grassy bank. There she began a familiar ritual of hers—laying out food, explaining what everything was, and how she made it, and when we'd eat it. There was a lot—quiche, salads, and a flask of coffee to go with the pastries for dessert. She kissed me and was affectionate from the moment we sat down. I was confused—frightened but clearly enjoying her tenderness. I admired Marie's bravery and half-observed, half-succumbed to her courtship. Behind us the bushes rustled without any hint of a breeze and I leaned toward the noise. There was so much on my mind I barely registered the man in the thicket jerking off. Then a fat rat ran in front of our picnic and disappeared down the hill. We packed up and moved but still we couldn't get a minute's peace. We laugh every time we recall Marie's gallant attempt at seduction surrounded by rats and wankers. Regardless, I was beginning to feel safer with Marie again—my layers of protection were coming undone.

On July 23, the Vatican, under Pope John Paul the III, issued a letter to the U.S. bishops, which opposed civil rights protection for lesbians and gay men. This was in direct response to the anti- and pro-gay rights initiatives being considered on local and statewide levels across the United States at the time. It may have had as much to do with a Gallup poll amongst Catholics. The survey found that 46% of Catholics believed homosexuality morally acceptable and 78% said homosexuals should have equal access to jobs, like ng. The Vatican stated, "There is no right to homosexuality. There are areas in which it is not unjust discrimination to take sexual orientation into account, for example in the consignment of children to adoption or foster care, in employment of teachers or coaches, and in the military recruitment." The Vatican directly attacked any legislation that would protect lesbians and gay men and stated "homosexuality is an objective disorder" and the result of protective laws "may in fact have a negative impact on the family and society." According to the pope, homosexuals would avoid discrimination if they stayed in the closet and had no public life—then the fact of discrimination would be moot, because it would not arise; the Vatican's version of the American legal system.

That same month in 1992, at the Ancient Order of Hibernians national convention, it was decided that the AOH was out of the parade business for once and for all. Their conviction to dump the New York parade, and the ILGO controversy with it, was so solid that delegates voted to amend the Hibernian constitution. They were sick and tired of the New York upstarts and extremely worried about the legal debt the organization was accruing in its attempt to maintain its ban on ILGO. The AOH constitutional amendment prohibited any AOH division from sponsoring a parade or a public celebration. This decision left a big question mark over the future of the largest and most famous St. Patrick's Day Parade in the world, which the Hibernians had been running for over one hundred years. It also gave a group of opportunists in New York the big break they'd been waiting for—the chance to muscle in and gain control of the parade.

Behind the scenes Frank Beirne and the St. Patrick's Day Parade Committee's Vice-Chairman, John Dunleavy, secretly filed papers to incorporate the St. Patrick's Day Parade and Celebration Committee ensuring its autonomy and break with the AOH. The fact that the Irish Catholic fraternal order was no longer in charge should have made a difference, especially in legal terms, but it didn't, which didn't really surprise ILGO.

However, all the activity was exciting. I loved that ILGO, a new group of Irish immigrants, could cause so much chaos amongst the AOH, an old group of Irish men. We didn't know what to expect next ... we mistakenly thought we'd seen it all by now.

CHAPTER TEN

The Rise And Fall Of The Fixers

"Yesterday I dared to struggle. Today I dare to win."

– Bernadette Devlin

ROCK THE SHAM!

HE WORLD of the St. Patrick's Day Parade would go completely haywire before March 17, 1993. The next few months would produce judges with singing bow ties, secret meetings in the dark recesses of the chancery and the birth and death of the "fixers." It all began on October 27, 1992 A three-judge panel at the New York City Commission on Human Rights surprised everyone, not least ILGO, by overturning Judge Maldonado's original recommendation. They ordered the Hibernians to allow ILGO to march in the upcoming parade. The commissioners disagreed with Maldonado's analysis and concluded that ILGO should march given the sufficiently secular nature of the annual Irish celebration on Fifth Avenue. We were stunned.

There was an uproar. The AOH was furious. The media attacked the decision dubbing it a First Amendment travesty. *New York Newsday* used the ILGO as KKK analogy asking "Would anyone force a civil rights group to let David Duke (white supremacist and former Klan leader) march in a parade honoring Martin Luther King Jr.?" Again the New York press failed to acknowledge ILGO was Irish. Our insistence that we not be annihilated was so threatening it united the most unlikely forces against us, crossing all boundaries, from race and ethnicity to class and gender with no regard for political, religious, and moral beliefs. So the notoriously right-wing Pat Buchanan could rant about ILGO and the liberals at *The New York Times* could say, "Martin Luther King Jr. could not have been compelled to let the Ku Klux Klansmen march with him." The message was clear—Irish lesbians and gay men were repugnant, lethal, and insulting to everything Irish. The logical deduction then is that all lesbians and gay men must be contained to maintain order and decency Nevertheless, here we were in the midst of all this craziness; the Human Rights Commission had reversed its decision and it was looking like 1993 would be the year ILGO would march up Fifth Avenue on St. Patrick's Day. It still didn't feel like a flight of fancy to me—more like it was long overdue.

The parade chairman, Frank Beirne, and his lawyer, Jacob D. Fuchsberg, responded to the new situation with great haste and filed a notice of appeal within two days of the commission's final order. Judge Alice Schlesinger of the New York State Supreme Court was assigned the appeal. Beirne named the commission, the national, state, and New York County AOH, the AOH parade committee of which he was chairman and ILGO as defendants By the end of the week there was talk of canceling the 1993 parade. Al O'Hagan, a prominent Hibernian, told *The New York Times*, "Right now, for the first time in over 200 years, there will not be a St. Patrick's Day Parade in New York City." We were a little perturbed. ILGO wanted to join the parade, not see its demise. However, if the AOH was willing to cut off its nose to spite its face, that was its business.

Waiting in the wings was a group of Irish-American "leaders" who rapidly took center stage. By early November they had a brand new parade committee, organized by lawyer Brian O'Dwyer, the son of the ex-City Council President and former grand marshal, Paul

O'Dwyer, whom we knew had sound political beliefs and a lot of integrity. Unfortunately Brian O'Dwyer and his colleagues, most of whom were New York Democrats, were not cut from the same cloth. This new parade committee, which we dubbed the "Hynes group," because Democratic Brooklyn District Attorney Joe Hynes was one of its central movers and shakers, was given a nod by the National AOH, which issued yet another statement announcing its disinterest in sponsoring parades. The Hynes group said ILGO could march in their parade.

Ignoring his expulsion from the AOH, Frank Beirne continued to act like a bona fide member. After all, he and Dunleavy had secretly incorporated their parade committee so the AOH in fact was no longer involved in the event on Fifth Avenue. So, he set about organizing the 1993 parade as if everything was normal. He booked a room in the Roosevelt Hotel for Tuesday, November 17, and sent out invitations to all the groups who had participated in the previous year's parade. Brian O'Dwyer invited people to attend a meeting at his law office on Duane Street on Wednesday, November 18. Both meetings were set up to plan the same parade—this was becoming ridiculous.

John Cardinal O'Connor was angry and he would get angrier yet. In an editorial in *Catholic New York*, the official paper of the Archdiocese, Mayor Dinkins, the Human Rights Commission, and ILGO came under attack. The timing was impeccable; it was published right before the AOH and the Hynes group parade meetings. It stated:

> That the Catholic-Irish community stands to lose such
> a glorious tradition is sad, obviously. What is even sadder
> is the set of circumstances under which the loss will take
> place; the belligerent insistence of a hostile group that it
> must be part of this celebration, under its own terms, and
> the dangerous, offensive meddling of the City of New York—
> and its mayor—in a private religious matter.

The Archdiocese clearly interpreted the city's action as interference. It conveniently failed to acknowledge the city's obligation and compelling interest to assert its laws, one of which protects lesbians and gay men from discrimination. Apparently, the Archdiocese didn't recognize the conflict inherent in its own meddling in the public policy of the city, in public schools for example, where religion supposedly holds no sway. Clearly 1993 could be the year when ILGO got to march as our own contingent in the St. Patrick's Day Parade and everyone was feeling it.

ROCK THE SHAM!

The cardinal, who always maintained he had no power or influence over the Hibernian parade, was furious at being left out of the loop. His position was being undermined, or questioned, by "leaders" (the Hynes group) in the Irish-American community who for once had not deferred to him. If he could not depend upon his own, Irish-American Catholics to respect and bend to his will it might pose problems for him with other ethnic Catholics. Just as bad, though, was his lack of control over a small group of feisty and hopeful Irish immigrants, who were gay, and who had won the hearts of most New Yorkers as well as the support of the city's mayor.

While the cardinal may have been coy about his influence over the AOH parade, the Archdiocese has a steady history of interfering in public policy. Cardinal O'Connor consistently used the pulpit to push his political agenda. Nobody in power was willing to acknowledge or challenge him on his hypocritical and cynical abuse of religious zealotry to promote a political position. Every time O'Connor's politics were challenged he simply charged "Catholic-bashing" and everyone ran for cover. ILGO was not so naïve as to shrug off the Archdiocese with O'Connor at the helm. Unfortunately, other people thought they could, and in the end ILGO paid for their arrogance.

Over two hundred delegates attended Frank Beirne's meeting at the Roosevelt Hotel. The serving parade committee was re-elected with Beirne as chairman. The star of the night was attorney Jack Hale, who had been sent by the Archdiocese to keep ILGO from marching. Hale was no stranger to church/state conflicts—he had been around during the City Council debates on the Gay Rights Bill in the 1980s. Most recently Hale had been advising Mary Cummins, the right-wing Queens school board leader who was fighting the Rainbow Curriculum in the public school system and in whose district the first Lesbian Avengers action took place. The participants of the Roosevelt meeting left, feeling confident with the Archdiocese on their side.

The following evening several ILGO members attended the first Hynes group Parade Committee meeting at the downtown offices of O'Dwyer and Bernstein. About fifty people showed up: Reporters were left in the lobby to sit it out, waiting for hours for some news. Gerry Keogh announced he would start the meeting with a prayer. Sandy Boyer, from the Irish Arts Centre, and Mary Ann Wadden looked as surprised as I was. Brian O'Dwyer, one of the organizers, did not participate but mooched around in the background, appearing every once in a while carrying manila folders and disappearing just as quickly. Joe Hynes, the Brooklyn District Attorney, announced that he was there to lend his support. Also present were Irish Republican activists Vincent Conlon and Seán Mackin, radio show host Adrian Flannelly, Martin Galvin of Irish Northern Aid, as well as several prominent lawyers in Irish circles and many disaffected AOH members. There were few women, besides those of us from ILGO.

Much of the discussion centered on saving the parade. There was also a lot of talk about whether or nor ILGO should in fact be allowed to march. Then Seán Mackin made a fiery speech and received much warm applause when he said it was about time the parade was brought into the twentieth century. It was obvious there was a core group with a plan in place. They'd met before this first "official" meeting. The Keogh brothers, Galvin, Mackin, O'Dwyer, his cousin Seán Downes, a bunch of active AOH men who hated Frank Beirne, and Joe Hynes with several of his Assistant District Attorneys, were running the show.

It is ironic that the only group who was ever presumed to have "an agenda" in this huge controversy was ILGO. But the agendas were flying at the Hynes group meeting. Everybody there, save ILGO and a few independents, wanted control of the New York parade for very particular reasons. Some simply hated Frank Beirne. Some held political beliefs and convictions that were not being addressed sufficiently in the Irish community or Washington, so the parade would be a good vehicle for them. Others were hacks and opportunists who wanted to run the show to further their political careers. There were genuine people present too who wanted to work towards a meaningful and inclusive parade on Fifth Avenue in future years, but sadly they were not part of the self-appointed "leadership."

Before leaving the meeting I approached Gerry Keogh and asked how they intended to deal with Cardinal O'Connor. He told me to relax—the cardinal would not be a problem. I asked him if he understood the relationship between the Archdiocese and the lesbian and gay community, or understood O'Connor's hostility towards lesbians and gay men. Keogh was completely confident and led me to believe everything was taken care of. The men of the inner circle considered themselves well-versed in the sophisticated politics of New York City. It remained to be seen what they understood and how far they were willing to go. We went to the pub with our friends, Sandy Boyer and Marianne Wadden. Seán Mackin was there too and Sandy said it would be worth our while speaking with him to get him on our side. Marie and I had a conversation with Mackin, Marie asking again about the cardinal because she knew this group didn't know what they were dealing with, but Mackin was nervous; he did not want to be seen talking to us. He gave us no assurance whatsoever about supporting ILGO. It felt so typical it was depressing.

On November 23, 1992, the President of the New York County AOH, Timothy Hartnett, filed an affidavit in support of Frank Beirne's petition to reverse and vacate the Human Rights Commission's decision: "Constitutional protection is not reserved for zealots. It is not only the Nazis and the KKK and the gay groups that have the right to shape their message." Further on the document argued: "Heterosexuals who engaged in unseemly public physical displays would be treated no differently than homosexuals." But what is seemly for heterosexuals is not acceptable in homosexuals. As Frank Beirne said in his deposition, "We got complaints that there was girls holding hands." An AOH police department employee reported, "I saw what appeared to be a lieutenant of the New York City Police Department holding hands with another male." So the AOH's claim, then, is that two heterosexuals holding hands is offensive to them—which, of course, is untrue. Hartnett stated: "Anyone who did what ILGO did in 1991—were they a collection of heterosexual Gaelic virgins—

would never be invited back." All ILGO did was march. The AOH was becoming expert at manipulating commonplace anti-gay hostility to their advantage.

On December 17, ILGO filed response papers to the legal briefs submitted to Judge Alice Schlesinger. Our argument was that the proceedings were moot (legally insignificant because of having already been decided or settled). The AOH had made it clear through press statements and a constitutional amendment that they were no longer sponsoring parades and the commission's order was directed at the sponsors of the St. Patrick's Day parade. Nobody knew who the 1993 sponsor was because the permit had not yet been awarded. Through the court cases the New York parade was being transformed into a religious procession, the idea being that, under the law, hatred of lesbians and gay men is a legitimate religious position deserving constitutional protection. The crucial questions were, would the AOH (or the new incorporated Parade Committee run by Beirne and his side-kick, John Dunleavy) be allowed to redefine its message, willy-nilly, to suit its current agenda? And to what extent, if any, was the law willing to protect the freedom of speech and associational rights of lesbians and gay men who chose not to be closeted? The year was coming to a close and the holidays fast approaching.

Marie and I continued to struggle to sort out our relationship, and it was taking its toll. Marie was beginning to feel hopeless. One morning I would wake up full of new resolve to take the leap and trust Marie again. The next day I'd be running for cover. She was worn out dealing with constant rejection. Sensing her waning spirit sent me into a panic. The more anxious I became the further away the answer seemed from my grasp. I kept telling myself to calm down, to think it through rationally. But I was terrified, not rational. I desperately wanted to say, "Yes, let's do it." But I couldn't. Marie had done everything humanly possible to win me back. She'd taken care of me when I allowed her to, she'd left me alone when that was what I needed, she understood my anger and pain, and she accepted me the way I was. But I was not as brave or sure as she was. Marie booked a flight to Ireland for the Christmas break and I stayed in New York. While Marie was away, she decided it was over—there was nothing more she could do. Without her I realized how empty New York was, and her brief absence over the holidays changed everything for me. It seemed sudden but it wasn't. While Marie was in Clonlara, County Clare, deciding our relationship was over, I was in New York knowing that I was still in love with Marie and ready to dive back into a new relationship with her.

On January 3, 1993 I went out to JFK to meet Marie. This time I was on time. American Trans-air, flight number 637, arrived. My stomach heaved at every swing of the automatic doors in the arrival hall. I stood on my toes and strained my neck to get a clear view, convinced I was going to miss Marie. Behind the doors hundreds of people lined up for customs and, behind them, people drowsily waited for their bags at the conveyor belts. A couple of times I rushed forward, thinking I'd seen her, but it always turned out to be someone else. I paced back and forth, never taking my eyes off the doors. The pacing was making me feel manic so I stopped. I wished I could smoke even though I was already light-headed and would probably pass out after one drag on a cigarette. I watched other people's relief as they spotted their loved one pushing a trolley of suitcases into the buzzing terminal. I loved the ritual of awkward hugs, pats on backs and children sneaking unnoticed under rails and clambering around someone's legs. There she was! It was a few seconds before Marie spotted me. A big smile spread across her face. I carelessly and uncharacteristically shoved through the crowd to get to her. We hugged and Marie pulled back, took a good look at me and said she was very surprised to see me at the airport. I didn't know why. Marie was anxious to get out of the building to have a cigarette—she'd been deprived now for nearly seven hours. I joined her and if I lost consciousness now it didn't matter—Marie was home. We were back together at last.

By January the ILGO working group was meeting very regularly, several times a week. I tried to maintain a clear separation between the parade and my day job. Every once in a while Eileen and I inevitably had to sort out an ILGO problem, and then I'd go right back to work. She came to check in with me on the fourth floor each morning. Rick had made some business changes and Eileen and I no longer worked in the same room, nor was she my boss now. Eileen was open about the personal details of her life, my opposite in that regard. She told me she never quite knew what was going on in my head or what I really thought. This was not unusual because I was close with few people and chose very carefully whom to trust. I was also under the false impression that I actually told people a lot about myself when in fact I was extremely reticent. I'd always been a little wary of Eileen. Now especially that our lives were so enmeshed at work and with ILGO, it felt particularly smart to keep some distance.

Like many of us Eileen found working in the ILGO parade group extremely frustrating. In tandem with our distinct emotional vulnerabilities and foibles, there were personality clashes and power plays. The nearer the day of the parade drew, every past slight or grudge resurfaced anew, fresh and vigorous. We were under tremendous pressure and had to make huge efforts to be patient. Minor irritants drove me crazy, like someone not paying attention, asking the same question repeatedly. I resented people's need to be reassured and even though I understood why someone might be acting out, it infuriated me, wasting so much time. Outright hostility frightened me though and there were times in ILGO when people clearly hated each other. We had our share of bullies and Eileen was one of them. Eileen had so much energy, was clear in her views, and had no time for people who couldn't grasp what we were talking about no matter how often the concept was explained—of course it drove her nuts. But she undermined those in the group she had no respect for, which was almost everyone. Nobody ever had the guts to confront her or anyone else who was being overbearing. The typical response was for the wounded party to announce that they were leaving ILGO. Always prepared, I jumped in to listen and empathize, trying to cajole them back—we couldn't afford to lose anyone. My approach to working with difficult people came from what I learned growing up. If there was a way to manipulate destructive emotional energy to minimize the damage, I found it. This didn't seem controlling or negative to me; rather it was the only response I knew. Our work was extremely difficult. Being gay meant we were dealing with constant rejection and hatefulness from outside, which exacerbated old rejections, ridicule, humiliations and hurt. As a group we rarely acknowledged how painful our work in ILGO was. Miraculously, given the forces amassed against us, the least of which at this time was our internal dynamic, we managed to keep going.

Eileen began to express an interest in getting more people involved in the ILGO parade working group and suggested some friends she had worked with in the past. Having more people involved was a great idea but the particular people Eileen wanted weren't appealing; some had dubious histories as activists in the gay community and they had never showed any interest in anything Irish. I knew Eileen believed if she convinced me all would be well in ILGO—the group wouldn't follow her but would be more inclined to trust my judgment. I listened to her and made no commitment. Eileen didn't give up easily though and the idea would emerge again. The parade group settled, knowing we had a hard slog ahead before our third parade in 1993. There was a decent-sized crew, with Marie, leaving her Lesbian Avenger work for a while for ILGO to coordinate all the details and activities for March 17 from her office job at NYU. Along with her we had Paul O'Dwyer, Eileen Clancy, John Voelcker, Catch Keeley, Tom Kieran, Lucy Lynch, Brendan Fay, Patricia Nora Ryan, (who was simply known as Ryan), and Sheila Quinn who had recently joined in, rather tentatively.

We met at Voelcker's apartment in Gramercy Park. He had enough mugs to go round and the tea would be brewing in a huge leaking ceramic pot as we arrived minutes apart from each other. We brought cookies, slices of pizza sometimes, and Tom always came with a bunch of bananas. Our routine was to report on everything that had happened during the previous week, discuss what needed attention, and then draw up our calendar for the week ahead. Everything had to be meticulously covered, from attending other meetings, getting the word out by flyer distribution and posters, to making phone calls, photocopying, and licking stamps for mailings. We did interviews and spoke to other groups and individuals to encourage them to support us. We cut clips from newspapers about the parade. We talked to anyone who might have information about what was going on within the AOH, the Hynes parade group, or the city's political machine. Money was always an issue because we never had any, so we organized fund-raisers and what we couldn't get for free, like photocopying at work, we paid for out of pocket. We had one five-minute break. While everyone else lined up to use the bathroom, the smokers huddled in John's hall by the elevator bank and sucked on cigarettes until we were called back inside. We sat on whatever was available, from couch to hard-backed chairs to the floor, taking notes, doodling, listening, sparring, falling asleep, concentrating, strategizing, and thinking about being at home in bed.

On Wednesday, January 6, 1993 we started the year by attending the Hynes group meeting at O'Dwyer and Bernstein's to see what they were up to. The pressure of being polite to ILGO had become too much for some people. Every time I spoke, which was rare, many people in the room physically recoiled. I often felt I had just reeled off explicit details of my sex life or announced ILGO's plan to take up arms. We were not supposed to speak. When heads jerked violently in any direction in response to meeting my eyes, I stopped making eye contact and noticed I was even reluctant to look at my friends in ILGO after a while. Fortunately for me, there were ILGO people present as well as Sandy Boyer, and the handful of straight Irish women and men who didn't expect my head to do a 360-degree swivel at the very moment they had plucked up the courage to take a look at THE LESBIAN. But for their humorous confirmations about how bizarre the meetings were, I would have had grave misgivings about my level of paranoia. None of this was funny. The meetings of the Hynes Parade Committee were so dehumanizing I couldn't explain, intellectualize, or rationalize the experience to make it bearable. Dealing with people who hate you is one thing; sitting among people who don't think you're human is impossible. And yet we were doing it never knowing if it would be worth it in the end.

On January 7, Mickey Carroll at *Newsday* reported that Steven McDonald, the New York City cop who had been paralyzed on the job by a bullet, would be the Grand Marshal of the Hynes Parade Group and hinted that City Hall had assured this group of the permit. McDonald later responded saying he had not been asked to be the Grand Marshal and felt like he was being used. He was right. This didn't say much for the political savvy of the new Irish leaders.

Two days later the police commissioner, Raymond Kelly, handed the St. Patrick's Day Parade permit to the Hynes group. The Hibernians threatened a religious war, boycotts, and court proceedings. We relaxed. It began to sink in; ILGO would be marching. The Hynes group talked about lengthening the parade by one hour to include all groups on the now famous waiting list. They promised to put on the best parade ever. The mayor said not only had he made his views known to the police commissioner, but he had made his views known to the world, firstly by marching with ILGO in 1991, and then by refusing to attend the parade in 1992. All the hoopla was exciting and made the prospect of our marching all the more real. Almost everyone in our group was happy. We saw an end in sight. Marie worried that it wasn't over yet and I was so desperate to believe it was I blocked that anxiety from my mind. Of course she was right; it was far from a done deal.

Just two days later, on Sunday, January 10, the cardinal let a mighty roar from the pulpit. At long last all the political players were showing their hands. Without a trace of irony, he asked during his speech: "Do the mayor and police commissioner agree to this arbitrary transformation from the religious to the political? Will other religiously related activities become equally vulnerable to arbitrary politicization in this land which boasts of its tradition of separation of church and state?" He said Catholics would not be treated as second-class citizens, nor would they be silent. The congregation applauded his speech.

ROCK THE SHAM!

Amongst them were the AOH Parade Chairman, Frank Beirne, and Vice-Chairman, John Dunleavy. When O'Connor was leaving, one of his monsignors turned to Beirne and gave him the thumbs up, which didn't seem very holy.

In response, Paul and Eileen were quoted in *The New York Times*. Paul told the truth when he said, "The argument that it is just a religious celebration never came up other than as a means to exclude us." Eileen, sharp as ever, went for the jugular with her exquisite observation: "It's remarkable that a religious leader should crusade for the right to discriminate against a class of people and then complain bitterly when it's not allowed." Mary Holt Moore, the 1991 Grand Marshal, made the ludicrous assertion that the mayor would lose votes amongst the Irish Catholic population, as if Irish Catholics had voted for him in the first place. The Hynes Parade Group called for unity, rather timidly.

The editorials were predictable, except that the *New York Post* introduced a new analogy, ILGO as the Palestinian Liberation Organization, the St. Patrick's Day Parade as the Salute to Israel Parade. It also stated it was likely the Archdiocese would pull the Catholic schools, colleges and marching bands that participated in the parade if ILGO marched. A Sean Delonas cartoon, also in the *Post*, had an entirely different viewpoint: it looked towards the parade in the year 2000. Fifth Avenue was bereft of spectators; a lone marcher in a kilt held a placard that read, "Heterosexual, sex-in-the-dark, man-on-top, no birth control contingent." The cardinal all alone on the steps of the cathedral was waving frantically at nobody.

Judge Schlesinger would not be ruling on the Human Rights Commission decision now because the Hynes group had the permit and were allowing ILGO to march so there was no longer any case. However, Alice Schlesinger had her own personal agenda and after speaking with Ernest Mathews, the AOH attorney, and our lawyers, she decided to pursue a meeting at the Chancery with Cardinal O'Connor. We had no idea what the judge was up to, except perhaps a piece of the action, and her desire to get embroiled was a curiosity especially since the lawsuit was now moot. We didn't pay much attention—ILGO was set to march and that was all that mattered.

However, the next day ILGO was summoned to the judge's chambers. Eileen, Catch and I were able to attend. Our lawyers, Clare O'Brien and Paul Wickes joined us. The judge's law clerk showed us into Schlesinger's room. We sat in a semi-circle in front of the judge's large desk. There were framed photos of her family amongst the thick legal volumes and files. She entered and sat down behind the heavy desk, which immediately swallowed her up. She was slight, dark-haired, and very friendly. Paul Wickes made the introductions. The State Supreme Court Judge spoke very matter-of-factly, as though what she was reporting was mundane. When she told us she had already visited the Cardinal I was suddenly infuriated and didn't understand exactly why. I gripped the wooden arms of my chair and braced myself. Judge Schlesinger informed us that in order to resolve the dispute ILGO would have to sign a statement disavowing the ACT UP (Aids Coalition to

Unleash Power)/WHAM (Women's Health Action Mobilization) Stop the Church action, which took place in 1989 before ILGO ever existed. Thousands of protestors had turned up outside St. Patrick's Cathedral and many activists inside were forcibly removed and arrested for interrupting the mass. They were protesting the Archdiocese's interference in safe sex and HIV/AIDS education and prevention as well as its virulent opposition to abortion and the use of contraception. The cardinal had never gotten over that action. It was as if he had felt immune from the outside world because of the very massiveness of the cathedral and the Stop the Church action had put an end to that. O'Connor no longer felt secure in his cathedral to freely practice his political interference and lobbying. And now ILGO was being asked to issue a statement saying we did not condone the destruction of church property. My body tensed more and I forgot to exhale. We would also have to say that we respected the Catholic Church's right to say that homosexuality was immoral and sinful. We would have to state we respectfully disagreed with the Catholic Church's teaching and tenets regarding homosexuality. I felt like my head was filling up with rushing water and had to battle to hear what this judge was telling us. She explained there was a difference between disavowing an act while not disavowing the people who had acted. Then I realized why I was furious—Alice Schlesinger had sat with Cardinal O'Connor discussing us and coming up with these ridiculous suggestions. It was all so casual, the easy flow of words, the story, the edge of excitement she couldn't hide. We were being asked to say that ILGO and the entire lesbian and gay community were immoral perverts. We were being asked to be divisive and to betray the only people who supported us. We were being instructed to agree with inhumane and unethical teachings and tenets that sometimes killed us, and to top it all, we were supposed to give up the bit of power we had—the power of anger that enabled us to act against this type of institutional annihilation. The room suddenly became unbearably oppressive and sinister. I wanted to lie down and sleep. I dug my nails into the chair to help me stay alert. I rarely felt such pure rage.

Judge Schlesinger believed her suggestion that ILGO march with a new banner containing our acronym only, as opposed to the fully spelled out name of the group, was something we should consider too; but the cardinal and the two monsignors at the meeting had no opinion either way regarding this idea. She said the cardinal was very upset and extremely preoccupied with how he was being perceived. The Catholic Church could not be seen to be condoning homosexuality, she explained on his behalf. He felt like he was the victim in the parade controversy, she confided. I had stopped exhaling again. From the top of the cathedral steps in 1991, the judge reported, Cardinal O'Connor had heard "We're coming for your children" being shouted at the reviewing stand, never mind that it was fourteen blocks away! I began to wonder if I was hallucinating. My ears buzzed, then blocked up, as if wads of cotton had been inserted into them. Who did this woman think she was? Just like the Hynes group, Judge Schlesinger thought she was going to "fix" this fight. Just like the Hynes group she didn't have a hope in hell because she had no idea what was at stake. Had she understood anything she would have decided against calling ILGO into her chambers. Clearly, she didn't even realize how comfortable she was with the cardinal's hatred of lesbians and gay men.

When the frigid air hit me on the street my body didn't react. I wondered what Judge Schlesinger was doing now. She might be powdering her nose in the bathroom. Maybe she was tidying her desk and getting ready to go home. She could have been on the phone to the pope, for all we knew. I remember half-walking and half-running against the fierce wind to Ellen's, a diner on Broadway, where we would sit with Clare and Paul to discuss the twenty minutes that had just passed. I did not want to stop at Ellen's. Instead I wanted to continue plodding through the slush until it calmed me. Paul Wickes had said something that outraged Eileen but I was not able to listen to her, nor did I want to. I wanted to scream for her to get away from me. The cardinal felt victimized! That had to be some kind of sick joke.

We sat shivering at the table listening to our lawyers urging us to consider the solutions that had been suggested. We could re-work the wording to avoid compromising ourselves. I wasn't paying much attention anymore. I was remembering Marie's caution. She never believed ILGO would march in the 1993 parade because she didn't trust the Hynes group. I wondered why all this was happening when all indications were that ILGO was set to march. The attorneys needed to know if ILGO could enter into some kind of discussions, in good faith, on the grounds of what had been proposed by Judge Schlesinger. They must have been out of their minds. As usual, they wanted an answer the next day.

We traipsed to Daisy's restaurant in the West Village and caught up with Paul, Marie and Ryan. They listened to our story, growing paler by the minute. We made phone calls and arranged a meeting later that night in Eileen's apartment in the East Village where John Voelcker and Tom Kiernan joined us. It was a good meeting. We were together. We did not want to march in the St. Patrick's Day Parade at any cost. There was nothing more to discuss and no basis for entering into another set of bogus negotiations. We felt proud of ourselves.

So the leaders of the Hynes parade group had got what they had always wanted — control of the New York parade. Now, instead of focusing on running the big event, they were back-peddling. At a press conference on Thursday, January 14, they called on the cardinal to intervene in order to avoid a boycott of the parade because of the inclusion of the Irish Lesbian & Gay Organization. As Richard Perez-Pena at *The New York Times* pointed out, "The appeal to the cardinal was surprising because he used the pulpit of St. Patrick's Cathedral to assail the permit process and the inclusion of homosexuals." A few days later I returned a phone call from Seán Mackin, a central member of the progressive Hynes group, the same man I had spoken to in the pub after their very first meeting. We talked at length but within the first few minutes of the conversation I knew it was all over. The new group was about to drop their inclusive policy and ILGO with it. Mackin was nervous, speaking rapidly, hardly letting me get a word in. He kept repeating, "The news is bad." He explained that the National AOH was having an emergency meeting in St. Louis and any AOH member involved in getting ILGO into the parade, or who intended to march in a parade with ILGO, would be disciplined. Given that the national board of the AOH was no longer interested in parades this was an interesting statement. Of course, the bulk of the men involved in the new parade group were members of the AOH, albeit liberal members. Mackin said none of them were willing to risk disciplinary action over ILGO. I knew their agenda never had anything to do with supporting ILGO in the first place and that they simply used the conflict over ILGO's participation to try to gain control of the parade. They knew the city would not grant them the parade permit unless they said they would let ILGO march. Mackin said they had underestimated the cardinal. He conceded they probably should have sat down with ILGO and discussed it as Marie and I had wanted from the start—they had been warned by our questions at the very first meeting.

However, the so-called forward-thinking leadership of the Irish-American community didn't take ILGO, or our worries about the cardinal, seriously because they didn't believe ILGO was central to the dispute. They hadn't just underestimated the cardinal—they failed to understand everything because they did not know homophobia was what this political battle was about. What's worse, as soon as they figured it out, they dumped ILGO. Mackin was falling all over himself, telling me he was being honest, which he was, but it wasn't as if it was any consolation to ILGO. He was dishonest when he said he had no choice but to stay in the AOH. He didn't want to alienate "these people" because his work, and the cause of the Hynes group, that of Irish Republicanism, was too important.

The betrayal of ILGO by this group of leaders in the Irish community is unforgivable. They pandered to the most reactionary elements of their constituency and were unwilling to shift from their comfortable position, always feeling more politically astute and smarter than those they claimed to represent. They never had a vision for a more progressive Irish politics, and they certainly had no guts. It didn't matter so much that they did not understand what was going on in the beginning. What I cared about was where they would be standing when they eventually got a taste of what ILGO was up against. My mistake was to have had hope, to have believed their principles would include supporting lesbians and gay men. Even with Marie's constant warnings, and even though I tried to protect myself, I wanted our fears to be proved wrong. But the door was being slammed in our faces. There was no satisfaction in being able to say, "Yes, you should have listened to us," or "we told you so." The betrayal was devastating.

I put the phone back in its cradle, forgetting Mackin immediately. Instead I began formulating statements in my head about ILGO calling it quits. If we didn't, we risked losing even more. I was trying to figure out how we might sound strong and proud, not defeated. I was avoiding calling the others in ILGO to pass on what Mackin had told me. But I did call. When the job was done, I sat at Marie's table and cried for hours. Perhaps Seán Mackin was feeling bad too, but he still had his "pure politics" to keep him going.

The following day, Sunday, Cardinal O'Connor's homophobic speech from the pulpit of the previous week was read at every single mass in every single church in the New York Archdiocese. If anyone missed mass, it was also published in its entirety in *Catholic New York*. The rumblings were even felt as far away as St. Louis, where George Clough, National President of the AOH, overturned the AOH's constitutional amendment, once again putting the AOH back in parade business.

Officially, nothing had changed yet. Our "leaders" were strategizing about how to sort out the mess. On Monday, Brooklyn District Attorney, Joe Hynes, Congressman Peter King (an upstate right-wing Republican), Sean Cudahy of the AOH, and Adrian Flannely, radio show host, met with Cardinal O'Connor. Afterward, they all agreed there would be one parade and rejected any notion of partition, an old Irish problem. We didn't know what this meant but we knew we were witnessing the slow death of our dream to march in 1993.

That night ILGO met as usual. For a change I acknowledged how upset I was. I said we had put up with enough. We had sat in too many rooms with people who hated us, thought we were weird, perverts, child-molesters, crazy, sick, spoilers, and even accused us of being "paid British agents!" We had listened. We were polite. I'd had enough. I suggested we call it a day. To my surprise a lot of people agreed, but they worried about the timing. Eileen disagreed strenuously; she did not think it was a good idea at all. I knew it was a terrible plan but I was looking to be talked back into the fight. I needed someone to tell me why we couldn't give up, why we had to continue. I was aware of the risk of suggesting we call it a day and very glad when Eileen challenged the suggestion. We had a discussion and decided to continue. There was never any talk of quitting again. I felt much better.

The final meeting of the Hynes Parade Group was astounding. The only redeeming fact for ILGO was we would never have to sit through another one again and that was not to be scoffed at. We sat and watched, waiting for the excuses. Instead we were presented with passionate and sentimental speeches. Man after man got up to recite his civil rights, human rights, and radical political credentials. The atmosphere was heavy with mutual admiration as they bonded over past glories. They referred to each other as "brother" with warmth and sincerity.

At last the Keogh brothers got to the point. They reminded us that the group had formed with the intention of saving the tradition on Fifth Avenue when it seemed the AOH was out of the parade business. Now that the AOH made it clear that it was still in charge, the Keoghs said the permit should be handed back. This caused a bit of a debate because some people wanted to stall until the National AOH made its position abundantly clear, when it couldn't have been clearer. Others worried that it wouldn't look good for the mayor, who had taken a great risk awarding the permit to them. There was no way they could approach City Hall again for favors if they bowed out now, they argued. This was very serious business indeed. I had a question. I asked them to explain themselves. Why had they given the impression they were taking the high moral ground in organizing an inclusive parade when obviously they had neither principles nor integrity? My attitude was very upsetting to them, they said, their feelings were hurt.

It was good for us to hear Paul O'Dwyer, not ILGO's Paul, but the once powerful Irish leader, state it was disgusting to see Irish people discriminating against Irish people, given our history. But he was an old man now and unfortunately there was nobody in this group of men to replace him. Undaunted, the charade continued with speeches of praise for the mayor, the cardinal, Joe Hynes, and each other. It was pathetic.

Except for a few more grunts and groans the Hynes group dissolved. They had thought they were just moving in on the parade. They thought they'd be able to carry whatever political banners they wanted. They believed they would bring the parade into the twentieth century. The truth is they could have, but they didn't have the political backbone. Instead, they capitulated to the political agenda of the Archdiocese. They cared little of the world outside of their parochial power base, which, they decided, was where they wanted to stay. In the end they got rapped on the knuckles and ended up with nothing but red faces. They needed a scapegoat. Even though it was all over I was still getting faxes, messages, and phone calls from Gerry Keogh asking ILGO to make a statement condemning "irreverence involving houses of worship, religious objects of veneration or beliefs" and "recognizing the authority of the Roman Catholic Church." When the group eventually took an official vote, 7 were in favor of handing the permit back to the city, five against; there were four ILGO representatives at the meeting and four of those five were ILGO votes—only one non-ILGO person stood with us. The Hynes group issued a press statement: "Partition, or two parades, is not acceptable, because partition destroyed Ireland, and two parades would destroy the unity so important to our community."

One moment everything looks good, the next thing we know we're planning for the most likely scenario, not marching in the parade. Eileen began quoting Martin Luther King, Jr. at our meetings and said our only response now should be an act of civil disobedience. This was new language and the group didn't necessarily trust where it was coming from. After a lot of discussion we decided we wanted an action where as many people as possible could support us. We knew lots of our supporters could not, or would not risk arrest. Because we were an immigrant organization we also had to take our member's immigration status into account in our decision making. But I also remember not completely understanding the concept of civil disobedience, even considering it a bit daft. During my activist days in Ireland one thing was clear—avoid getting arrested at all costs. Maybe Eileen picked up on that difference and that's why she was quoting Martin Luther King, Jr. all the time. Back then I would have been stunned had I known what would actually happen on March 17, 1993.

Even though the Hynes group handed back the parade permit, the Police Department had not yet reissued it to another group. The AOH filed a lawsuit to have the permit

ROCK THE SHAM!

awarded to them. The case was assigned to Judge Leonard B. Sands in Federal Court. It was reassigned when Sands volunteered a conflict of interest—he was a close friend of Mayor Dinkins. On January 28, at an AOH parade meeting attended by four hundred people, the crowd applauded wildly when it was announced that the case was to be heard by a Nixon appointee, Judge Kevin Duffy. It was reported that Judge Duffy was known to wear a bow tie on St. Patrick's Day that played the tune, *When Irish Eyes are Smiling*.

> *When your sweet lilting laughter's like some fairy song, And your eyes twinkle bright as can be:*
> *You should laugh all the while, And all other times smile, And now, smile a smile for me.*

Clearly, Judge Kevin Duffy found he had no conflict of interest.

ROCK THE BLOCKS

I'D RATHER FIGHT THAN SWITCH!

PRE-ACTION
MEETING
FRI, MARCH 15, 8PM
LESBIAN & GAY
COMMUNITY CENTER
208 W 13TH ST
NEW YORK CITY

IRISH
LESBIAN
AND GAY
ORGANIZATION

IRISH LESBIAN & GAY ORGANIZATION
ST. PATRICK'S DAY PROTEST MARCH
SATURDAY, MARCH 16, 1996 • 9:00AM SHARP • 42 ST & 5th AVE
THEN RAGE AGAINST THE PARADE! ROCK THE BLOCKS! 11-5PM
ILGO HOTLINE 212-967-7711 x3078

THIS POSTER BROUGHT TO YOU BY
DYKE ACTION MACHINE!

ROCK THE SHAM

nakes

"A friend in power is a friend lost."
— Henry Adams

The Grass

ROCK THE SHAM!

AFTER THE 1993 parade I was never again shocked by what people and institutions did to try to stop ILGO from doing what it believed was right. At least now, with just four weeks to go, we knew where we stood—we would not be marching in the St. Patrick's Day Parade; instead we would march to protest our exclusion. Thinking all we had to deal with now was organizing our peaceful demonstration was a mistake. On Sunday, February 21, ILGO hosted a Queer Bingo fundraiser at Anseo, an Irish pub on St. Mark's Place in the East Village. The usually dark bar was flooded with light as a camera crew from the national news magazine show, *60 Minutes*, filmed. Morley Safer had already interviewed us so the bingo was for atmosphere.

For once Aldyn was not serenading us—instead he was our caller. Ryan was ILGO's prize collecting queen. She had scoured the streets of SOHO and the East and West Villages, cajoling businesses, restaurants, cinemas, and stores into donating gifts. Aldyn gingerly spun the plastic globe of our fragile toyshop bingo machine, waiting for the next lucky red number to pop out. Marie stuck it on the pegboard. "G 5," Aldyn shouted, "G is for Gay, and G is for Gaelic." People groaned or marked the number. As the game progressed, a hush fell over the bar with everyone concentrating, heads bent over cards, pencils ready, shoulders tense. "N 17. N is for Nancy boy!" At last someone rose to their feet, in triumph, and roared "Bingo!" This would be good television.

Queer Bingo was forgotten by the following morning, Monday, February 22, when Judge Kevin Duffy heard arguments in the Hibernians' suit to secure the parade permit for the 1993 St. Patrick's Day Parade. Duffy was robust and larger than life. He seemed fair and asked lots of questions of each side. We sat through the AOH's ILGO routine as they lied again about the 1991 parade and ILGO's alleged "manifestly sexual behavior with members of the same sex." I was astonished when AOH lawyer Ernest Mathews admitted the parade waiting list was a sham, or in his words, a "ruse." In previous lawsuits he had been categorical about the list's authenticity, and AOH witnesses had sworn to it, under oath. In fact, Mathews had relied heavily on the waiting list in 1992, and Judge Pierre Leval had fallen for it hook, line, and sinker. He had based his decision on the integrity of the list, stating that he could not jump ILGO over the groups waiting ahead of us. It was only when Judge Duffy pressed Mathews, asking him if the waiting list was a waiting list to nowhere that Mathews told the truth; "Yes," he responded. Lies told under oath are usually considered perjury, but this didn't seem to bother Duffy or Mathews. I wondered if Judge Leval felt duped or humiliated and thought probably not.

The power and arrogance of the institutions ILGO did battle with was phenomenal. At last I began to understand that the AOH and the Church, with the backing of the court, could do whatever they wanted and get away with it. I left 40 Center Street knowing we hadn't a hope in hell but wishing, as always, that the system would work for us this time. Judge Duffy said he would make a decision as soon as possible.

Snakes In The Grass

We didn't have to wait long. Just over a week later, on Friday, February 26, New York City came to a stand still. Judge Duffy handed down his parade decision in favor of the Hibernians on the same day the World Trade Center was bombed for the first time. The phone was hopping at work. Duffy's order lambasted the Human Rights Commission, invoking George Orwell's *Nineteen Eighty-Four*:

> *The commission sought to dictate how the parade*
> *sponsors would express their thoughts. Such activity*
> *(telling citizens what they must think and how they*
> *must express themselves) is something one would*
> *expect from the "Thought Police" described by George*
> *Orwell.*

Kafka would have been my literary analogy, especially when Judge Duffy went on to state, "This court holds no brief for either side in this controversy. However," he continued, "everyone should recognize that the undermining of the freedom of any individual is the undermining of the freedom of us all." But wasn't it the existence of ILGO that was being constantly undermined? As individuals, lesbians and gay men have been consistently denied the freedom to say who we are and be treated equally.

The city was ordered to grant the AOH the permit to conduct the 1993 parade. Frank Beirne responded by urging marchers to bring their rosary beads to pray for everyone, including gays, lesbians, and people with AIDS. Mayor Dinkins said from Tokyo, "My position was that I had hoped that the court would rule that the parade would be inclusive. The court has determined otherwise and I will go along with the law." We were a little perplexed by his remark but did not dwell on it. The city lawyers announced they would not appeal the decision and ILGO vowed to be on Fifth Avenue with everyone else who wished to celebrate on St. Patrick's Day. Judge Duffy may have ruled that discrimination against lesbians and gay men is lawful but in our view that didn't make it acceptable.

The *Irish Echo* published a sanctimonious editorial in its next issue:

> *From the parade organizers, we asked that they find*
> *a way to make the event a true reflection of the diversity*
> *of the Irish community. From the members of ILGO,*
> *we asked that they continue to press their case to the*
> *organizers and to their supporters within the Irish*

PREVIOUS SPREAD: The C.D. Rebels – so radical and so wrong. Eileen Clancy is wearing glasses in front row on far right. © www.carolinakroonphotography.com

ROCK THE SHAM!

community, and not to involve the city. From the
mayor, we asked that he allow the Irish to work
through problems themselves.

Those who had claimed to support ILGO in the Irish community had just dumped us.
ILGO had tried to maintain contact with the AOH but the AOH refused to talk with ILGO.
We had done everything in our power that was ethical to try to solve the problem, without
the help or support of one single organization in the Irish community. That is not to say
there were no people of influence and integrity in the Irish community who supported us,
but these people were few and far between. We politely sat through meetings and listened to
bigots, fixers, and liberals and we did it with dignity. The Human Rights Commission sued
the AOH as it was compelled to under the law. The mayor marched with ILGO in 1991 as
he should have and had every right to. The Hynes group (Irish-American Democrats) had
more involvement with the city than ILGO ever had. The editorial implied that the Irish
community is a law unto itself, beyond the scope of the law of the city, or at least, that it
should be. Once again, the New York elite of Irish America misunderstood this fight. The
Echo didn't seem to have a grasp on city politics. Otherwise, it would have known Mayor
Dinkins' initial involvement was a calculated political decision to win back the support of
New York's lesbian, gay, transgender and AIDS activist community, whom he'd disappointed.
His marching with ILGO had nothing to do with the Irish community. Queers had voted for
David Dinkins, not Irish people.

Now, in ILGO, we spent hours discussing and debating exactly what to do on St.
Patrick's Day. After many meetings we decided against a civil disobedience action, which
Eileen promoted, and instead announced our plan to hold a peaceful protest march from
59th Street down Fifth Avenue to 42nd Street. The demonstration would begin at 9am, two
hours before the St. Patrick's Day Parade kicked off. We believed more people could safely
participate in a march. Decisions didn't always go the way we all wanted them to go, but
the group had always stuck together, give or take a hiccup or two, once a decision had been
made; that was how it worked. When ILGO chose to file a lawsuit, even though it was a very
contentious issue and not a unanimous decision, everyone weighed in behind it. Now that
we were losing in court, it may have been the wrong decision. But the few of us who were
vehemently opposed to trying our luck in the legal system did not turn on the group when
we didn't get our way. Unfortunately, Eileen did not share this philosophy.

We held a public meeting at the Lesbian and Gay Services Center so we could answer
questions about our plan. Rather than honor the group's decision not to organize a civil
disobedience action, which would involve arrests, Eileen sat in the front row sulking and
refused to participate. The meeting was tough; we were so used to Eileen's energy and
determination and her incredible motivational skills in public and with the media. The
group depended upon her hugely as she was such a central figure by now. But at this

meeting we got our first glimpse of the activists Eileen had talked about bringing into ILGO to "help" us. Now, that our plan to hold a protest march was set, they were openly hostile. They challenged ILGO's decision, which was not up for debate—it was ILGO's place to decide how to respond to the AOH and the court's ruling. But at every turn, Eileen's "friends" undermined ILGO's right to act in a way we believed appropriate, thus making it clear their beef was with ILGO and not any of the institutions ILGO was standing up to. In their opinion, ILGO was not radical enough. They had come to our community meeting to be divisive because they had a plan of their own.

Marie and I began to suspect that Eileen was up to something—we feared she wasn't just angry and upset but working behind the scenes against ILGO. Eileen talked to me a little at work but during our parade meetings she sat in silence and morale in the group was very low. Marie asked John Voelcker, who was closest to Eileen, if he knew what her plan was and he was genuinely perplexed by the inquiry. Then we began to hear rumors that another gay group was planning a St. Patrick's Day action of their own. That was fine with ILGO—so long as we could be assured that what we were doing would not be disrupted or interfered with, given our responsibility for those who chose to support us—any group could do whatever it wanted.

Marie called Maxine Wolfe and Sarah Schulman, with whom she worked closely in the Lesbian Avengers. Both Marie and I wanted to know what experienced activists thought about what might be up. We met in the Violet Café and as soon as we began to air our fears and anxieties I realized I had been in a daze from panic; once our fears were out in the open I began to feel grounded again. Maxine and Sarah listened and passed no judgment on ILGO's plan. They were calm and practical. They weren't in ILGO and didn't have to sit through our meetings so they could give us an outsider's perspective. We met a few more times for coffee and it was Maxine's and Sarah's availability, wisdom, and support that held us together. I knew our job was manageable again.

Finally, the rumors were confirmed. Another action for St. Patrick's Day was indeed underway. Marie confronted Eileen at our next meeting and asked if she knew what the other group's plan was. Eileen said she couldn't tell us anything about it. The tension in the room was brutal and sad. Everyone now knew something was amiss. We could not speak openly anymore because we worried about Eileen's loyalty and feared she might be reporting back to a hostile group. However, ILGO had many enemies, and had dealt with far more powerful foes. We set about sorting out the mess.

I called people I'd heard were involved in the other group to try to get some information. ILGO wanted to be assured that their action would not thwart our goal for St. Patrick's Day. However, nobody could or would give me that assurance. I was blown off with arrogance and sarcasm. I was told there would be no mistaking the action but nobody would say whether or not it would take place in the middle of ILGO's protest march. A friend in the Lesbian Avengers called to let me know she had been invited to a secret planning meeting;

she gave me the details. Ironically, with only a few weeks to go to St. Patrick's Day, our biggest headache turned out to be a gay activist group intent on obstructing ILGO.

Sheila Quinn and I met before going to the secret meeting. At least we could ask them to settle our fears by agreeing to maintain a distinction between what ILGO was doing and what they were doing. After all, they had come to every community meeting we had held and we weren't hiding anything. Sheila and I were turned away at the door. We were told that the meeting was for invited guests only and not just for anyone who felt like attending. We stood in the lobby of the building on Broadway, flummoxed. As we stood and argued and cajoled, people slunk past, had their names ticked off the elitist list, before quickly disappearing upstairs. I wondered if Eileen was up there already. The three bouncers at the door told us they could not give us any assurances about keeping the actions separate. Again I asked if we could just go up for a couple of minutes to tell the gathering what our worries were. I was told no because I was "not involved." That did it—I blew a fuse: "I have been involved in this since 1991. When did you get involved?" We left. All we could do now was make sure we continued to publicly state exactly what ILGO's plan was and to make sure our marshals knew to look out for an action within our march in order to keep everyone safe.

Every time I think nothing else can happen it happens and the next hurdle came as a complete surprise. ILGO was suddenly put under intense pressure by the city and the Police Department to call off our protest. They offered us any location in New York but Fifth Avenue. We stuck to our plan. Fifth Avenue was central to our message: if we weren't going to be allowed in the parade we were certainly going to be on Fifth Avenue on St. Patrick's Day, protesting. Being anywhere else was meaningless—it was the parade on Fifth Avenue we were barred from. In the middle of this battle Eileen called Paul, her nemesis in ILGO, one week before St. Patrick's Day, and told him she had decided to leave the group. John Voelcker, Eileen's closest ally and friend, was bowled over and very hurt. He had not believed she would betray ILGO. I worried about coping at work and was glad Eileen and I had separate offices. To this day, Eileen doesn't understand why people in ILGO felt so betrayed. She said it was clear that we didn't mind other actions taking place and that she had done nothing wrong by leaving and going with this other group. But Eileen was a leader in ILGO and even if she felt very torn about what to do in 1993 it did not mean that the rest of us had no right to feel truly betrayed by her.

We got back on track because we didn't have any choice. In fact Eileen's leaving was a huge emotional relief because along with her went the bad feeling in the working group. We could never replace her or the schmoozing and networking that seemed second nature to her. We spent a little time licking our wounds and pulled together again without having to be wary or watchful. During the day I ignored Eileen except when we had to communicate about work. Rick didn't know what was going on and I was too furious to even attempt an explanation. I managed by choosing to despise Eileen, to cut her out rather than feeling hurt, confused, or too upset to keep going, until the parade was over for one more year.

Snakes In The Grass

Then a very odd thing happened. The director of the Lesbian and Gay Anti-Violence Project (AVP), called me at work to ask ILGO to reconsider our plan to have a protest march. He explained he had not wanted to make the call but told me several major AVP donors had pressured him. Paul began to get similar calls from the "gay male leadership" in New York—the "Homocrats." Matt Foreman, of the AVP, said he understood completely if ILGO refused the request but he had to be able to tell his people he had made the call. Only the previous year he had spoken eloquently at our rally in Sheridan Square. This was an omen; something was foul in our world ... again.

Unknown to us at the time, the police commissioner, Ray Kelly, had sent a letter to O. Peter Sherwood, the Corporation Counsel (city legal representatives), on Friday, March 12. Kelly's letter stated, "It is imperative that we seek immediate judicial intervention and obtain an order restraining ILGO from proceeding south on Fifth Avenue as they propose." The police commissioner was allegedly worried about public safety. However, Peter Sherwood was not convinced such drastic action was warranted yet because he knew about the strange phone calls ILGO was receiving from gay "leaders." He responded, "I am advised that concentrated efforts are proceeding to persuade ILGO and its supporters to avoid conducting their march in ways that would present the potential for confrontation."

After work on Friday, only four days before the parade, we had a meeting at Ryan's apartment on Eldridge Street. Ryan was excited when I arrived. She told me that Paul was on her phone, talking to the mayor, who had called her apartment looking for him. We passed through the kitchen into Ryan's living room, where Paul was silently nodding his head, listening. Our eyes met, he understood the question in mine. He raised his eyebrows and shrugged in response. He looked washed out and exhausted. He turned his back and nodded at the wall, trembling a little. The conversation lasted about ten minutes. As people arrived and were filled in on what was going on, they sat in silence; we listened to Paul's end of the conversation, waiting for it to finish. When Paul hung up, he just stood there, lost. I hugged him. He kept saying, "I can't believe this." All else had failed, so the mayor called to make it clear he did not want us to go ahead with our planned march.

On the heels of David Dinkins' call, the phone rang again. It was the mayor's office; this time to tell us that Deputy Mayor Bill Lynch, along with Debra Pucci, and Jan Parks, was coming to Ryan's to talk. Ryan laughed aloud with a bit of a cackle and immediately ran off to the kitchen to boil the kettle again. In the middle of all this commotion Lesbian Avengers were buzzing the door downstairs to pick up posters and buckets of wheat paste to do the rounds that night. Ryan's apartment was already full of people when Bill Lynch, Debra Pucci, and Jan Parks arrived.

Lucy and Trish sat on the bed. The rest of us sat on the floor and on any available surface. Lynch took an armchair while Debra and Jan stood beside him. Ryan fussed about and asked the visitors if they'd like tea. Bill Lynch wanted to get down to business so Ryan couldn't get him to say whether or not he wanted milk and sugar. She sized him up and decided he probably took both and handed him a mug. He was in full swing until he too' his first mouthful. It turns out he's a diabetic. He left the mug of sugary tea on the floor Afterward we figured Ryan must have had some insight into what was about to take plac and teased her about trying to poison him.

Deputy Mayor Bill Lynch was furious. None of us had ever seen him like this. Debr and Jan were silent for most of the visit. He asked us to reconsider our plan. He was probabl furious that the mayor's phone call hadn't done the trick and that he'd had to come all th way to a Lower East Side tenement to bully us into submission. He was emphatic about wha a big mistake ILGO was making. He said that this was "Big P...politics" now and that w had better not screw up. According to him, "Big P...politics" meant that if ILGO went ahea as planned with our protest march, we would be responsible for screwing up any hope th lesbian and gay community had for winning domestic partnership rights, the state-wide Ga Rights Bill, and acceptance of gays in the military. He said if we insisted on marching, th blame for the failure to implement these policies would lie at our feet. This wasn't just abou our small group, he said, but the larger picture. He continued to hector us with this type c rhetoric for about fifteen minutes, not allowing anyone else to speak. I thought it was al very interesting. I knew City Hall wanted us to back down and take the fall to take pressur off the mayor. I knew it was all about politics, not "Big P...politics," but city politics, and th upcoming mayoral election. This parade issue was too hot for Dinkins now. Irish-America Democrats had screwed the mayor by buckling under pressure from Cardinal O'Connor handing back the permit and deciding not to run an inclusive parade. David Dinkin expected ILGO to pay because he didn't want to look bad. ILGO was supposed to give u now to make New York City's mayor look good and possibly, not to split the gay vote.

Some of the others debated with Bill Lynch, back and forth, and he continued to try t make us feel like we were doing something naive and dangerous. But the only stupid thin we'd done that night was let Lynch into Ryan's apartment. I told him I understood wha he was talking about but disagreed with his analysis, and said that ILGO would not bacl down because we believed what we were doing was right. I made it clear we would not b taking the fall for anyone. The color rose in Marie's cheeks and I knew she was furious. Sh launched in and accused Lynch of using ILGO as a political football just like everyone els had. She told him he had a nerve coming here and telling us how to organize and what ou strategy should be. That put an end to the visit.

Throughout our battle to march in the parade and our refusal to be dispossessed o our Irish and gay identities, we have been consistently asked to back down for the sake o all kinds of causes and interests. Now, the mayor, a politician who claimed to support u and who compared marching with us in 1991 to marching in Selma during the civil right movement, was asking us to give up our integrity. Nobody, it seemed, understood what thi battle meant for ILGO—we were out and not about to go back into the closet or apologize t anyone for our dedication and bravery. But City Hall wasn't done. As we would find out, i had one final card up its sleeve.

After Lynch left we battled each other to get a word in edgeways. I was upset that several people had been moved and impressed by what Lynch had said, and not surprised that others had been thoroughly intimidated. But it didn't take much to clear up what had transpired. Lynch was doing his job, protecting the mayor, but barking up the wrong tree. We would have our protest march as planned. The AOH said ILGO should not be allowed to march the route we had chosen because they did not want us marching past St. Patrick's Cathedral. Our demonstration should be banned, they said, because it would cause a skirmish between ILGO and the people coming out of mass on St. Patrick's Day. Their charge of public disorder was completely unfounded unless they knew something about the mass-goers that they weren't revealing. AOH lawyer Ernest Mathews was his usual charming self as he expostulated on ILGO's planned demonstration: "Once again, it shows that they are trying to co-opt our audience. Many people arrive to the Avenue early to get good spots, and others are busy setting up the different bands and marching units. It's a shame they'll have to look at these clowns going by... They're calling for a boycott, well, let's see just how many people do boycott." We certainly would see.

The death-threats began to mount up on our hotline and Marie got a call from a terrified worker at Gay Men's Health Crisis who had gotten a message telling him their building would be bombed because of ILGO. I received hate mail at work, with a red 'X' slashed across a picture of my face from the newspaper and threats scrawled on both sides of the page. Even the AOH parade committee used our telephone hotline service to listen to our recording, once forgetting to hang up the phone while they commented. We saved the message and played it for everyone at our next meeting for some light relief.

On the Sunday before the parade we met to watch the *60 Minutes* broadcast. There was a lot of screeching and laughing. There was also some gasping and swearing! I didn't know what to make of it because I couldn't concentrate. Marie was gently teased for wearing lipstick and being the ILGO glamour girl. It was odd to see Eileen and for her not to be in the room watching with us, especially when she revealed that Jack Hale, the cardinal's lawyer friend, was related to her—they were cousins. We laughed with delight as we watched Hale's reaction to this news. Morley Safer enjoyed himself immensely and there were lots of camera angles of him smiling sardonically and smugly at the silly Hibernians. Everyone seemed to be pleased enough with the show, except Marie. She said it was treated like a family squabble without any depth or context. After the show, we had a brief meeting and went home to finish whatever work still had to be done by Wednesday, St. Patrick's Day.

The next morning the mayor pulled his wild card. He had come full circle and now turned on us; ironically, he used an old tactic that had been used against civil rights marchers during the movement in the 1960s. The city wanted a restraining order to keep ILGO off Fifth Avenue; they were prepared to go to any length to ban our protest march. The so-called leadership of the Irish community had abandoned us. The legal system never considered extending the same constitutional rights to ILGO as it had to the AOH. The Church opposed us, and now the mayor and city government stood with them all, against ILGO. And meanwhile, we had a group of so-called radical activists in the gay community telling us that we weren't doing enough. With the combined weight of these mighty institutions coming down on us I figured we had to be doing something right.

On March 16, the eve of St. Patrick's Day, we appeared in court and confounded everyone because we didn't fight the restraining order. Clare had noticed a flaw: the city only wanted ILGO banned from marching southward on Fifth Avenue. We had decided that marching in protest was our goal and marching northward on St. Patrick's Day would suffice. Given our history in the courts we would have lost anyway. Later in the day we would make our announcement. That afternoon we sent out a press statement saying we would be holding a press conference at 5pm at The Center. At the conference, which was packed, we announced our plan to hold our peaceful protest march at 9am starting at the New York Public Library on 42nd Street going up Fifth Avenue, rather than down, to 59th Street. There was no injunction against us doing this. In a couple of hours we were due back at The Center for our pre-action meeting at 8pm.

But we had been caught out. The corporation council had been tipped off about the oversight in the injunction and the city lawyers found a judge to hear their case even though the courts were closed. They were awarded a final and all encompassing order banning ILGO from marching anywhere and in any direction on Fifth Avenue on St. Patrick's Day. Where they were successful in seeking out an after-hours audience with a judge, ILGO was not. So, by the time of our pre-action meeting, we knew there was an injunction in place against the protest. If we proceeded in organizing it, we would be charged with criminal contempt, a misdemeanor, which carries a possible sentence of one year in jail.

Right before the pre-action meeting the ILGO parade-working group met and completely changed our plan for the next morning. Lesbians and gay men across the city were furious at the length Mayor Dinkins and the courts had gone to stop us from having any voice on St. Patrick's Day. There was no question in anyone's mind about what to do. ILGO would march regardless of the injunction—this was civil disobedience.

Our pre-action meeting was spirited and full of energy and excitement. Katherine O'Donnell and Helena Crotty stood to take a bow. They had traveled from Cork in Ireland to support ILGO. Katherine was one of the organizers of the first lesbian and gay contingent in the parade in Cork, where her group won a prize for best new entry. Lesbian and gay groups were set to march again in Cork, as well as in Dublin and Galway. Bernie Hegarty, an Irish lesbian living in London, had also come to New York for St. Patrick's Day.

The room was packed to capacity. Our marshals, most of whom were Lesbian Avengers, went through the routine. Everyone should bring some form of identification, preferably photo ID with a home address. We should wear warm clothes and gloves that covered the wrists for protection against handcuffs. Maxine loved to bring food to share, candy, fruit, cigarettes, and water if practical. Throughout the room people stood when they remembered something, everyone's tips adding to the list of dos and don'ts. There was such a buzz I forgot all the horror of the previous months, even the past week, and was enjoying myself. We were told not to bring penknives or anything that could be construed as a weapon. There was a quip about lesbians and their Swiss Army knives. Long earrings and jewelry in general wasn't a great idea because it could get caught in clothing. If we had anything we valued at all we were told to leave it at home. We learned that enough medication should be brought in a prescription bottle and some left for safety with the ILGO support crew. We filled out support sheets so we wouldn't get lost in the system if we were arrested; someone would be watching out for us. Then everyone present made an important decision collectively about what information we would give to the police to take care of each other and avoid letting the cops single people out, like people with HIV or AIDS or people who were not citizens or documented immigrants. We would give our names, addresses, and dates of birth—all that was legally required. Everyone was on a high, except Eileen's group, who called themselves the CD (Civil Disobedience) Rebels.

The CD Rebels were furious. The last thing they wanted was to be seen to be doing the same action as ILGO—quite an identity crisis for them. Even Eileen later admitted that they were in a bit of a quandary now (although she claimed we never said we were going to do a civil disobedience—so why the dilemma?) so they decided to wait until the morning to see whether or not they would support ILGO. We let them splutter for a bit and made our final announcement to a cheering crowd: "Despite the injunction, ILGO and our supporters will still meet on the steps of the New York Public Library at 9am and from there march up Fifth Avenue." The CD Rebels would decide not to support ILGO, which was never their intention, and they made one final attempt to hurt us with Eileen leading the way.

The ILGO working group met again briefly with the marshals, support and legal teams to make sure everything was covered. We added the finishing touches to our posters and hugged each other good night, happy and tired. Marie and I walked to a Mexican restaurant down the street to do an interview for the Irish documentary Linda Cullen was working on with RTE, the Irish broadcasting corporation. It was close to midnight and we were exhausted. We ended up hanging out with Linda and the crew for a couple of hours. Back out on 13th Street, the night air was frigid. Snow that had turned dirty gray was packed high along the curb. It was already St. Patrick's Day. At 14th Street we hopped on a waiting L train and were in Marie's apartment in Williamsburg in 20 minutes. Marie set the alarm for 7am. So as not to forget anything we placed plastic bags full of posters on the floor in front of Marie's hall door, along with our identification, cigarettes and cash. The ILGO banner went on top of the pile. We both slept soundly.

"Anyone in a free society where the laws are unjust has an obligation to break the law.

CHAPTER TWELVE

We're Here! We're Queer! We're Irish – Get Used To It!

ROCK THE SHAM!

ON THE STREET Marie slipped her arm through mine and we kept up a brisk pace to the subway station. I loved when we linked arms because of the intimacy, the pleasurable feeling that I was protecting Marie, and because it reminded me of the women walking the streets of Dublin. Drizzle covered us with tiny dots of moisture, which sometimes caught the light of a passing car and sparkled, making us look like we were covered in dew. This was real Irish weather.

The first obvious sign that something out of the ordinary was anticipated on Fifth Avenue was the overwhelming police presence. When Marie and I emerged from the bowel of the 42nd Street subway station there were cops everywhere—it felt like walking onto the movie set of a post-apocalyptic New York. Hundreds of police stood in rows along 42nd Street. They sat in vans parked bumper to bumper, waited on horseback and motorcycles and seemed prepared for whatever might happen, in their riot gear. We stood still for a moment, to take in the scene, and to get our bearings. I put my hat on to cover up my bright red hair, but continued to feel conspicuous passing police officers huddled at the intersections on our short route to the New York Public Library. Lots of people were already gathering on the steps when we arrived. It was raining now.

We stood around, at odds with our environment, and as always not knowing how to fill in this awkward time before the demonstration began. I moved slowly up the steps a little, hauling two plastic bags of posters behind me, nodding and smiling at friends and strangers. I took sips of people's tea and coffee, being less anxious now than I had been in previous years about bladder explosions, and more worried about being dehydrated. As usual, I did not want to talk to anyone, but needed something practical to do before I got too agitated. Marie was soaked, rain dripped from her hair and the tip of her nose. We made our way up the library steps towards the main entrance of the building. It was nice and quiet and dry there. I found clean cardboard and had spare markers in my pocket so I got down on my hands and knees between two massive concrete pillars, turned my back on the spectacle below, and started making posters.

ILGO's marshals had arrived that morning long before any of us. They busied themselves scouring the entire area of the library, noting where the police and their barricades were situated (which was everywhere), making plans and decisions about when and where ILGO would move out onto Fifth Avenue. As soon as our comrades in ILGO figured out where we were, they joined us. We went through the alphabet, trying to figure out which of the thirty-two counties in Ireland we hadn't remembered because we wanted each one spelled out in bold letters on our posters. Eventually reporters found us too. They snapped shots, did interviews, and hovered. I had put my foot through the handles of the plastic bag that kept our banner safe and dry and kept it firmly pinned under me. Paul tipped my shoulder and I looked up at him, and at Clare O'Brien, our lawyer. We hadn't seen her since the morning before, in court, which seemed so long ago. She told us about her after-hours efforts (with f all people, Norman Siegel of the NYCLU) and failure, to get an appeals court judge to overturn the injunction. I got to my feet. Tears welled up in Clare's eyes as we spoke, which couldn't bear. I think this was the first time I realized how important the issue was for Clare and how upset she was by what had happened. I turned away to look at what I'd been avoiding. The vast area in front of the public library was milling with people, all the way down each level of steps and out to the edge of the sidewalk. Unhooking the plastic bag from under my foot, I prepared to go out into the rain and down nearer Fifth Avenue. The police switched on a powerful sound system and began to read out the court order, word for word: Paul O'Dwyer, Anne Maguire and John Voelcker, in their capacities as leaders of the Irish Lesbian and Gay Organization, and 'John Doe' and 'Jane Doe' (said names of 'John Doe' and 'Jane Doe' being fictitious, their true names being unknown to plaintiff), being individuals or organizations who plan or intend to or in fact gather on St. Patrick's Day, March 17, 1993, to march south on Fifth Avenue," and on it went, eventually announcing that if we did not disperse, we would be arrested and charged with criminal contempt. The crowd began to boo and chant, drowning out the amplified warning so we never got to hear any further threats. The time for us to make our move was very near. Alexis Danzig, one of our marshals, warned everyone that if they stepped out into the avenue they would risk arrest, which was the normal action to take as not everyone was aware of the Federal injunction, or aware that they would be risking arrest, and we didn't presume that everybody at the library that morning had been at our pre-action meeting the night before. However, for some reason, Eileen Clancy told me recently that she construed this as meaning ILGO had made a deal with the cops because Alexis used a police mega phone to make the announcement. ILGO has no history of making deals with the Police Department—not since Eileen and John Voelcker had made one the previous year and got screwed. The only time anyone in ILGO ever had anything to do with the police was when the cops arrested us or refused to give us a permit. In light of Eileen's activist experience, I don't understand how she could have mistaken a marshal's warning, which is par for the course at a protest, as an affirmation that a deal had been struck between ILGO and the NYPD.

We huddled on the sidewalk close to Fifth Avenue for an on-the-spot press conference. As soon as Paul began to speak we were surrounded and squashed. The media frenzy began. Reporters and photographers hemmed us in, and the politicians scurried for a spot in the limelight beside ILGO. My heart began its familiar thud against my ribs and I could hear it beating in my ears, faster and faster, louder and louder. Each breath became an enormous effort. I had been having panic attacks for years but never knew what they were—the frightening woozy sensation was just a part of the parade business. The banner was trapped

ROCK THE SHAM!

against my hip and we were so tightly packed I couldn't free my arm to shift it. It looked like there were thousands of people on the steps.

Politicians were shouting, because there was no amplification, about why they had turned out on this St. Patrick's Day to support ILGO, regardless of the city's injunction. spotted Jan Parks from City Hall. The last time we had seen him was in Ryan's apartment on the Lower East Side when Bill Lynch bullied us with his "Big P...politics" speech. I wondered if Jan would get fired for showing up. I felt a shift. There was something going on out on Fifth Avenue—there were people out there. My panic attack peaked at last; my vision blurred and misted over draining the color from everything. The pounding in my head dulled all other noise in the world. It felt like my heart was going to burst out of me like the creature in Alien. Through this haze I saw Ernest Mathews, the AOH lawyer, standing close by, watching I remember wondering, *What's he doing here?* But my attention quickly returned to the commotion out front. And then I saw Eileen.

There she was, on Fifth Avenue, arms frantically waving directions as she shouted and roared at whoever was there with her. I couldn't hear what she was saying. Beside me a woman bellowed, "Where's the banner? Who has the fucking banner?" I think it was Maxine Seeing Eileen shook me because, for some reason, I had assumed she would not show up What was she doing? One moment we were listening to politicians at a press conference seconds later I was pulling the banner out, passing it down the line of ILGO people, as we were being rushed out onto Fifth Avenue. I never realized what was happening but Eileen was trying to get people out onto Fifth Avenue before ILGO made a move. For years I was in denial about this until everyone I asked told me that my version—Eileen was trying to make the CD Rebels wait so ILGO could lead the way—was false. ILGO people repeatedly told me that Eileen was leading the CD Rebels out onto Fifth Avenue to take over ILGO's march and I didn't believe them.

But now ILGO was being pulled out on to Fifth Avenue by Lesbian Avenger marshals Maxine kept shouting, "If you support ILGO, wait and march with them." It was chaotic The CD Rebels were shouting too. They roared, "Charge!" at the police. But people heard Maxine and waited to fall in behind ILGO.

My eyes did not leave that front line of marshals. I knew they were in control of the situation. I stared at filmmaker, Su Friedrich, the marshal directly in front of me, and did everything she said, trusting her completely. At the other end of our long green banner Ryan and Eileen screamed at each other. Questions flew in and out of my head at once. Why did the Rebels want to charge the police? Was everything going to be all right? Would people know what was going on, would the cops go berserk? My hands squeezed the fabric of the banner but I couldn't feel anything. The disturbing images of the previous minute, seeing Ernest Mathews on the steps of the library, Eileen Clancy in the middle of Fifth Avenue and Bill Monahan shouting "Charge!" flashed in front of me. I was scared.

Fortunately, the chaos was short lived. Within a minute or two, the marshals had

We're Here! We're Queer! We're Irish – Get Used To It!

Tom Kieran, Paul O'Dwyer, Catch Keeley, Councilman Tom Duane, Marie Honan march in protest despite federal injunction, in 1993 © *Donna Binder*

BELOW: Me and Marie, Sheila Quinn, Lucy Lynch, Brendan Fay and Tarlach MacNiallais © *www.carolinakroonphotography.com*

regained complete control and ILGO was marching very slowly on Fifth Avenue toward 42nd Street. We didn't know where the CD Rebels were but they were not in front of us anymore. I inhaled and exhaled and took a long look ahead of me, relaxing. We were safe now. I looked at the line of experienced activists guiding us along the route—Maxine Wolfe, Sarah Schulman, Carrie Moyer, Phyllis Lutsky, Alexis Danzig and Su Friedrich, amongst others, led ILGO up Fifth Avenue. They held hands or linked each other as their bodies moved with determination and power. They were strong and beautiful.

Directly beyond the marshals were hundreds of reporters, photographers and TV crews. Behind us people were singing. Rain poured down. "What are they singing?" I asked. "We Shall Overcome," I was told. "We're Here, We're Queer, We're Irish, Get Used to It!" reverberated about us. I joined in with that chant—it felt more appropriate.

Beyond the intersection at 42nd Street, rows of police officers waited for us. I looked over my shoulder and saw Trish, whose eyes peeked out from a scarf she had wrapped around her head and face. She had not planned on being arrested. "Trish?" "I had to do it," she said. "I couldn't stay when I saw you all going, when I saw Lucy going." Then she remembered she had no identification, nor was she legally living in the United States. "Oh my God! What will I do?" I told her what she knew I would: "It'll be all right." In front of her, Lucy, beaming as always, held on to the banner beside Sheila Quinn.

People sang and chanted, waved their homemade, sodden placards in the air: "Ancient Order of Hate," "Brits out of Ireland; Bigots out of the parade" and "First Amendment Menace—Dinkins." Following us along the sidelines, hundreds of supporters roared, "The whole world is watching." In 1993 this was an international news story and months after the event, newspaper clippings in several languages continued to turn up in our mail box, sent by people who'd been away and had seen photos of the march in the foreign press. At the intersection at 42nd Street, a single strip of police tape spanned the entire width of Fifth Avenue. This piece of plastic symbolized the end of the line for our protest march. The avenue ahead was a frozen zone, clear of the public and traffic. At the frozen zone's ending point a solid wall of New York City law enforcement waited for us. The marshals stopped. The protest came to a standstill. Again, we heard the amplified police warning of arrest over a loudspeaker. We chanted even louder now to drown out the threat. Our eyes were on that yellow police tape, the line not to be crossed.

For the first time that morning the marshals turned around and faced us, still holding hands. We watched them intently, staring into their eyes, clutching our banner that said who we were, the Irish Lesbian & Gay Organization. I had an urge to reach over and touch Su, the marshal standing inches away from me. They let go of each other and let their hands fall to their sides. Without a word to us or each other, they broke rank, divided into two groups, each slowly and deliberately moving to one side of Fifth Avenue in a movement that looked like it had been choreographed and practiced for this exact moment. This left the way ahead clear. We knew what to do.

A hush fell over us for one moment. I put my hand over Marie's and Sheila's, holding the banner with them, and then we marched straight ahead, through the police tape. A massive roar rose from those marching behind us and from our supporters on the sidelines, and it continued as everyone on Fifth Avenue walked on over. We had done it. When we could march no further because of the wall of police, we sat on the ground.

Marie turned and kissed me. We felt very proud of ourselves. Sheila was trembling and I remember murmuring into her ear, never letting go of her hand. When I looked behind me I couldn't believe how many people there were. Now I wanted a cup of coffee and a cigarette, even something to eat. The chanting rose to a crescendo and seemed to be coming at us from all directions. I saw Mary Ann Wadden far away, standing on the library wall, waving a placard I couldn't read. Marie passed me a lit cigarette. Catch had already smoked halfway down hers. Tarlach hadn't taken a breath, he was so busy shouting and pounding the air, his fist clenched. At the far end of the banner smoke rose up around Ryan, and Tom Kieran sat quietly beside her. John Voelcker, looking cheerful again, chatted to Tom Duane, the only openly gay and HIV-positive city council member, who was on his hunkers not getting his backside wet. Most of the marshals joined us. This was an unusual turn of events because marshals did not normally get arrested. But this was not a normal situation. Sarah Schulman told us her brother Charlie was there because he was furious about the injunction. He said he was an American and that "they can't do this to Americans." I wasn't sure if he meant it was okay to do it to immigrants but didn't ask. Adrian O'Byrne's brother, Brían, came to support him and ended up out on Fifth Avenue with Adrian.

While we sat in puddles in the middle of the street Katherine O'Donnell, who had traveled from Cork to be with ILGO, was watching from the sidewalk. She had to be restrained from marching out on Fifth Avenue with us by her friends. She explained that after the initial burst of excitement and exhilaration she felt seeing us break through the tape her mood quickly changed:

> *I found it hard to stop crying—I think it was seeing the brave*
> *burst of you marching. You all looked wonderful to me—I*
> *forgot what was going to happen. It came as a real shock to*
> *see the police pulling you off the road. I couldn't understand*
> *why you couldn't march. ... I was frustrated and raging.*
> *Then seeing these fuckers coming up the street shouting, 'Go*
> *home you faggots,' was really weird because they looked*
> *like my brothers and cousins.*

Rob Cates, a big bear of a man who worked in the same building as Eileen and me, said he left when he couldn't stop crying. Clare O'Brien watched with Linda Cullen who was there to finish up the documentary for Irish television. Linda had to send her crew off to cover the event without her direction because she was so sad she was unable to work. She stood with Clare, both quietly weeping.

A fellow behind me shouted, "David Feinberg, famous gay writer, is getting arrested." I don't know if Feinberg was mortified, but I would have been. The word also went out that Tony Kushner, Pulitzer Prize-winning author of *Angels In America*, was with us. The boys were very excited.

Then the cops moved in. They had thick white plastic cuffs and hauled stretchers behind them. Sheila had a vice grip on my hand. One by one the police picked off people beginning with the banner holders up front. Few of us had any idea what it was going to be like to be arrested because this was our first time. I held on to Sheila for as long as was possible and talked to her while she was lifted, hands cuffed behind her, onto a stretcher. We'd be with her in a minute I reassured her. Marie was next. She let out a low-pitched roar as her arms were yanked behind her and the cuffs roughly pulled into a lock on her wrists. I wanted to cry out but talked to her instead—she didn't seem to hear me. I've never felt so lonely in all my life. Marie was raised up by several cops and lifted to a stretcher. All the while people were chanting and cheering and telling those being arrested that they were wonderful and fabulous. I sat unable to do anything while Marie's head disappeared amongst a sea of cops.

A cop squeezed my arm, bent down and asked me if I was going to get up and walk. I said "No." He shouted, "Stretcher!" above the din. With that both of my arms were pulled up behind me and the sleeves of my leather jacket, which I'd pulled down over my wrists and held in the palm of my hand like I'd been told to during our pre-action meeting, were wrenched from my grasp. I felt the cuffs going on my skin and with a swift upward jerk the cop pulled them into place. I was grabbed under my arms and by my ankles, lifted and then pushed flat down on my back on the stretcher. All my weight was on my cuffed wrists and the plastic bit into them. I tried to shift to my side but was pushed on my back again. The stretcher was in the air, a cop at each end. It felt precarious and I had visions of myself toppling off, face first, with no hands to break the fall. I didn't look at the cop I could have looked at, who was holding the stretcher at my feet. I lay my head down and looked at the cloud-filled sky and the tops of skyscrapers.

Even though it was cold and wet I began to perspire. The cops carrying me seemed to be walking back and forth for too long. I could hear shouts, "Not here! Over to the other one!" The cops moved off again and I concentrated on staying put, on the stretcher. "No, no, this one," another cop yelled and off we went again. My eyes hadn't strayed from the gray mass of clouds above Manhattan. Then I heard them direct the police officers to the "male" wagon. The tour continued and I was taken to the van where the men were being loaded. When I heard, "Is it male or female?" I stopped looking at the sky and used the cop's belly behind me to prop my head up. There were cops everywhere I looked—standing around looking busy or bored. Cops watching me or paying no attention at all. I began to panic and asked what was going on. There was no response. My eyes darted from left to right, searching for anyone who was not in uniform. Finally, I saw a face I knew, far away. Carolina Kroon, a photographer and a Lesbian Avenger, was watching and snapping shots. She waved at me, with a serious expression, and I knew it was going to be okay. She could see me.

Eventually I was deposited at the first of the many "female" police vans that would cart us to the Seventh Precinct. I saw Marie and Sheila and Lucy sitting inside the windowless wagon. The stretcher was lowered to the ground. Both cops were now at my head; they lifted the stretcher and pushed it up to a vertical position in one fell swoop. The sensation of suddenly being upright gave me an intense and unexpected dose of vertigo. My feet jarred against the pavement and several cops grabbed me before I fell headfirst into the metal steps of the van. The police took two Polaroid snaps before whooshing me up into the wagon. Everyone shuffled up the bench so I could sit by Marie. She was silent and didn't acknowledge me. I knew she was terrified. I whispered to her and kissed her head. Eventually, she blurted out with a mixture of anger and pain that she thought something had happened to me.

Slowly the van filled with women and we sat, arms strained and confined behind our backs by the cuffs, on two long benches across from each other. Catch was very quiet but Lucy and Trish chatted. Sarah Chin and Kris Franklin joined in the conversation and when our van was so full women were sitting on our laps, the doors were slammed shut, leaving us in darkness. Several cops stood in the front compartment with the driver—a square of light poured through a grill in the partition that separated us from the police. When the engine started a cop pulled the metal shutter across the grill and cut off our bit of light and air. Once in motion we balanced ourselves against each other with our feet and did our best to keep the women without seats secure on our laps. Then, we all sang "Happy Birthday" to Trish.

We wanted to know where we were going. We shouted inquiries through the wall—"What precinct are you taking us to? Where are we now?" After complete silence we got our answer: "We're taking you to the East River." I got a fright but other women shouted back appropriate responses to such a threatening comment.

The women who were arrested on March 17, 1993 were taken to the 7th Precinct at Pitt Street while the men were brought to Central Booking. We knew a lot of people had been arrested but we still hadn't heard how many. After sitting in the van for half an hour at the precinct we were led through iron gates into a yard and from there to the main building. In a large sunlit reception area, on our way to the cells, we passed the CD Rebel women. We had no idea then where they'd been arrested but later learned that they had run up Fifth Avenue and were arrested around 47th Street. Eileen Clancy later told me that she had tried to get people out onto Fifth Avenue because she saw hoards of police marching our way and not because she wanted to take over ILGO's action. We agreed that the non-communication between the Rebels and ILGO was a huge blunder. ILGO made every effort to communicate with the CD Rebels and was rebuffed at every turn. The Rebels organized on a paranoid level of secrecy but they did attend every one of our public meetings. Speaking again to Eileen did

ROCK THE SHAM!

not convince me that the Rebels were the only activists at our final pre-action meeting in 1993 who failed to understand that ILGO was going to march in an act of civil disobedience despite the city's injunction. So, my conversation with Eileen hasn't much changed my mind about what took place on March 17, 1993. I continue to believe that the CD Rebels were responding to ILGO and not to the powers aligned against us.

Our vanload was the first ILGO crew to arrive at the precinct. We were marched in single file through drab institutional corridors, a few filing cabinets and rickety old tables lined the walls, to a windowless room with two holding-pens, or cages. There, still handcuffed, we lined up for more photographs. The police asked us to take our hats off and we laughed at the absurdity of the request, having no free hands.

The cops putting us through the motions were mostly rookies, something they were quick to tell us, and had never booked or printed people before. They were nervous and got very flustered when we began shouting for the cuffs to be removed—they were being watched by their supervisors. But some of the cuffs were fastened far too tightly, already causing nerve damage, and some women's hands were swelling and turning purple. We complained loudly and didn't let up. Eventually a couple of timid men came in with a pair of scissors. But they couldn't fit a blade between plastic and flesh because there was no room and when they eventually found someone whose cuffs were a little looser, the scissors snapped. More vanloads of women arrived, more needed their cuffs removed and so there were more noisy demands from us. The cops weren't lying when they told us they hadn't the proper tools to remove the cuffs but an experienced sergeant managed to get the hang of using scissors. It took him over two hours to get through us all.

Both holding-pens were completely full of women by then, but there were women we knew had been arrested who were missing. They were sharing cells in another part of the jail. Our names were called out and the metal door was unlocked and re-locked each time one of us left. I was told to empty my pockets and place everything on a brown-topped Formica table. The contents were listed and put into a large envelope. Then, unlike everyone else, I was ordered to take off my leather belt and to remove the laces from my Doc Marten boots—they were making sure I wouldn't try to hurt myself. My jeans dropped to my hips and the bottoms dragged along the wet floor.

Once everyone's pockets were emptied, the long slow process of finger printing began. One by one we were called from the pens to answer questions and have our fingertips rolled in ink for three sets of prints. The police officer, wearing surgical gloves, rolled out black ink on a long rubber strip, took each finger separately in her or his hand, pressed it down and then rolled it expertly from left, round to right in the marked square on a form. The thumbprint was last. This was repeated twice more and by the last set I knew to relax the joints in my fingers and to let the officer guide my fingers rather than trying to do the job myself. We were led to a deep metal sink to clean off the excess ink with scouring powder.

Even though it had been previously agreed we would only give information we were legally obliged to give—our name, address and date of birth—people were talking up a storm, some out of fear and others because they forgot. We reminded everyone again and when we told people that some women there could be singled out because of immigration status everyone understood. But the cops continued to ask the questions anyway: "Are you married? What weight are you? Do you have any tattoos?" Later we heard that when city council member Tom Duane was asked his height he responded, "With or without heels?"

The process was laborious and we knew we would not be released until after the parade was over. We settled down. Women sat on the floor in smaller groups and chatted. There wasn't room for everyone to sit, so we took turns. I spent a lot of time watching while other women were being finger-printed. In one corner a woman sat poring over schoolbooks—she had an exam the following morning. Chewing gum, candy, carrots, nuts, and pieces of fruit were passed around.

First in from outside was Bill Dobbs, who was acting as a legal observer. He came and asked if everything was okay. Shortly after Dobbs left with his notebook a cop came through asking for me. He said there were lawyers outside who wanted to talk to me. Marie was still upset and asked me not to leave because she was worried it was a set-up. But I convinced her it was okay because it was probably Paul. The cop unlocked the gate and led me out to the corridor where Paul stood with the famous civil rights lawyer, Bill Kunstler. Kunstler lunged at me, throwing his arms about me and lifted me off the ground in a bear hug. I was completely taken aback and laughed out loud. He told me his daughters had been arrested (with the CD Rebels) and proudly announced that one of them was only fourteen years old. He was charming and dramatic and, I thought to myself, probably a hard man to live with. Paul was enjoying himself. He said well over 200 people had been arrested and so far, everything was going smoothly. When I returned, the relief on Marie's face made me feel awful. I promised her I would not leave the pen again. Trying to get all those women to hush up for a minute to pass on the news wasn't easy. But when they heard how many people had been arrested the cheer bounced off the concrete blocks of the walls and took my breath away.

The bathroom was at the end of a block of double cells, in a tiny single cell with iron bars, no door, and no toilet seat—just a filthy bare bowl. We lined up in single file against the wall and waited our turn, talking to the women in each cell as we moved up the queue. Our police escort kept shouting, "No talking!" but everyone ignored her; what was she going to do, someone quipped, arrest us? We passed on any information we had to Maxine, Sarah, and Carrie Moyer, who stood together behind bars.

Cora Roelofs was sitting on the floor of her cell. We smiled at each other and then laughed out loud. I'd met Cora years before in Bewlys, a café in Dublin, when she was sixteen or seventeen and I still lived in Ireland. Her big sister, my friend Sarah, had bowled me over and won my heart when we first met at a women's conference in 1980s when it seemed every sentence she spoke began with, "As a lesbian..." Those were the days when neither Cora nor I were saying we too were lesbians. We'd both come a long way and I loved the connection we had, the threads that bound our lives together, made us who were are and finally, made being here on this day, together, so right.

Meanwhile, at Central Booking, the men were singing show tunes! By the time the cops at Pitt Street began to release us in dribs and drabs all the men were free. In the early evening of St. Patrick's Day, the parade on Fifth Avenue long over, we walked out into the freezing darkness, to be greeted by cheers and applause. The ILGO support team had been waiting outside all day. Of all the commitment and energy required to pull off a good and a safe action, support work is probably the most thankless. Leaving jail and being welcomed out by women and men who've been thinking and worrying about us, have cups of tea and coffee waiting, and look absolutely delighted to see us is the best part. Everyone reacts differently. While I love being greeted, I also find it intensely mortifying to be cheered but other people bow, curtsey, punch their fists in the air, or wave a hand or nod with cool nonchalance. Regardless of how people respond in that moment, everybody loves the support crew. Their jobs were not over yet. They had to collect our desk appearance tickets on which the charges against us were listed along with a time, date, and place for our first court appearance. These tickets would make up ILGO's defendants' list.

A group of us got the train into the East Village and went to Haveli's on Second Avenue for an Indian meal. I sat beside the Irish women who had traveled from Cork and London and asked them what the day was like for them. They said it was amazing, and sad, and freezing cold—they had also waited for us outside the police precinct. In the middle of dinner they took off to do an interview with a reporter they'd met earlier that morning. We had a delicious meal and were fussed over by so many waiters it verged on harassment, and relaxed for the first time in months.

News of the parade began to filter in. Once again, the parade formation committee physically ejected Division 7 of the AOH by holding up the parade and forcing them off Fifth because of their original invitation to ILGO in 1991. Even though Division 7 had been exonerated by a higher power within Hibernian ranks, the New York parade organizers refused to allow them to march. The Gay and Lesbian Equality Network in Ireland issued a press statement, "We marched today in Ireland to reject the Ancient Order of Hibernians claim that our national day is a celebration of narrow-minded Catholicism."

Later that night I sat squashed between people in a dark corner of Crazy Nanny's, a lesbian bar on Seventh Avenue, watching my friends and ILGO supporters dance up a storm. The owners of Nanny's had made a point of inviting us there after the parade to feed us and help us wind down. We could also watch the news on a big screen. People always tried to drag me up onto the dance floor, not understanding, or caring in their great relief and the buzz in the air, that I was much happier sitting still, at last. I just wanted to be quiet and watch and admire them all having fun, talking, eating, doing whatever they were doing. So on March 17, 1993, I sat and watched. At the far end of the DJ's booth people stood around hot plates, eating the corned beef, potatoes, and cabbage that the bar provided for us. The huge screen over the dance floor showed our demonstration and the arrests at news time and people shrieked when they saw themselves or their friends. I unconsciously rubbed my swollen and bruised right wrist—a reminder of the plastic handcuffs and so much more.

Everything changed after 1993—the St. Patrick's Day Parade in New York was never referred to without lesbians and gay men being mentioned in the same breath. Indeed, lesbians and gay men became such an intrinsic part of the day that the organizers of the parade may as well have let ILGO march. However, that hasn't been their decision. Over time, the players have changed but many of the details have remained unchanged. From 1993 through to the year 2000 ILGO and our supporters have been through much the same ritual on March 17 each year. Our arrests are followed by numerous court appearances. Often, the court cases are only resolved, if at all in any given year, a few months before the next St. Patrick's Day protest. On each of those St. Patrick's Days, I wondered how long it was going to take before we got to meet for a meal and some fun, after having marched in the parade with our banner, in the land of the free, and the home of the brave.

"Yes, when we're not sodomizing each other under the cathedral and trying to destroy the Roman Catholic Church in all its manifestations, we try to bring down Western civilization by playing bingo. That's what we do to make money on relax on a Sunday afternoon."

– Paul O'Dwyer, ILGO,
The New Yorker, March 1993

CHAPTER THIRTEEN

Moving Right Along: 1993-2000

ROCK THE SHAM!

N APRIL 2000, at dinner in Meriken, celebrating ILGO's tent anniversary, I officially retired from my activist role in the group. I wa hopelessly exhausted and hadn't an ounce of creativity or energy to kee me going. Everyone from the 1991 parade working group in ILGO ha long since moved on and I was the only original member left. Susa O'Brien and Cecilia Dougherty were also leaving as they had plans to liv in Ireland. The others at the dinner were supportive and understandin if not a little sad—it was the beginning of the end and we all knew it.

Since 1993, close to 600 arrests have been made at ILGO's St. Patrick's Da demonstrations. ILGO has not been allowed to march in protest of our exclusion from th parade since 1992 and never again marched in the St. Patrick's Day Parade after that firs in 1991. Nothing...yet everything...changed; while ILGO cannot march or protest withou risking arrest I've met young people who think St. Patrick's Day is a gay holiday! I have tol this story covering only the first two years (and three parades) of ILGO's fight. Much ha happened in the meantime but the main political, legal and ethical questions and position were established during this two-year period and have remained basically unchange However, it is worth explaining some of what did take place in the intervening years to th present day.

David Dinkins lost the mayoral election to Rudolph Giuliani on November 2, 199 Giuliani won a second term in 1997 and continued Dinkins' legacy of arresting ILG protesters each year. (In fact, according to the city's official website Giuliani considere "Upholding City's Denial of Parade Permit" to ILGO as one of its proud "accomplishments" ILGO tried to highlight the insidious nature of this policy as we knew it would not stop a us, and of course it didn't. As usual, violating the rights of the LGBT community is not take seriously. Ironically, the NYCLU, who paved the way to ban ILGO from ever being on Fift Avenue on St. Patrick's Day, eventually began to rely on citations from ILGO's litigatio history to defend the rights of other organizations! So, along with a host of new politician there were new lawsuits, new judges and new lawyers. Most important of all were the ne people, who, year after year, took on the work of ILGO. It was their contribution, especiall as the years accumulated, that was most challenging. Without their dedication, tenacit and creativity, ILGO's struggle would not have continued into a new century.

Back in 1993, on the heels of the St. Patrick's Day arrests, dubbed by Matt Foremar then of the Anti-Violence Project, as "the largest mass arrest in the history of the gay/lesbia liberation movement in NYC" our small group was faced with more work. We had to fin lawyers to represent us in criminal court, coordinate defendants' meetings and make sur nobody fell through the cracks. Months after the arraignment of all 228 defendants i Criminal Court Judge Dynda Andrews found those arrested with ILGO (and not the radic CD Rebels) guilty of criminal contempt, resisting arrest, and disorderly conduct. In he final decision and order, Andrews stated she would not grant ILGO's motion to dismiss th

ILGO supporters tell Cardinal Spellman's secret. © *Donna Binder*
PREVIOUS SPREAD: Sal Cecere, arrested in 1994, was made to wait until his trial in 1998 to tell it like it was © *Donna Binder*

charges in the interest of justice, because:

> *Dismissal of these cases would have an extremely detrimental impact upon the public's confidence in the criminal justice system since it would imply that persons may defy court orders virtually at will... the real victim of the violation of the court order is none other than the integrity of our judicial system...*

I remember wondering if the public was as confident in the legal system as Judge Andrews, and given ILGO's experience so far, the position that the court had integrity seemed ridiculous. The arbitrary nature of this "integrity" would shortly, and for once, work

ROCK THE SHAM!

Our lawyers, Paul O'Dwyer and Mary Dorman, with John Francis Mulligan © *Alice O'Malley*

in ILGO's favor.

We took advantage of the upcoming mayoral election by initiating a "Drop the Charges" postcard campaign directed at Mayor Dinkins. The card's headline read, "Don't assume that you have the lesbian and gay vote on November 2." We demanded the charges against us be dropped. We stood on street corners and outside of political events and asked people to sign cards, which we then mailed to City Hall. To complement this we also targeted Robert Morganthau, the Manhattan District Attorney with a "Drop the Charges" petition.

Maxine and Ann Northrop went downtown at lunch hour to the heart of the city's administration. We were surprised to see Ann Northrop at our meetings because she was a CD Rebel. To her credit she put up with our formidable anger and suspicion of her after the CD Rebel's assault on ILGO. Maxine and Ann strategically settled themselves outside of the District Attorney's office to collect signatures for the petition. People lined up, eager to add their names. We later heard that Robert Morganthau was furious and didn't leave the building all day. Word on the lawyer grapevine was that the ILGO case was particularly unpopular at the DA's office and nobody wanted to prosecute it. The direct action tactic worked. Right before Election Day, we were summoned to appear before Judge Andrews again. She informed us that the District Attorney had decided to drop all the charges against us. Andrews, no longer fearing the demise of the entire judicial system, didn't bat an eyelid as she sealed the cases forever. After this everyone knew for sure the legal system, like the Archdiocese, and every other institution ILGO ever dealt with, was political and corrupt at its core.

The following year, 1994, 102 people were arrested at ILGO's action but this time the charges were dropped in the interests of justice. Judge Robert Sackett stated our arrests were a "blatant denial of First Amendment rights." Unlike his predecessor, his harshest criticism was directed at the city administration and the NYPD; his order further stated, "To allow such convictions to occur would be to encourage further undermining of constitutional safeguards by those charged with their protection." In his order Judge Sackett said ILGO should apply for a permit for our pre-St. Patrick's Day Parade protest. The City, furious and outraged by Sackett's attack, appealed this ruling and so began our long journey with our lawyers, Paul O'Dwyer and Mary Dorman, to the Second Circuit Court of Appeals, and from there to Washington where ILGO requested, and was denied a hearing, by the United States Supreme Court. The process was slow and cumbersome and the Sackett case would not be put to rest until our trials in 1998 when many of those arrested four years earlier no longer lived in New York, or the United States. The only legal victory ILGO achieved was in the Second Circuit Court of Appeals when ILGO's Paul O'Dwyer and ILGO lawyer Mary Dorman won the argument which stated clearly that going limp and refusing to walk did not constitute resisting arrest. This was an important precedent for all street activists as charges are often harsher than warranted as a means to make people fearful of protesting and demonstrating in public. However, this victory didn't actually mean that ILGO members and other activists haven't been charged with resisting arrest; quite the opposite has happened, especially in more recent years. ILGO members are currently involved in a class-action lawsuit stemming from our arrests in March 2000, when instead of being issued with a bench warrant where we'd be processed and let go, everyone was put through the system which meant we were kept overnight as harassment for daring to be a presence on Fifth Avenue on St. Patrick's Day. It didn't seem possible that the NYPD policy could get worse under Mayor Bloomberg, but it has.

Back when we were preparing for the fifth year of our battle with the AOH and now, also the NYPD and Mayor Giuliani, we decided to take Judge Sackett's order at face value and applied for a permit to march two and a half hours before the Hibernian parade. We sent our application in October, five months before the parade in 1995. We were treated to a classic run around by the police who refused to respond. No matter what letters of inquiry we sent, or how many phone calls we made, they refused to give us an answer. We had no other option but to force a "yes" or "no" out of them. Paul and Mary Dorman drew up the legal papers and ILGO went to Federal Court to compel the Police Department to respond

Fifth Avenue, St. Patrick's Day, 1994... one hundred and one good people are arrested. From left: Susan O'Brien, Brendan Fay, and P.N. Ryan © *Donna Binder*

to our permit application. This was the beginning of the "permit" phase of ILGO's history in the legal system.

Judge Keenan, who presided over the 1995 hearing, handed down quite a work of art on March 15. Even though he had clearly established that there was no other day for Irish people quite like St. Patrick's Day he concluded:

> *ILGO can conduct a parade and trumpet its message*
> *on another day. Indeed, Irish history, tradition and*
> *culture are not so drab and sterile as to permit of only*
> *one hero—St. Patrick.*

Keenan's order went on to painstakingly list the names, dates, and places of birth of some thirteen Irish men ILGO might "trumpet" our message to. His top six were Michael Collins, Eamon de Valera, James Joyce, Charles Stewart Parnell, George Bernard Shaw, and

isa Fane has her marshal's armband secured by Maxine Wolfe in 1995. So much serious hought, commitment, and dedication went into every single ILGO protest.
• *Morgan Gwenwald*

)scar Wilde. Judge Keenan noted with some excitement, "The proximity of the birth dates of 'ollins, deValera and Wilde is particularly striking. Why not parade on the weekend nearest ᴐ their birth date?" I was surprised Keenan had not included Cardinal John O'Connor on is list.

Once again, the law was supremely confident in its right to create and then limit LGO's message and how ILGO should define itself. Judge Keenan was telling us that our ational holiday shouldn't be that important to us. He was obnoxious and arrogant enough ᴐ throw out names of men (not one woman appeared on his list) that ILGO could and hould celebrate in order to get over this dispute. In other words, he completely ignored our rgument; he made us invisible and silent by ignoring who we were, what we wanted and ʹhat our message was. Judge Keenan, however, had no qualms telling us what he'd like to ᴇe and hear from us. No other group would be treated this way—a Christian denomination ʹould never be asked to give up December 25, Christmas Day, because Christianity isn't so Jrab" as to permit such a narrow definition of itself.

ROCK THE SHAM!

Holding the banner in 1995: John Voelcker, Assemblywoman Deborah Glick, Sheila Quinn, Susan O'Brien, Marie Honan, Councilman Tom Duane and me © *Bruce Manning*

ILGO's journey through the courts has been dismal and depressing. The Police Department's excuses for not granting us a permit to protest hours before the St. Patrick's Day Parade have been wide and varied. First, they said they were unable to guarantee our safety; that the potential for anti-gay violence from onlookers was too great for the NYPD. However, a year later, they eventually admitted they would be well able to protect us if they wanted or had to. In 1995, Luis R. Anemone, NYPD Chief of Department, cited traffic congestion as the reason ILGO was not granted a permit. The reason ILGO didn't get a permit to protest in 1996 was a "physics kind of thing," according to Lieutenant Cirillo of the Manhattan south precinct. He explained it would be "impossible to have two parades in one place at the same time." But ILGO wanted to march hours before the St. Patrick's Day Parade, not at the same time. It may have taken the NYPD several years to figure out which excuse would seem legitimate in a courtroom but once they found it they stuck to it. This does not mean that it is what they actually practiced because there are examples and instances where two and sometimes even three events, including parades, take place around the same time, in the same area and on the same day in the city. What it was really about was not allowing ILGO march past St. Patrick's Cathedral, Cardinal O'Connor's territory.

'm arrested, again, in 1995... sometimes St. Patrick's Day could be the saddest day of the year.
© *Saskia Scheffer 1995*

The Irish-American Gay, Lesbian and Bisexual Group of Boston (GLIB) fared no better n the courts in the end either. Their case was heard by the United States Supreme Court n 1995 and the vote was unanimous—the organizers of the Boston parade did not have to nclude GLIB. Naturally, 1993 didn't see the end of the "fixers" either. Later on, in 1995, we had the City's Comptroller, Alan Hevesi, throw himself into the mix. He had the arrogance to discuss ILGO and our strategy at one of his Lesbian and Gay Task Force meetings attended by leaders of many of the city's lesbian and gay groups—but not ILGO. Alan Hevesi decided, with the unanimous approval of the gay task force, to approach Cardinal O'Connor to broker a deal without first consulting ILGO. According to one of his liaisons, the comptroller is an intellectual and just loves to engage in ideas and discussion and that was supposed to explain what happened.

John Francis Mulligan, Susan O'Brien, both of whom had joined ILGO after our 1993 protest, and I went to meet with Hevesi to sort out what he was up. We were treated to a ten-minute monologue and resume of the comptroller's positions on gay and Irish issues. The tone was akin to Bill Lynch's "Big P...Politics" speech and was just as condescending. Hevesi had spoken to the cardinal and told us he didn't know that the Hynes group had been in

The 1996 parade – Rock the Blocks Rules! © *www.carolinakroonphotography.com*

BELOW: Me and Marie with Susan O'Brien, Rena Blake in 1996... ILGO marches in protest, as our exclusion from the parade continues. © *www.carolinakroonphotography.com*

touch with Cardinal O'Connor in 1993 or that Judge Alice Schlesinger had also paid a visit. Clearly Hevesi was up to something; we needed a bit of time to figure it out.

Shortly after that meeting I got a call from the comptroller's office to invite me to a one-on-one lunch with Hevesi, just the two of us, man-to-man-like. I explained that ILGO never worked in this way. Of course the whole episode ended with the comptroller being furious and attacking ILGO when we had figured what he really wanted was to march in the St. Patrick's Day Parade and get the kudos he believed was his due for his work on behalf of the peace process in Ireland. He wanted ILGO's boycott lifted and went about it in an underhanded and cynical way. Had he paid any attention to the history of the dispute he would have known that ILGO would not fall for the move. Regardless, ILGO fought on. Rock the Blocks! is what we called our action in 1996. The parade fell on a Saturday so we figured we'd get more people out to join us. We lobbied and cajoled groups to take up space along the parade route to voice their feelings about the continued ban on ILGO from the parade. It was beautiful. That morning ILGO attempted, once again, to march in protest on Fifth Avenue where we were stopped and arrested; but the protest didn't end there. All along the parade route, while the parade passed by, groups of ILGO supporters did street theater, sang, chanted, handed out leaflets, danced, held placards and banners above the crowds, and talked to spectators about why they were there. Circus Amok, visible from great distances as they walked on stilts, waved colorful flags and sang to spectators:

Fags can march in Dublin
Dykes can march in Cork
Today we're gonna Rock the Blocks
For justice in New York

The Radical Faeries, waving wands, chanted, "Bring back the snakes. Drive out the cops." The Lesbian Herstory Archives battled with the police to take up space along the parade route. ACT UP handed out green condoms while students from Columbia, Barnard and NYU retorted to the mean spirit of a few young men who roared, "Queers go home!" with "WE ARE HOME!" The Worker's World Party banner read, "Brits out of Ireland - ILGO in the Parade." Jews for Racial and Economic Justice held their small banner over the blue police barrier so everyone who marched by in the parade saw them. When Gerry Adams, despite Sinn Féin's alleged support of lesbian and gay rights, passed the reviewing stand in his bigoted parade my sister Cathy and Elizabeth Meister were waiting there; he watched as they unfurled their ILGO banner, which we had stayed up till four in the morning making with Erin Kelly, Elizabeth's girlfriend. A friend from Queens had been given two free tickets to the reviewing stand and passed them on to ILGO and Cathy and Elizabeth loved the idea of unfurling a banner for Adams. But they had to fight to get a seat with Elizabeth claiming that Cathy was her cousin who had come all the way from Ireland and they had to be let in—they

ROCK THE SHAM!

It's 1996, and it's okay for teenage girls to march with rifles but lesbians are still banned!
© www.carolinakroonphotography.com

had tickets and everything. After much cajoling and pleading the AOH man broke down and allowed them access. They found seats and made friends immediately with everyone sitting around them, cooing at and holding their babies. When Elizabeth and Cathy stood to display the banner their new friends helped them to get it unfurled! Of course, when the parade spectators saw that it was pro—ILGO and challenging Adams, Cathy and Elizabeth almost got throw out on to Fifth Avenue with Gerry—brave ladies.

The Anti-Violence Project, dressed as doctors and nurses, handed out flyers and Lysander Pucci's church group, St. Clement's Episcopal showed up to support us. Dotted along the route of the parade people on their own held up signs with shamrocks and pink triangles and their own message on them. Protesters, some of whom were ILGO members, John Francis Mulligan, Emmaia Gelman and four others were arrested in the parade when they unfurled their Irish Lesbian and Gay Freedom Fighters banner in the middle of the Manhattan College contingent. John Francis and Emmaia, along with one or two other ILGO members, including Cyrus Tavadia who joined our group when he was still in high school continued to infiltrate the parade up until 1999 unfurling banners as Irish Lesbian and Gay Freedom Fighters and later, Irish Queers. They have been doing actions ever since, some involving arrests but more recently they've concentrated on more cultural interaction with parade spectators. John Francis Mulligan says, "Irish Queers continues in a long tradition of progressive anti-imperialist, anti-racist, Irish Republican activists that accept no half measure of freedom."

Each year since 1993, after all the hoopla was over we still had to traipse in and out of court many times, taking off work or school. After years I lost track of how many times ILGO and those arrested with us on St. Patrick's Day had appeared in court. I'd forgotten the judges' names and faces there had been that many. Back in 1993, I was on top of all the legal ins and outs and knew exactly who all the players were. Since then there have been so many cases that the arguments, judges, courtrooms, lawyers, and rulings have overlapped and bled into each other in my mind leaving me only with an overall impression of our experiences.

There have been as many unforgettable moments in courtrooms as there were elsewhere in this story. In community court following the 1998 arrests the judge, who was quite elderly, shouted about how six million people couldn't just come into the city to disrupt everything. City Councilman Tom Duane talked to the judge about the history of civil disobedience during the civil rights movement to explain why ILGO risked arrest each year. The judge's response was that he knew nothing about the civil rights movement and they were probably trying to get six million people to disrupt the city too and that they should all be arrested! Marie said this judge was completely bonkers; he hadn't a clue what was going on in or outside of his courtroom. When he eventually realized that ILGO hadn't rounded up six million protesters to disrupt the entire city he wanted to know why we hadn't made that clear in the first place!

At trial ILGO defendants have been found guilty of disorderly conduct on the basis of a police officer's testimony about the annual Dyke March in June. This officer painstakingly explained how we gathered in Bryant Park, walked, first on the sidewalk on 42nd Street and then entered Fifth Avenue and took up several lanes, disrupting traffic, and marched downtown to Washington Square Park. We told the judge he was testifying about an entirely different event and that it was clear the officer couldn't distinguish between a lesbian march in the late afternoon heat of June and the early morning St. Patrick's Day protest at the end of winter. The judge didn't think this mattered.

Through the years in ILGO's small parade working group, with much turn over in who was involved and when, our political difference and styles have been invigorating at best, extremely destructive at worst. While I agree that the personal is political, I also think it's the first step in being an effective agitator, not the be all and end all. ILGO was often divided and eventually two separate camps emerged—the "radical" and the "old school." I was part of the latter, being more concerned with strategically building upon our past actions rather than self-consciously determining what action might seem most radical or personally gratifying. In new and often younger members ILGO was infused with a "queer" sensibility and it was assumed by "queers" that they were inherently more "radical". If ILGO voted to do one thing they seemed to automatically find the decision suspect. This was a new tension and one I hadn't bargained for.

I have never approached activism self-consciously measuring how radical or not it might be—I think long and hard and then argue for what I consider is the best and most effective action to take. Ironically, in 1995, most of the "queer" activists in ILGO originally believed it was okay for Gerry Adams to march in the St. Patrick's Day Parade because his cause was far greater (i.e., more radical) than ILGO's. I didn't agree. I thought Adams had many options the most radical of which would have been to join ILGO's protest. I am very wary of anyone who categorizes everything, save anything related to lesbian and gay liberation, as more "radical" and by extension, more meaningful and valid. I am not saying that many issues at different periods in history should and do take precedence but never at the cost of going back into the closet. So, if it was okay for Adams to march why did ILGO member, Marion Irwin, so courageously challenge him in hostile territory at a huge rally in Gaelic Park? Because our right to be who we are is the most basic and fundamental right in life.

Rather than stand their ground and do battle within the group those members who believed ILGO was consistently making the wrong political decisions began to operate as "outsiders." Even physically, at our meetings, they sat outside of the main group. It is intensely irritating and undermining to have a running commentary from the "outside" to remind us, year after year, that we are not good enough. Of course, being an outsider means not assuming any responsibility for what ILGO is or does; it's a very comfortable and safe place to be—neither radical nor powerful in the end. While I would love to report that our differences have been fascinating and challenging, I can't. That said, it is quite an achievement that we continued, irritated, cranky and often very angry with each other, to fight the good fight.

ILGO was truly fortunate to have steady and committed activists like Susan O'Brien, who much to her horror ended up having to testify in Federal Court as an ILGO witness during our trial in 2000. Cecilia Dougherty, a brilliant experimental video-artist began documenting ILGO's actions with a fantastic crew each year so that we have the most incredible video archive of our later protests. Lisa Springer and Richard McKewen, the best-humored person ever, joined, too, during the terribly difficult years after 1993 and took on several roles within ILGO, varying their work from year to year and learning from those in the group who had done the job before. People whose paths would never have crossed otherwise were drawn to ILGO. Lisa Fane and Sal Cecere came after working at GLAAD, the Gay and Lesbian Alliance against Defamation, and went on to organize ILGO's media and support for years. Maxine Wolfe, one of the Lesbian Avenger leaders, made sure we had

Putting your body on the line and fighting for your liberation is often a joyful experience...
Maxine Wolfe is arrested in 1997 © *Saskia Scheffer*

their support every year. Sarah Schulman spent a whole year on her own contacting law firms and law professors across the city until she found someone who would tackle what ILGO was up against in the legal system. Jacqueline Charlesworth at Paul, Weiss, Rifkind, Wharton & Garrison talked to some partners and in 1996 filed a suit against the Mayor, the City of New York and its Police Department for violating ILGO's constitutional right to protest before the parade on Fifth Avenue—the "permit" case. Deciding to use the deep resources of a corporate law firm, over Mary Dorman and Paul, who had originally started this legal action was just another betrayal, this time on ILGO's part. This is the case that eventually went to a jury trial in 2000.

Anne Stott worked with ILGO for several years and made a documentary with Sally Sasso titled Rock the Sham. We had used this slogan on several of our posters to publicize our actions in the mid-1990s. The artist Carrie Moyer designed ILGO's poster every single year without fail. Jenny Romaine organized musicians, or as we called it, "The Jenny Romaine Band," and my memories of being arrested are filled with their music. Alexis Danzig, Amy Bauer (who has come out of activist retirement on several occasions for ILGO) and Phyllis Lutsky, among many others, have trained our marshals and prepared us for civil

ROCK THE SHAM!

disobedience through the years, with Maxine coordinating. Marlene Colburn worked the main phone each year at ILGO's support central—none of these women are Irish but they believed in what ILGO was doing. So many Irish and Irish-American people have worked in ILGO's parade group since we began, so many others on the day, or in the lead up to our protest, giving their time, experience, love, and intelligence and all contributing to ILGO's battle and history. It was this determination and loyalty and work that maintained ILGO's will to keep fighting. In the late 1990s, Noreen Dean Dresser and Ann Duggan joined and continued to bring new views and voices to the group, sometime not very popular ones, but they also took the banner to the parade for years after ILGO's tenth anniversary in 2000. ILGO, for all intents and purposes no longer existed after the tenth anniversary. But this small group stayed put on the sidelines of Fifth Avenue, with spectators, and protested as the parade passed by. Unfortunately, even though Mayor Bloomberg, who took over after Giuliani's second term, marched in the Fifth Avenue parade without conscience, some people representing ILGO attended a breakfast the mayor had invited them to. This would never have happened during the years beginning in 1991 through March 2000. And then there was Seán McGouran of the Northern Ireland Gay Rights Association (NIGRA). Every year, he organized a picket, or some form of protest, in support of ILGO, outside of the American Embassy in Belfast. He kept in constant touch with me through those old blue air-mail letters and also by sending me NIGRA's newsletter, *Upstart*.

Two years before our final hurrah in 2000, Sal Cecere, a tall and handsome strawberry blond, who did a lot of ILGO's media work, stood in front of Judge Pickholz, a stern grey-haired woman, on the fourth floor of New York City's criminal court at 100 Center Street on May 2, 1998. Our trials were over at last and as defendants we had the right to address the court before sentencing. The courtroom was cold and depressingly drab. This was where Judge Sackett's case from 1994 ended up after its journey through the appeals process. Mary Dorman and Paul O'Dwyer very graciously returned as our lawyers despite the fact that ILGO had unceremoniously dumped them in favor of a big corporate law firm.

Judge Pickholz was paying attention. She gazed directly at Sal as he stood before her. He took a deep breath, began to speak and without any warning, burst into tears. Everyone was shocked. I shifted uncomfortably on the bench for a moment. But Sal was not put off. He didn't stop, or apologize, or blow his nose. He sobbed, explaining this was the first time he had ever been able to tell his story of what St. Patrick's Day was like for him. His work was important to him, he explained, so he talked about his new job, working with young people, telling us it was depressing trying to instill a sense self-worth and pride in them and half-laughed, half-cried that he, a gay man, was trying to do it. He told the court his mother no longer came to ILGO's protest on March 17 because she got too upset watching him being dragged off to a police wagon and he in turn was upset because it was so painful for her.

The dingy courtroom was still. I was crying now, and cursing Sal for making me forget what I was going to say in front of the judge before she sentenced us. But none of that mattered now anyway; Sal was saying it all. Feeling the sadness of what we go through every year on St.

Demonstrating in 1997 – without laughter and a sense of humor, we would be doomed. The ed rose showed my support of Bernadette McAliskey's illegally jailed daughter, Róisín. Also pictured is John Voelcker. *From ILGO Files*

BELOW: Susan O'Brien used to be shy, then she joined ILGO – with Lisa Springer and Cyrus Tavadia in 1997 © *Cecilia Dougherty*

ROCK THE SHAM!

It's good to be out of jail again and on our way home – released arrestees, the support team and our legal observers, in 1997 *From ILGO Files*

Patrick's Day is a rare occurrence; we're all so intent on just getting through it. But Sal made us face how painful it is. However, what made it unbearable for me was that Sal was speaking into a vacuum; he didn't have the audience he deserved. There to hear him was Judge Pickholz, a smattering of court officers, and the stenographer who had been expressionless throughout the trial but who now sweetly nodded with empathy as she tapped out Sal's words. The pair of blond assistant district attorneys were no longer so sure of themselves. I couldn't see how Mary and Paul were reacting because they sat with their backs to us at a table up front. The only other people in the courtroom were the dozen or so ILGO defendants out of the original one hundred and one who had been arrested on March 17, 1994. We were all found guilty of disorderly conduct and given unconditional discharges and a $45 fine. The district attorney had sought ten days of community service as our punishment for walking 100 yards protesting the bigotry of a bunch of Irish men.

From the beginning ILGO's battle to march was immediately commented upon by a host of media. Along with all the articles and reports there were cartoons and editorials every year. Right after the very first parade Dana Carvey, of *Saturday Night Live* did a St. Patrick's Day Parade skit in which he played Paul—it wasn't funny. Mad TV took over from *SNL* with their less obnoxious gag in 1999. Gays marched in Springfield's parade in 1997 in *The Simpsons* and Smithers made a silly reference to it on a separate episode back in 1995. ILGO and the parade has been written about by people as disparate as beat poet Allen Ginsburg to right wing activist and two-time conservative presidential candidate, Patrick Buchanan. We've had politicians and famous people arrested with us. Tony Kushner, author of *Angels in America,* was first arrested with ILGO in 1993 and continued his support of our cause for years. Through Tony, Vanessa Redgrave joined ILGO on the steps of St. Patrick's Cathedral along with some members of the Five Lesbian Brothers and Michael Cunningham, in a torrential downpour, to announce ILGO's plans for St. Patrick's Day, in 1995. Kenneth Cole plastered fancy posters across the city in support of ILGO in an advertising campaign

ROCK THE SHAM!

Practicing our chants in a hall packed with activists the night before our 10th anniversary demonstration, in 2000. From left: Noreen Dean Dresser, me, Lisa Springer, Ann Duggan, and Emmaia Gelman. © *Margaret O'Flanagan*

for his shoes. Even this year, in February 2005, I smiled all the way into work after seeing a display of rainbow cookies lined up beside green shamrock cookies at Once Upon a Tart where I get my coffee on Sullivan Street every morning. Our battle to be who we are is part of popular culture and this explains why younger people could possibly perceive St. Patrick's Day as a gay holiday.

The stories that inspire and have always inspired me most are the everyday stories, like Sal's, or much earlier on in ILGO, Peter Kellegher's, which he wrote about in ILGO's great newsletter in 1991. Peter was the young man who was afraid at first, never uttering a word at our meetings, running away before anyone could talk to him and then he began to embrace who he really was and it transformed his life. Clearly we'll never hear the vast majority of the stories that could and will be told but there are enough for us to know what we did for all those years was meaningful for many people even when most of the institutional power bases, including some academics (not Lucy McDiarmid who came to our protests) told us we were pretty much ineffectual while fawning all over David Dinkins for marching with us nce. (And this without ever interviewing anyone in ILGO).

I was asked years ago when I thought ILGO would be invited to march, banner and all, n the St. Patrick's Day Parade and my response was the year 2020; I'll be fifty-seven years ld. I thought about the question, and even though 2020 is far off in the future, fifteen years f this battle have already passed. While I was actively involved, I approached the work oping that each year would be the magic one. ILGO came a long way for a group that began vith the bulk of its immigrant membership in the closet; we've had an incredible impact. But I still think back to the days when people came to our meetings and were afraid to tell us their names or where they came from in Ireland and wonder where they are now and vhat happened to them. I wonder about all the Irish lesbians and gay men who never even nade it to ILGO and know their numbers far exceed the numbers who did. I think about ur losses—all the men who passed through ILGO, or turned up to protest on March 17, that ve lost to HIV and AIDS. Looking over a list of people who pledged to march behind our banner for our tenth anniversary, I spotted Stanley Rygor's name. Stanley came to our céilí t Sheridan Square on St. Patrick's Day in 1991 with his son Robert, and played Irish jigs and eels on his accordion when Mayor Dinkins joined us the day after we had marched together ll those years ago. Now Stanley comes to so many events in Robert's memory, still grieving is loss. I wonder about David Dinkins too, because I can't reconcile what I saw in his eyes n 1991 with his turn against ILGO in 1993—it doesn't make sense.

Before ILGO's tenth anniversary protest march Steve Rawlings, Diane Knox and Matthew Press of Paul, Weiss, Rifkind, Wharton & Garrison tried our case for a permit before a jury and lost. The jury decided against ILGO relying on a point of law which argued hat ILGO did not have a right to the same audience as the St. Patrick's Day Parade. This vas like a repeat of the Human Rights Commission case. The jury believed everything ILGO vitnesses had said. They didn't believe the police witnesses, and went so far to say they hought the police were liars. Still, that wasn't enough—their decision had nothing to do vith justice or fairness or a humane and ethical reading of the law. It was in their hands and hey chose to rely on an instruction that could have been interpreted either way. They took he easy, and I believe, the cowardly, way out. The jury turned out to be no different to any udge, conservative or liberal, that ILGO had come across on this journey, which was very upsetting.

However, we had other things on our mind. Fifty-seven women and men were set to ome to New York from all over Ireland for the protest on our tenth anniversary. Having a arge group of lesbians and gay men come from Ireland to march with us had been a dream f mine—that it happened was moving and inspiring. I thought finding accommodations or the visiting protesters would be a nightmare but it wasn't—lesbians and gay men across he five boroughs called us and offered their homes. On the eve of ILGO's tenth protest, our uests from Ireland were officially welcomed to New York City by the Manhattan Borough President, C. Virginia Fields. The following day, March 17, fifteen of them were arrested

ROCK THE SHAM!

On the eve of ILGO's 10th anniversary protest, in 2000, some of the gang pose after our pre-action meeting. This photograph makes me happy. Back row: Siobhán Twomey, Cecilia Dougherty, Susan O'Brien, Marie Honan, me, and Paul O'Dwyer. Front: my sister Cathy, Emmaia Gelman, and my brother Seán. © *Margaret O'Flanagan*

FOLLOWING PAGES: 1997 poster, Come Sin With Us, and 2000 poster, How Do You Want To Do This? *Courtesy of Carrie Moyer*

(including my brother Seán from Dublin) by New York City police officers.

Hillary Clinton, now a New York Senator, marched with the Hibernians while sh was campaigning, breaking the Democratic Party's boycott. In part she was able to do thi because of a St. Patrick's Day parade in Queens, co-founded and organized by Brendan Fa and his group the Lavender and Green Alliance, because it included gay people. So Clinto was able to say she marched with "the gays" in Queens and now she's marching with "th Irish" on Fifth Avenue. Politicians for the most part are a lousy bunch—not one politicia who supposedly supported us turned up at our protest when they no longer held office The only politico who turned out in support of ILGO, year after year, was the Reverend A Sharpton, a recent presidential candidate. Even Matt Foreman, along with the main LBG'

Democratic Party organizations, supported Hillary Clinton instead of demanding that she not march. Everything had changed and nothing had changed. These political positions would have been queer blasphemy only a few years previously. However, seeing as Bill Clinton had moved so far to the right during both administrations, leaving the door wide open for George Bush to take over, why expect Homocrats to remain to the left of their leaders (which would be the center at this time in history)? I do expect that those who have appointed themselves as the gay leadership to have the intelligence and ethics to value our lives instead of putting us in even more danger, and for what? A little personal power? Their policies and actions are certainly not improving the lives of the poor, young, sick, single, people of color, immigrants, or the vast majority of gay people in this country.

I am almost fifteen years older since marching that first and only time in 1991. I don't have a mop of bright red curly hair anymore. I lost a very dear friend—and after the death of my Aunt Mary in Dublin, decided at last, much to Marie's relief, that I was never going to be moving back to live in Ireland. I had had a fantasy of going "home" for years but finally realized that New York has become my home. Sometimes I feel jaded and depressed, but that's part of my personality as well as the world we inhabit. In the long run I always regain my hope, especially after a much needed break from serious and consistent activism. Now, as I finish writing this book in October, 2005 I'm ready again. I love the idea of building on what has gone before us. I love the creativity and ingenuity it takes to continue the fight for lesbian and gay liberation, never in a vacuum, but in the world we all inhabit. I even love waking in the middle of the night with what I fancy is the best idea I've ever had only to realize, the next morning, that perhaps it wasn't such a brilliant plan after all. But sometimes those semi-sleepy, semi-conscious moments are truly wonderful. I wish everyone who did activist work got this buzz from it. What motivates me is also what keeps me alive—hope, rage, love, fear, cynicism, anger, humor and a solid belief that what we're all doing together is absolutely worthwhile. I still get that same old buzz I got when I was a young woman all those years ago in Dublin, sitting around Anne Speed's fireplace with a bunch of women, creating something out of ourselves that is so much bigger than any of us individually.

Lesbians and gay men can march in parades throughout New York and the United States on various holidays. We can march in parades in Ireland on St. Patrick's Day. We can't march in the Indian Independence Day Parade or the Pulaski Day Parade in New York but have in the Filipino, Puerto Rican, and African-American parades (the latter had lesbians and gay men marching before ILGO existed). The truth of it is that it's not about the marching. We want to live openly as who we are and are insisting that we not be penalized for it. Where we find hostility we name it and then challenge it. In ILGO's case we just happened to be in the right place at the right time. We were faced with a challenge that we accepted having no idea where it would take us, what would be asked of us, what might be lost and gained. But we took it on nonetheless, like so many have before us, because we believed we could change the world.

SEVEN DEADLY SINS
7
SEVEN YEARS & COUNTING

COME SIN WITH US

Be **GREEDY** and take Fifth Avenue!

Don't be a **SLOTH**!

Show your **ANGER** and **PRIDE**!

CD & MARSHALL TRAINING
SUNDAY
MAR. 9 • 2 PM
LESBIAN & GAY COMMUNITY CTR
208 W 13 ST

ST. PATRICK'S DAY DEMONSTRATION

PROTEST WITH THE IRISH LESBIAN AND GAY ORGANIZATION

MONDAY • 9AM MARCH 17, 1997

GATHER ON THE STEPS OF THE NEW YORK CITY PUBLIC LIBRARY 42nd STREET AND FIFTH AVENUE

FOR MORE INFORMATION, CALL THE ILGO HOTLINE 212-967-7711 x3078

Make the AOH green with **ENVY**!

Show your **LUST**!

Don't be a **GLUTTON** for punishment!

PRE-ACTION MEETING
SUNDAY
MAR. 16 • 8 PM
LESBIAN & GAY COMMUNITY CTR
208 W 13 ST

7 YEARS AND COUNTING

196

HOW DO YOU WANT TO DO THIS?

SITTING OR STANDING?

The food will stink. The cops will be mean. But, all your life, you'll know you stood up (or sat down) for what you believe. Join us on our tenth anniversary for our biggest, most furious protest yet. March with the Irish Lesbian & Gay Organization against homophobia and our exclusion from the St. Patrick's Day Parade.

BE ONE OF 2,000 PEOPLE TO RISK ARREST.
ST. PATRICK'S DAY • FRIDAY, MARCH 17, 2000 • 9:30 AM
MEET AT SOUTHWEST CORNER OF 59TH ST & FIFTH AVE
TO PLEDGE TO JOIN US OR FOR MORE INFORMATION:
ILGO HOTLINE 212-967-7711 x3078 • www.ilgo2000.com

2000 IN 2000

IRISH LESBIAN AND GAY ORGANIZATION

ARE YOU THE ONLY ONE NOT COMING?

Where They Are Now

Catch Keeley and **Lucy Lynch** moved back to Ireland but Lucy is on the move again and passed through New York like a whirlwind recently. Catch initiated and helped organize the second International Dyke March in Dublin in 1998 which Marie, Maxine and I attended. She returned to New York for ILGO's tenth anniversary demonstration. **Sheila Quinn** moved, too (she currently lives in Brussels), as did **Marion Irwin, Adrian O'Byrne, Rena Blake, Margey** and several other ILGO members. **Susan O'Brien** and **Cecilia Dougherty** opened the very successful Anthology Books in Dublin. (www.anthologystore.com).

Sal Cecere lives in Los Angeles where he temps at Outfest and works as an actor. He was chosen to play Twenty Minute Man by Robert de Niro in *Analyze That*. He has appeared on *Frasier* and *Judging Amy* on TV and has worked with many theatre companies. Sal got frustrated feeling angry and disillusioned and moved from ILGO to working with kids and people with HIV. He's single so check him out. (www.salcecere.com)

Eileen Clancy worked with the Irish Parades Emergency Committee (www.ipecobservers.org) documenting police activity during the Orange Order's marching season in the north of Ireland. In New York she is currently involved in I-Witness (http://iwitnessvideo.info), which was organized following the mass arrests and illegal detention of almost 2000 protesters here during the Republican National Convention. I-Witness collected and logged hundreds of video tapes as evidence which resulted in the dismissal or acquittal of 400 cases.

Lisa Fane works as the director at Radio City Entertainment. She traveled to Pennsylvania for five weekends campaigning for John Kerry during his presidential bid. She lives with her partner Maggie, and the funniest looking dog ever—Lily. Lisa is primarily focused on spiritual studies and practices Siddha Yoga meditation.

Brendan Fay left ILGO in 1994 to set up the Lavender and Green Alliance, a gay Irish and Irish-American group and not, as some mistakenly believed, an environmental gay group. He co-founded a small inclusive St. Patrick's Day Parade in Queens. Brendan runs a civil marriage trail to Toronto based upon the freedom trail during slavery in the US. He is working on a documentary about Father Mychal Judge, who died on September 11, 2001 at the World Trade Center.

Marie Honan is currently a Ph. D. candidate in Modern European History at NYU. Her topic is public health and tuberculosis in Ireland at the turn of the last century while Ireland was under British rule, and eventually partitioned when the south of Ireland became a republic. She has taught at NYU and worked on several research projects. She works part-time at the New York

ROCK THE SHAM!

at the New York Society Library

Emmaia Gelman, who worked closely with John Francis Mulligan in Irish Queers, is now a student of urban planning at MIT in Boston.

Peter Kellegher, the young man who transformed before our eyes after several silent months of attending our Saturday meetings, moved, too. He is a world traveler and uses Dublin as his base. He sends me postcards from across the globe and always asks, "Is the book finished yet?"

Fr. Bernard Lynch wrote a book, *A Priest on Trial*, about his experiences in New York following a charge of sexual abuse by a student. The case was thrown out of court and Bernard was fully exonerated. He is a psychotherapist and currently lives in London with his partner.

John Lyons moved to Los Angeles in 1998. He works in the entertainment industry as an actors agent in his own business, The Austin Agency. He has a son, Arjuna, who is the love of his life. He is a keen gardener and horseman and limits his current political activism to local environmental issues.

Tarlach MacNiallais has worked in New York with disabled adults for twenty years. He also runs a program at the Mexican Consulate teaching English. He will be leaving New York next July with his partner to travel. After two years they plan to live in County Down, Ireland.

I work as an editor of archival film at Getty Images. During the process of writing this book I caught the writing bug and I'm currently working on my first novel, about sisters, the murky relationships between the living and the dead, in a very strange Irish family.

Richard McKewen graduated law school in 2001 and clerked for Judges Constance Baker Motley and Judge Kermit Lipez. Following a two-year clinical teaching fellowship at Georgetown he now works for the Consumer Protection Bureau of the Federal Trade Commission. He dreams of owning a cocktail lounge.

Keith Moore moved to Texas and has lived in Houston for the past several years. He has his own business in the home décor industry, still laying those carpets!

John Francis Mulligan is a queer activist in New York City. For every St. Patrick's Day Parade since the year 2000 John Francis has organized many different types of protests including interrupting the parade and being arrested, to cultural events along the parade route. Good man!

Paul O'Dwyer has his own law practice in New York and concentrates on advocating for the rights of gay men, lesbians and HIV-positive persons to seek asylum in the United States, and can often be found in the higher courts throughout the country arguing to change the laws.

Lisa Springer is a writer. She currently works full-time for New York University at the American Language Institute, where she teaches English as a second language. She has a son and lives with her partner.

Cyrus Tavadia works as a special agent for the Geek Squad. He also does PR work for the computer company and has appeared on TV shows including *The Apprentice*, *Queer Eye for the Straight Guy*, and *Good Morning America*. He fixed computers at Madonna's most recent concert tour! He lives in East Harlem, makes music, looks out for his father and because he joined ILGO when he was in high school he can't believe he's twenty-eight already.

In 1996 **John Voelcker** retired from activism for a decade. Shortly thereafter, he donated his ILGO archives to the New York Public Library. He has worked in internet media and now runs a media consulting practice in New York. He sits on the Board of the Medius Institute (founded 2005), which coordinates, promotes and advocates for basic research into issues that affect the mental, emotional and physical health of gay men.

Maxine Wolfe retired from her teaching job at the graduate center of CUNY and divides her time between activism, family, friends, The Lesbian Herstory Archives (www.lesbianherstoryarchives.org), her garden, yoga, cooking, making pottery in her basement and traveling to countries she's always wanted to see or to visit friends.

Mary Dorman is still practicing law in New York City, suing people (at every opportunity) in positions of authority and entities that abuse power. As she says, "She wins some and wins some."

Cathy Maguire works as a curator and designer and has had shows at Bard, FIT, Pratt and the Cooper Hewitt. She gave birth to Liam English on August 17, 2005 and lives with her partner, Peter, in Pennsylvania.

It came as no surprise when **Clare O'Brien** made partner at Sherman & Sterling in 1995, where she continues to work in Mergers and Acquisitions. She has two daughters, a six-year-old and five-month old baby girl, and currently lives in New Hampshire with her husband.

In 2003 **Paul Wickes** left Shearman & Sterling to join the New York office of Linklaters, an international law firm based in London. He is now Linklaters' U.S. Managing Partner.

Rick Prelinger lives and works happily in San Francisco with his wife, Megan. Both are dedicated to the Internet Library which provides access to digital materials to researchers, historians and the general public free of charge. He made a feature-length collage film, Panorama Ephemera, in 2004. At the Internet Archive check out Rick's film collection. (www.archive.org/details/prelinger)

David Dinkins is a Professor in the Practice of Public Affairs at Columbia University's School of International and Public Affairs. He is also a Senior Fellow at the Center for Urban Research and Policy. Most recently he has been involved in an advertising campaign to combat colon cancer. The caption above his blue hospital gowned-body reads, "I was man enough to take the test."

Bill Lynch traveled to South Africa for the country's first free election, as an advisor to Nelson Mandela, who subsequently became the nation's first black president. Lynch is President of Bill Lynch Associates, a political consulting and lobbying firm. He worked on John Kerry's Presidential campaign.

Joe Hynes remains the Brooklyn District Attorney.

Frank Beirne was reinstated as a member of the Ancient Order of Hibernians the week before he died in December 1996. *The Irish Voice* reported that on his death bed several Hibernians tried to get him to sign an apology to the AOH, which he refused or was incapable of doing.

Cardinal O'Connor died of brain cancer on May 4, 2000.

ROCK THE SHAM!

The Ballad of ILGO: Two Miles of Hate

(Words by Tarlach Mac Niallais and Eilis Heller, 1991—to tune of Jim Larkin)

In New York City in '91, around the time of St. Patrick's Day
The AOH planned a big parade, as to who could march they had the final say
Ireland to them means leprechauns, and green beer and green berets
It doesn't mean jailed Republicans, or kids in wheelchairs, or Irish gays.

'We don't want no Joe Doherty sashes, they won't look good in our parade."
Then Frankie Beirne and his gang of Fascists, threw out the piper who'd worn Joe's name.
Then Steve McDonald and kids disabled, wanted to march in their wheelchairs
The AOH said, "You are not welcome, and we don't care if it seems unfair."

'We have our rules and our regulations, they're cast in stone and we cannot sway.
If we let you in, Lord who knows who'll follow, Oh, God forbid we'll have to let in gays."

Then Anne Maguire and the Irish gay group, they'd filed their permit and made it clear
ILGO demanded to be included, The AOH said, "We don't want queers."
Bold Mayor Dinkins, he stood his ground, he held his head up with dignity
He said, "Gay people can march beside me, I won't be part of this bigotry."

Two miles we marched, two miles of hatred, with spittin' cursin', insults and jeers
I've never heard oh so many death threats, while drunken eejits hurled cans of beer.

The Mayor stated it brought back memories, of Alabama back in the days
When Dr. King he faced down the bigots, and the Ku Klux Klan they held their sway.
Well I've seen Paisleyites and National Fronters, and UVF and UDA
To tell the truth, I have rarely seen hate, like the hate I saw on St. Patrick's Day

We walked the gauntlet, with heads held high.
Proud Irish women and Irish men.
We're gay and Irish, we won't be beaten, you bet your life we will march again.

ROCK THE SHAM!

Ancient Order of Hibernians National Board

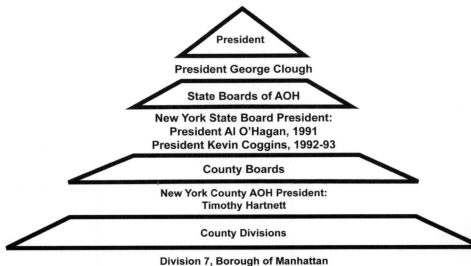

President

President George Clough

State Boards of AOH

**New York State Board President:
President Al O'Hagan, 1991
President Kevin Coggins, 1992-93**

County Boards

**New York County AOH President:
Timothy Hartnett**

County Divisions

**Division 7, Borough of Manhattan
(one of hundreds of divisions that make up the AOH membership across US)**

ROCK THE SHAM!

Simple Legal Chronology 1991-2000

Case taken by the Human Rights Commission (HRC) Against the AOH.
ILGO signs on as interested Party with Sherman & Sterling lawyers, Clare O'Brien and
Paul Wickes, 1991.
Judge Rosemarie Maldonado presides.
HRC, and by extension, ILGO loses.

ILGO (Sherman & Sterling) sues City and Police Department in Federal Court to Prevent
AOH from holding a discriminatory Parade or to prevent the NYPD from issuing such a
parade a permit, 1991.
Judge Pierre Level presides.
ILGO loses.

After talks with City Hall the St. Patrick's Day Parade Permit is issued to the AOH State
body over the New York County Division. AOH State promise to hold an inclusive parade
with ILGO included.

Human Rights Commission overturns Judge Maldonado's Recommendation and finds in
favor of ILGO, 1992.

AOH Parade Committee goes to State Supreme Court with case and Judge Alice
Schlesinger presides.
ILGO says case is moot as ILGO will be marching in 1992 parade.
Judge Alice Schlesinger visits the cardinal anyway.
AOH State Board, the new permit holder, backs down from allowing ILGO to march.

Hynes group forms and the Dinkins Administration and NYPD award them the 1993
St. Patrick's Day Parade Permit. AOH sues in Federal Court for return of permit.
Judge Kevin Duffy presides.
City loses and Hynes group returns permit.
New incorporated St. Patrick's Day Parade Committee is formed and they get the permit
and vow never to allow ILGO to march.

Mayor Dinkins and NYPD take out injunction against ILGO's promised protest march,
1993. Several hundred ILGO arrestees found guilty of criminal contempt, resisting arrest
and disorderly conduct.

Following arrests in 1994 Judge Robert Sackett dismisses charges against ILGO arrestees in the interests of justice and instructs ILGO to apply for a protest permit, stating that we should be granted one as was our constitutional right.

New York Police Department refuses to give ILGO a decision on whether or not to award ILGO permit to protest on Fifth Avenue on St. Patrick's Day in 1995, hours before the parade begins. ILGO sues in Federal court to compel NYPD to respond to our protest permit application with Paul O'Dwyer and Mary Dorman as our lawyers.
Judge Thomas Keenan presides.
We called this the Permit Case.
ILGO loses.

Mary Dorman and Paul O'Dwyer file papers in the Second Circuit Court of Appeals. ILGO loses and ILGO wins. The Second Circuit Court of Appeals rules that going limp does not constitute resisting arrest during a demonstration – this ruling applies not just to ILGO but to every demonstrator who goes limp or refuses to walk to a police wagon. ILGO loses right to permitted pre-parade protest.

ILGO dumps Paul and Mary for large corporate firm with lots of resources. Jacqueline Charlesworth leads the team at Paul, Weiss, Rifkind, Wharton & Garrison in Permit Case. Judge Koeltl presided and decided against ILGO. However, upon Appeal he was ordered to grant ILGO a jury trial which took place before the St. Patrick's Day Parade in the year 2000. Steven Rawlings, Diane Knox and Matthew Press tried the case. ILGO lost.